FINANCIAL SERVICES

FINANCIAL SERVICES

Khushboo Manoj

CENTRUM PRESS
NEW DELHI-110002 (INDIA)

CENTRUM PRESS

H.O.: 4360/4, Ansari Road, Daryaganj,
New Delhi-110002 (India)
Tel: 23278000, 23261597, 23255577, 23286875

B.O.: No. 1015, Ist Main Road, BSK IIIrd Stage,
IIIrd Phase, IIIrd Block, Bangalore-560085 (INDIA)
Tel: 080-41723429

Email: centrumpress@gmail.com
Visit us at: www.centrumpress.com

Financial Services

First Edition, 2011

ISBN 978-93-80921-11-2

PRINTED IN INDIA

Printed at Mehra Offset Press, Delhi.

Contents

Preface

Financial services refer to services provided by the finance industry. The finance industry encompasses a broad range of organizations that deal with the management of money. Among these organizations are banks, credit card companies, insurance companies, consumer finance companies, stock brokerages, investment funds and some government sponsored enterprises.

The financial services industry represented 20 per cent of the market capitalization of the S&P 500 in the United States. Financial Services companies have one thing in common: the new face of competition.

The evolution of technology and the rise in computer literacy are redefining the nature of money and transforming the financial services industry. This book explores the future of the financial services industry, giving readers an idea of the kinds of institutions and services that will survive in the early twenty-first century.

Author

1

Introduction

MEANING

Financial services refer to services provided by the finance industry. The finance industry encompasses a broad range of organizations that deal with the management of money. Among these organizations are banks, credit card companies, insurance companies, consumer finance companies, stock brokerages, investment funds and some government sponsored enterprises. As of 2004, the financial services industry represented 20% of the market capitalization of the S&P 500 in the United States.

The term "financial services" became more prevalent in the United States partly as a result of the Gramm-Leach-Bliley Act of the late 1990s, which enabled different types of companies operating in the U.S. financial services industry at that time to merge. Companies usually have two distinct approaches to this new type of business. One approach would be a bank which simply buys an insurance company or an investment bank, keeps the original brands of the acquired firm, and adds the acquisition to its holding company simply to diversify its earnings.

Outside the U.S., non-financial services companies are permitted within the holding company. In this scenario, each company still looks independent, and has its own customers, etc. In the other style, a bank would simply create its own brokerage division or insurance division and attempt to sell those products to its own existing customers, with incentives for combining all things with one company.

BANKS

A "commercial bank" is what is commonly referred to as simply a "bank". The term "commercial" is used to distinguish it from an "investment bank", a type of financial services entity which, instead of lending money directly to a business, helps businesses raise money from other firms in the form of bonds (debt) or stock (equity).

Banking Services

The primary operations of banks include:

- Keeping money safe while also allowing withdrawals when needed
- Issuance of checkbooks so that bills can be paid and other kinds of payments can be delivered by post
- Provide personal loans, commercial loans, and mortgage loans
- Issuance of credit cards and processing of credit card transactions and billing
- Issuance of debit cards for use as a substitute for checks
- Allow financial transactions at branches or by using Automatic Teller Machines Provide wire transfers of funds and Electronic fund transfers between banks
- Facilitation of standing orders and direct debits, so payments for bills can be made automatically
- Provide overdraft agreements for the temporary advancement of the Bank's own money to meet monthly spending commitments of a customer in their current account.
- Provide Charge card advances of the Bank's own money for customers wishing to settle credit advances monthly.
- Provide a check guaranteed by the Bank itself and prepaid by the customer, such as a cashier's check or certified check.
- Notary service for financial and other documents

Other Types of Bank Services

- *Private banking*; Private banks provide banking services exclusively to high net worth individuals. Many financial services firms require a person or family to have a certain minimum net worth to qualify for private banking services. Private banks often provide more personal services, such as wealth management and tax planning, than normal retail banks.
- *Capital market bank*: Bank that underwrite debt and equity, assist company deals and restructure debt into structured finance products.
- *Bank cards*: Include both credit cards and debit cards. Bank Of America is the largest issuer of bank cards.
- *Credit card machine services and networks*: Companies which provide credit card machine and payment networks call themselves "merchant card providers".

FOREIGN EXCHANGE SERVICES

Foreign exchange services are provided by many banks around the world.

Foreign exchange services include:

- *Currency Exchange*: Where clients can purchase and sell foreign currency banknotes.
- *Wire transfer*: Where clients can send funds to international banks abroad.
- *Foreign Currency Banking*: Banking transactions are done in foreign currency.

INVESTMENT SERVICES

- *Asset management*: The term usually given to describe companies which run collective investment funds.
- *Hedge fund management*: Hedge funds often employ the services of "prime brokerage" divisions at major investment banks to execute their trades.
- *Custody services*: The safe-keeping and processing of the world's securities trades and servicing the

associated portfolios. Assets under custody in the world are approximately $100 trillion.

INSURANCE

- *Insurance brokerage*: Insurance brokers shop for insurance on behalf of customers. Recently a number of websites have been created to give consumers basic price comparisons for services such as insurance, causing controversy within the industry.
- *Insurance underwriting*: Personal lines insurance underwriters actually underwrite insurance for individuals, a service still offered primarily through agents, insurance brokers, and stock brokers. Underwriters may also offer similar commercial lines of coverage for businesses. Activities include insurance and annuities, life insurance, retirement insurance, health insurance, and property and casualty insurance.
- *Reinsurance*: Reinsurance is insurance sold to insurers themselves, to protect them from catastrophic losses.

OTHER FINANCIAL SERVICES

- *Intermediation or advisory services:* These services involve stock brokers and discount brokers. Stock brokers assist investors in buying or selling shares. Primarily internet-based companies are often referred to as discount brokerages, although many now have branch offices to assist clients. These brokerages primarily target individual investors. Full service and private client firms primarily assist and execute trades for clients with large amounts of capital to invest, such as large companies, wealthy individuals, and investment management funds.
- *Private equity*: Private equity funds are typically closed-end funds, which usually take controlling equity stakes in businesses that are either private, or taken private once acquired. Private equity funds often use leveraged buyouts to acquire the firms in

which they invest. The most successful private equity funds can generate returns significantly higher than provided by the equity markets

- Venture capital is a type of private equity capital typically provided by professional, outside investors to new, high-potential-growth companies in the interest of taking the company to an IPO or trade sale of the business.
- *Angel investment*: An angel investor or angel is an affluent individual who provides capital for a business start-up, usually in exchange for convertible debt or ownership equity. A small but increasing number of angel investors organize themselves into angel groups or angel networks to share research and pool their investment capital.
- *Conglomerates*: A financial services conglomerate is a financial services firm that is active in more than one sector of the financial services market e.g. life insurance, general insurance, health insurance, asset management, retail banking, wholesale banking, investment banking, etc. A key rationale for the existence of such businesses is the existence of diversification benefits that are present when different types of businesses are aggregated *i.e.* bad things don't always happen at the same time. As a consequence, economic capital for a conglomerate is usually substantially less than economic capital is for the sum of its parts.

MARKET SHARE

The financial services industry constitutes the largest group of companies in the world in terms of earnings and equity market cap. However it is not the largest category in terms of revenue or number of employees.

It is also a slow growing and extremely fragmented industry, with the largest company, only having a 3% US market share. In contrast, the largest home improvement store in the US, Home Depot, has a 30% market share, and the largest coffee house Starbucks has a 32% market share.

TYPES OF FINANCIAL SERVICES

Financial services encompass a variety of businesses that deal with money management. These include many different kinds of organizations such as banks, investment companies, credit card companies, insurance companies and even government programmes. Financial services can also refer to the services and products that money management organizations offer to the public.

Banks are one kind of financial services organizations. Banks generally function by providing a sheltered and secure place for people to store their money. Usually, banks will invest their clients' stored money for the bank's gain, while paying a small amount of interest to those who keep their money in savings or checking accounts. Banks often provide a variety of financial services, including the issuance of loans, mortgages, checks, and credit cards. Some banks are known as private banks and offer services only to those who have a high net worth. Generally, private banks will offer a broader range of services to their clients than other banks.

Investment services, another type of financial service, generally deals with helping individuals and other entities invest their money in stocks, shares or funds. These services usually offer financial products for investors to buy, such as mutual funds. Usually, money invested with an investment service is managed by the service for the gain of the individual investor or a group of investors. Additionally, they may render professional advice to investors in exchange for payment. Insurance brokers or agents are companies or individuals that are hired to find appropriate insurance plans for their clients. Insurance providers offer plans which are designed to defer liability for the risk of loss from one entity to another in exchange for a predetermined amount.

This makes the second entity, typically an insurance provider, liable for any losses accrued by the first entity, typically an individual or company. Thus, a person will pay a health insurance provider, for example, a recurring fee so that the provider will be responsible for the payment of medical bills should that person fall sick or injured. Credit card companies are financial services companies which provide lines of credit to consumers in exchange for interest paid on the money consumers borrow when they charge a purchase to the card.

The card company pays for the purchase, but it does so by essentially issuing a high-interest loan to the purchaser. Other kinds of financial services include expert advisory services, where a financial expert will offer financial advice to clients, private equity funds, venture capital investors or angel investors.

SECURITIES TRADING

Securities trading financial activity involving transactions of property such as stocks, bonds, commodities, and currency. Although the trading of stocks and bonds dates back several centuries in many Western nations, the development of the securities industry since World War II has been sweeping. The advent of new technologies, particularly in computers and telecommunications, has brought about a new era in securities trading.

Traditional stock exchanges, while still vitally important in major cities around the world, now compete with such over-the-counter trading organizations as the National Association of Securities Dealers Automated Quotations. Nasdaq and other similar systems allow computerized trading, linking investors with brokers and dealers both on a domestic and an international level.

Such systems quote the highest bids and lowest asking prices on all securities, giving investors the opportunity to make optimum deals. In 1986, the London Stock Exchange created a computer-based network similar to Nasdaq with its deregulation move called "Big Bang."

It connected London to a group of international securities dealers, making the city's trading floor largely obsolete. In the United States, such over-the-counter trading was at least partially responsible for the problems associated with programme trading that arose in the 1980s and the collapse of the stock market in Oct., 1987. These events highlighted the weaknesses of computerized networks like Nasdaq. The 1980s were a decade of unprecedented volume and activity in securities trading because of technological innovation and new financial products. Securities fraud, particularly the insider-trading scandal, became a major issue.

Insider trading, or the private trading of securities based on information that has not yet been made public, became an issue in the mid-1980s with the prosecution of such investors as Dennis Levine and Michael Milken. Many contend that securities fraud of this sort has been a result of deregulation of the securities industry since at least the early 1980s, with an attendant relaxation of supervision by the U.S. Securities and Exchange Commission. The 1990s saw a renewed and accelerated effort by the SEC and other regulatory agencies to regulate the securities industry.

ONLINE TRADING

Online Trading has existed amongst people for ages and with the arrival of the internet, online trading is the buzzword of the day. With the internet as a platform it is very easy to trade in the instruments of your choice as and when you want.

Gone are the days when you actually had to make daily rounds of the stock exchange or go to your broker. Now you need not even make any calls but can simply trade as and when you want by the click of a mouse. There are several web sites online that allow you to trade on the stock exchange or the commodity exchange or any other case.

That allow online trading as brokerages and allow you to make your transactions using their web site. As any normal broker would do these web sites would also charge a small brokerage fee on your every transaction.

These days people want to be trading on every thing like stocks trading, commodity trading, currency trading, futures trading as well as on mutual funds and derivatives. Hence there are ample opportunities for people to invest and trade in something that would give you the desired results. The forms of trading can be done though an online brokerage. A key to trading successfully is to have good knowledge about what is happening around you. Yes many people try and predict what the markets are going to do next but every future prediction is based on the present.

And hence having the knowledge of what is happening and how is it going to impact the market is necessary to make good profits. You also need to diversify your investments. Hence you could invest a part of your total portfolio in stocks, another part could be dedicated to currency trading, another part could be used for commodity trading etc.

This is generally done by investors so that if one market or one form of investment is going through a bad phase then other forms of investments will keep the portfolio in balance. While trading it is important to remember that the markets can be a risky proposition and hence not all your wealth or income be dedicated to trading. It is also important to understand that the markets can be volatile at times or at times function in a very unprecedented manner.

And hence at such times it is important to have diversified your investments in order to minimize your losses. If you are not well aware of trading then do not worry for trading is no rocket science and definitely online trading is very simple to understand. This web site will tell you about the various online web sites where you can make an online trading account. Also the web site will throw light on what the different forms of online trading are.

DEMAT AND REMAT

The term Demat, in India, refers to a dematerialised account. For individual Indian citizens to trade in listed stocks or debentures. The Securities Exchange Board of India requires the investor to maintain a Demat account. In a demat account shares and securities are held in electronic form instead of taking actual possession of certificates.

A Demat Account is opened by the investor while registering with an investment broker. The Demat account number which is quoted for all transactions to enable electronic settlements of trades to take place. Access to the demat account requires an internet password and a transaction password as well as initiating and confirming transfers or purchases of securities. Purchases and sales of securities on the Demat account are automatically made once transactions are executed and completed.

ADVANTAGES OF DEMAT

The demat account reduces brokerage charges, makes pledging/hypothecation of shares easier, enables quick ownership of securities on settlement resulting in increased liquidity, avoids confusion in the ownership title of securities, and provides easy receipt of public issue allotments.

It also helps you avoid bad deliveries caused by signature mismatch, postal delays and loss of certificates in transit. Further, it eliminates risks associated with forgery, counterfeiting and loss due to fire, theft or mutilation. Demat account holders can also avoid stamp duty avoid filling up of transfer deeds, and obtain quick receipt of such benefits as stock splits and bonuses.

INDIAN MARKET SCENARIO

Indian capital market has seen unprecedented boom in its activity in the last 15 years in terms of number of stock exchanges, listed companies, trade volumes, market intermediaries, investor population, etc. However, this surge in activity has brought with it numerous problems that threaten the very survival of the capital markets in the long run, most of which are due to the large volume of paper work involved and paper based trading, clearing and settlement.

Until the late eighties, the common man kept away from capital market and thus the quantum of funds mobilized through the market was meager. A major problem, however, continued to plague the market. The Indian markets were drowned in shares in the form of paper and hence it was problematic to handle them. Fake and stolen shares, fake signatures and signature mismatch, duplication and mutilation of shares, transfer problems, etc. The investors were scared and were under compensated for the risk borne by them. The century old system of trading and settlement requires handling of huge volumes of paper work. This has made the investors, both retail and institutional, wary of entering the capital market. However, lack of modernization become a hindrance to growth and resulted in creation of cumbersome procedures and paper work.

However, the real growth and change occurred from mid-eighties in the wake of liberalization initiatives of the Government. The reforms in the financial sector were envisaged in the banking sector, capital market, securities market regulation, mutual funds, foreign investments and Government control.

These institutions and stock exchanges experienced that the certificates are the main cause of investors' disputes and arbitration cases. Since the paper work was not matching the rapid growth so there was a need for a better system to ensure removal of these impediments.

Government of India decided to set up a fully automated and high technology based model exchange that could offer screen-based trading and depositories as the ultimate answer to all such reforms and eliminate various bottlenecks in the capital market, particularly, the clearing and settlement system in stock exchanges.

A depository in very simple terms is a pool of pre-verified shares held in electronic mode which offers settlement of transactions in an efficient and effective way.

OBJECT OF DEMAT SYSTEM

India has adopted this system in which book entry is done electronically. It is the system where no paper is involved. Physical form is extinguished and shares or securities are held in electronic mode. Before the introduction of the depository system by the Depository Act, 1996, the process of sale, purchase and transfer of shares was a huge problem and the safety perspective was zero.

DEMAT CONVERSION

Converting physical holding into electronic holding. In order to dematerialise physical securities one has to fill in a

DRF which is available with the DP and submit the same along with physical certificates one wishes to dematerialise.

Separate DRF has to be filled for each ISIN Number:

- Surrender certificates for dematerialisation to your depository participant.
- Depository participant intimates Depository of the request through the system.
  - Depository participant submits the certificates to the registrar of the Issuer Company.
  - Registrar confirms the dematerialisation request from depository.
- After dematerialising the certificates, Registrar updates accounts and informs depository of the completion of dematerialisation.
- Depository updates its accounts and informs the depository participant.
- Depository participant updates the demat account of the investor.

DEMAT OPTIONS

Banks score over others Around 200 "depository participants" offer the demat account facility. A comparison of the fees charged by different DPs. But there are three distinct advantages of having a demat account with a bank — quick processing, accessibility and online transaction. Generally, banks credit your demat account with shares in case of purchase, or credit your savings accounts with the proceeds of a sale on the third day.

Banks are also advantageous because of the number of branches they have. Some banks give the option of opening a demat account in any branch, while others restrict themselves to a select set of branches.

Some private banks also provide online access to the demat account. So, you can check on your holdings, transactions and status of requests through the net banking facility. A broker who acts as a DP may not be able to provide these services.

FEES INVOLVED

There are four major charges usually levied on a demat account: Account opening fee, annual maintenance fee, custodian fee and transaction fee. All the charges vary from DP to DP.

Account-opening Fee

Depending on the DP, there may or may not be an opening account fee. Private banks, such as ICICI Bank, HDFC Bank and UTI Bank, do not have one. However, players such as Globe Capital, Karvy Consultants and the State Bank of India do so.

But most players levy this when you re-open a demat account, though the Stock Holding Corporation offers a lifetime account opening fee, which allows you to hold on to your demat account over a long period. This fee is refundable.

Annual Maintenance Fee

This is also known as folio maintenance charges, and is generally levied in advance.

Custodian Fee

This fee is charged monthly and depends on the number of securities held in the account. It generally ranges between Rs 0.5 to Rs 1 per ISIN per month. DPs will not charge custody fee for ISIN on which the companies have paid one-time custody charges to the depository.

Transaction Fee

The transaction fee is charged for crediting/debiting securities to and from the account on a monthly basis. While some DPs, such as SBI, charge a flat fee per transaction, HDFC Bank and ICICI Bank peg the fee to the transaction value, subject to a minimum amount. The fee also differs based on the kind of transaction. Some DPs charge only for debiting the securities while others charge for both. The DPs also charge if your instruction to buy/sell fails or is rejected. In addition, service tax is also charged by the DPs.

In addition to the other fees, the DP also charges a fee for converting the shares from the physical to the electronic form or vice-versa. This fee varies for both demat and remat requests. For demat, some DPs charge a flat fee per request in addition to the variable fee per certificate, while others charge only the variable fee.

For instance, Stock Holding Corporation charges Rs 25 as the request fee and Rs 3 per certificate as the variable fee. However, SBI charges only the variable fee, which is Rs 3 per certificate. Remat requests also have charges akin to that of demat. However, variable charges for remat are generally higher than demat.

Some of the additional features are as follows.Some DPs offer a frequent trader account, where they charge frequent traders at lower rates than the standard charges.Demat account holders are generally required to pay the DP an advance fee for each account which will be adjusted against the various service charges. The account holder needs to raise the balance when it falls a certain amount prescribed by the DP.

However, if you also hold a savings account with the DP you can provide a debit authorisation to the DP for paying this charge.Finally, once you choose your DP, it will be prudent to keep all your accounts with that DP, so that tracking your capital gains liability is easier. This is because, for calculating capital gains tax, the period of holding will be determined by the DP and different DPs follow different methods.

For instance, ICICI Bank uses the first in first out method to compute the period of holding. The proof of the cost of acquisition will be the contract note. The computation of capital gains is done account-wise.

OPENING AN ACCOUNT

Steps involved in opening a demat account First an investor has to approach a DP and fill up an account opening form. The account opening form must be supported by copies of any one of the approved documents to serve as proof of identity and proof of address as specified by SEBI. Besides, production of PAN card in original at the time of opening of account has been made mandatory effective from April 1, 2006. All applicants should carry original documents for verification by an authorized official of the depository participant, under his signature. Further, the investor has to sign an agreement with DP in a depository prescribed standard format, which details rights and duties of investor and DP.

DP should provide the investor with a copy of the agreement and schedule of charges for their future reference. The DP will open the account in the system and give an account number, which is also called BO ID. The DP may revise the charges by giving 30 days notice in advance. SEBI has rationalised the cost structure for dematerialisation by removing account opening charges, transaction charges for credit of securities, and custody charges vide circular dated January 28, 2005.

Further, SEBI has vide circular dated November 9, 2005 advised that with effect from January 9, 2006, no charges shall be levied by a depository on DP and consequently, by a DP on a Beneficiary Owner when a BO transfers all the securities lying in his account to another branch of the same DP or to another DP of the same depository or another depository, provided the BO Account/s at transferee DP and at transferor DP are one and the same, *i.e.* identical in all respects. In case the BO Account at transferor DP is a joint account, the BO Account at transferee DP should also be a joint account in the same sequence of ownership.

DISADVANTAGES OF DEMAT

The disadvantages of dematerialization of securities can be summarised as follows:

- Trading in securities may become uncontrolled in case of dematerialized securities.
- It is incumbent upon the capital market regulator to keep a close watch on the trading in dematerialized securities. The role of key market players in case of dematerialized securities, such as stock-brokers, needs to be supervised as they have the capability of manipulating the market.

- Multiple regulatory frameworks have to be confirmed to, including the Depositories Act, Regulations and the various By-Laws of various depositories.
- Additionally, agreements are entered at various levels in the process of dematerialization. These may cause anxiety to the investor desirous of simplicity in terms of transactions in dematerialized securities.

However, the advantages of dematerialization outweigh its disadvantages and the changes ushered in by SEBI and the Central Government in terms of compulsory dematerialization of securities is important for developing the securities market to a degree of advancement. Freely traded securities are an essential component of such an advanced market and dematerialization addresses such issues and is a step towards the advancement of the market.

2

Depository

INTRODUCTION

A Depository is an organisation which holds investors' securities in electronic form. The depository also provides services related to various transactions in such securities. A depository interfaces with its investors through Depository Participants.

Depository Participants maintain investors' accounts which are similar to Savings Bank/Current accounts with a Bank. Purchase and sale of securities can be done through demat account. Presently there are two depositories in India viz., NSDL and CDSL.

DEPOSITORY PARTICIPANT

In India, a Depository Participant is described as an agent of the depository. They are the intermediaries between the depository and the investors. The relationship between the DPs and the depository is governed by an agreement made between the two under the Depositories Act. In a strictly legal sense, a DP is an entity who is registered as such with SEBI under the provisions of the SEBI Act.

As per the provisions of this Act, a DP can offer depository-related services only after cbtaining a certificate of registration from SEBI. SEBI Regulations, 1996 prescribe a minimum net worth of Rs. 50 lakh for stockbrokers, R&T agents and non-banking finance companies, he should comply with the specified net worth criterion separately for each such depository. No minimum net worth criterion has been prescribed for other categories of DPs; however, depositories can fix a higher net worth criterion for their DPs.

BASICS OF DEPOSITORY

Depository is an institution or a kind of organization which holds securities with it, in which trading is done among shares, debentures, mutual funds, derivatives, F&O and commodities. The intermediatories perform its actions in various kinds of securities at Depository on the behalf of its clients. These intermediatories are called Dipositories Participants. There are basically two kinds of depositories in India. One is the National Securities Depository Limited and the other is the Central Depository Service Limited. Every Depository Participant needs to be registered under this Depository before starting operation or trade in the market.

BENEFITS OF DEPOSITORY

- Bad delivery eliminated
- Immediate transfer of shares
- No stamp duty on such transfers
- Elimination of risks that are normally associated in dealing with Physical certificates - loss/ theft/ mutilation due to careless handling/ forgery/ etc.
- Reduced transaction cost

HOW DO DEPOSITORY OPERATE

Depository interacts with its clients/ investors through its agents, called Depository Participants normally known as DPs.

For any investor/ client, to avail the services provided by the Depository, has to open Depository account, known as Demat A/c, with any of the DPs.

Demat Account Opening

A demat account is opened on the same lines as that of a Bank Account. Prescribed Account opening forms are available with the DP, needs to be filled in. Standard Agreements are to be signed by the Client and the DP, which details the rights and obligations of both parties. Along with the form the client requires to attach Photographs of Account holder, Attested copies of proof of residence and proof of identity needs to be submitted along with the account opening form.

In case of Corporate clients, additional attachments required are - true copy of the resolution for Demat a/c opening along with signatories to operate the account and true copy of the Memorandum and Articles of Association is to be attached.

SERVICES PROVIDED BY DEPOSITORY

- Dematerialisation is converting physical certificates to electronic form
- Rematerialisation, known as remat, is reverse of demat, *i.e.* getting physical certificates from the electronic securities
- Transfer of securities, change of beneficial ownership
- Settlement of trades done on exchange connected to the Depository

NO. OF DEPOSITORY IN THE COUNTRY

Currently there are two depositories operational in the country:

1. National Securities Depository Ltd. - NSDL - Having 95 Cr. Demat A/c as on 31-03-2010 - 300 DPs in India
2. Central Depository Services Ltd. - CDSL - Having 65 laks Demat A/c as on 31-03-2010 - 500 DPs in India

DEPOSITORY SYSTEM

The traditional system of dealing in shares involves dealing in Share Certificates with enormous paper work, getting the certificate duly endorsed in the buyer's name which is complex, time consuming and also involves various problems not only of bad deliveries of shares but also loss of share certificates in transit.

In the Depository System, the securities of a Shareholder are held in the electronic form by conversion of physical securities to electronic form through a process called 'dematerialisation' of share certificates and facilitates transactions electronically without involving any share certificate or transfer deed.

Here the transfer of securities takes place by means of electronic book entries.

The Depository system provides various other direct and indirect benefits as under:

- Bad deliveries are almost eliminated.
- The risks associated with physical certificates such as loss, theft, mutilation of certificate etc. are eliminated.
- It eliminates handling of huge volumes of paper work involved in filling in transfer deeds and lodging the transfer documents and Share Certificates with the Company.
- There will be immediate transfer and registration of your shares and you need not have to suffer delays on account of processing time.
- It leads to faster settlement cycle and faster realisation of sale proceeds.
- There will be a faster disbursement of Corporate benefits like Rights, Bonus etc.
- The stamp duty on transfer of securities, which is 0.25% of the consideration on transfer of shares in physical form is not applicable and you may incur expenditure towards service charges of the Depository Participant.
- There could be a reduction in rates of interest on loans granted against pledge of dematerialised securities by various banks.
- There could be reduction in brokerage for trading in dematerialised securities.
- There could be reduction in transaction costs in dematerialised securities as compared to physical securities.
- Availability of periodical status report to investors on their holding and transactions.

SEBI has initially prescribed that Financial Institutions, FIIs etc. have to deal with BPC shares only in dematerialised form, from 1-6-1998. SEBI has later prescribed that all settlements of trades done on Stock Exchanges in BPC shares must be in dematerialised form. However, the option to investors to hold the shares in physical form will continue. Depository system is playing a significant role in stock markets around the world and hence has become popular and prevalent in many advanced countries.

In India the National Securities Depository Ltd., promoted by Industrial Development Bank of India, Unit Trust of India, National Stock Exchange is the first depository and Central Depository Services Ltd, promoted by The Stock Exchange, Mumbai and Bank of India is another depository.

Investors have choice of two depositories now:

- National Securities Depository Ltd.
- Central Depository Services(I) Ltd

CONSTITUENTS OF DEPOSITORY SYSTEM

- Depository
- Depository Participants
- Share Registrar/Issuers
- Investor
- Clearing Corporation/Member

ROLE OF DEPOSITORY

The Depository performs its functions through a network of Depository Participants who interact with the Clearing Members and Investor.

The Depository carries out following functions through its participants:

- Enabling the surrender and withdrawal of securities through the process of demat and remat to and from the depository system,
- Maintaining investors' holdings in the electronic form through computers,
- Effecting settlement of securities traded on the stock exchanges.
- Carrying out settlement of "off market trades"
- Advising periodically to the Share Registrar/ Issuer about the beneficial owners of the securities.

ROLE OF DEPOSITORY PARTICIPANTS

Similar to brokers, who on behalf of a client in the stock market, a Depository Participant is your representative in the depository system. Financial Institutions/ Banks/ Custodian/ Stock Brokers etc. can become DPs provided they meet the necessary requirements and guidelines prescribed by SEBI. DP serves as a link between the investor and the Company through NSDL/ CDSL for dematerialisation of shares and other electronic transactions.

DP provides various services with regard to your holdings such as:

- Maintaining the securities account balances
- Enabling surrender and withdrawal of your securities to and from the depository.
- Delivering and receiving shares in your account on your instructions. Hence, shares bought by you on a stock exchange can be received directly in you account and similarly those sold by you can be delivered on your instructions.
- Keeping you updated with regard to status of your holdings periodically.

In the Depository System, BPC cannot entertain a demat request from you directly. You have to initiate the process only through a DP.

DEMATERIALISATION

Dematerialisation is a process by which your share certificates are taken back by BPC through your DP, checked and if found in order, demat is confirmed by BPC and then an equivalent number of shares are credited to your account held by DP in electronic form. The entire process of dematerialisation of share is required to be completed within a period of 15 days.

FUNCTIONING OF DEPOSITORY SYSTEM

OPERATIONS

The operation in a depository system is similar to the operation of money account in the Banking system. Like a bank transaction, share certificates are deposited in a depository and individual account is opened with the shares for which certificates are deposited. If anyone wishes to utilise the services offered by a depository, he has to open an account with the depository through a 'Depository Participant'. The Shareholder can transfer the shares between accounts without handling share certificates. It also leads to safekeeping of securities.

COSTS

Depending upon the services rendered by each Depository, the investors have to pay the charges for the services like account opening, account maintenance charges, transactions charges and custody charges etc. These charges differ between Depository Participants to Depository Participants and from Depository system also. Investors have to identify their own DP for their transactions of Dematerialisation.

HOW DO WE DEMATERIALISE ARE SHARES?

Activities involved in the Depository System are as under:

- Contact a DP of your choice to open an account.
- Make an application in a Dematerialisation Request Form alongwith the relevant share certificates. The DP will accept certificates registered only in your name.
- On receipt of DRF alongwith the original share certificates, the DP will send an electronic request to BPCs R&T Agent, through the Depository for confirmation of demat and simultaneously surrender your DRF and share certificates.
- BPCs R&T Agent is linked with the NSDL/ CDSL network though a V-sat connection. Your DP's request for demat is electronically received by BPCs R&T Agent through NSDL/ CDSL..
- When BPCs R&T Agent physically receives the DRF and your share certificates, it is verified and demat is confirmed to the Depository.
- The Depository will further confirm the demat to your DP.

- Your account will be credited by DP with the number of shares so dematerialised and the process is completed. On opening account, you will get an identification number called 'Client ID'. It serves as a reference for all your transactions with the DP. Thereafter you will hold the shares in the electronic form. You can get a statement of holdings and updation of your account after each transaction from your DP.
- When you open an account with a DP, you can buy or sell shares in electronic form without any paperwork and without payment of any stamp duty as in the case of traditional scrip-based transactions. You will be required to pay some charges for services offered by the DP. Hence it is advisable to get full details of service charges from the DP with whom you wish to open an account.
- You can now trade in depository mode through any broker registered with the National Stock Exchange and Stock Exchange, Mumbai but the necessary details of your account with the DP should be provided by you.
- In case of Public Issue, the applicant can specify the manner in which he wishes to receive his allotment. *I.e.,* in the form of physical certificates or in the electronic form. The Application Form will have a provision for this option. If you prefer to receive it in the electronic mode, you should mention your account number, name of your DP and Client ID number, so that it will be possible for you to receive allotment of shares directly into your account. In case of Public Issue of any security of issue size of Rs. 10 crore or more, security shall be issued only in dematerialized form.

FACILITIES UNDER DEPOSITORY SYSTEM

PLEDGING AND HYPOTHECATION FACILITIES

It is possible to pledge/hypothecate your share in electronic form by making an application to your DP. Similarly, you can also request for closure of pledge/ hypothecation. You can obtain the necessary details regarding pledge/ hypothecation from your DP.

FREEZING/LOCKING OF INVESTOR ACCOUNTS

If as a security measure, you desire to freeze/lock your account for any given period of time, you can advise your DP who shall take necessary action to freeze your account until further instruction from you.

RECEIPT OF CORPORATE BENEFITS

In order to enable the Company to calculate the benefits arising out of your holdings, the Depositories provides the download of beneficiary position, as on a given day to BPCs R&T Agent. For Example, if BPC announces dividend, NSDL/ CDSL will provide the download of beneficiary position with reference to the record date/book closure date and BPC will disburse the dividend to such Shareholder directly.

In case of Right/Bonus issue the distribution of share entitlements will be made in electronic form by NSDL/ CDSL based on the information provided by BPCs R&T Agent. Hence Shareholders will be given the option of receiving their share entitlements in the form of Physical Certificates or in the Electronic form with the Depositories.

BENEFITS OF DEPOSITORY SYSTEM

In the depository system, the ownership and transfer of securities takes place by means of electronic book entries. At the outset, this system rids the capital market of the dangers related to handling of paper.

NSDL provides numerous direct and indirect benefits like:

- Elimination of bad deliveries In the depository environment, once holdings of an investor are dematerialised, the question of bad delivery does not arise *i.e.* they cannot be held "under objection". In the physical environment, buyer was required to take the risk of transfer and face uncertainty of the quality of assets purchased. In a depository environment good money certainly begets good quality of assets.

- Elimination of all risks associated with physical certificates- Dealing in physical securities have associated security risks of theft of stocks, mutilation of certificates, loss of certificates during movements through and from the registrars, thus exposing the investor to the cost of obtaining duplicate certificates etc. This problem does not arise in the depository environment.
- No stamp duty for transfer of any kind of securities in the depository. This waiver extends to equity shares, debt instruments and units of mutual funds.
- Immediate transfer and registration of securities - In the depository environment, once the securities are credited to the investors account on pay out, he becomes the legal owner of the securities. There is no further need to send it to the company's registrar for registration. Having purchased securities in the physical environment, the investor has to send it to the company's registrar so that the change of ownership can be registered. This process usually takes around three to four months and is rarely completed within the statutory framework of two months thus exposing the investor to opportunity cost of delay in transfer and to risk of loss in transit. To overcome this, the normally accepted practice is to hold the securities in street names *i.e.* not to register the change of ownership. However, if the investors miss a book closure the securities are not good for delivery and the investor would also stand to loose his corporate entitlements.
- Faster settlement cycle - The settlement cycle follow rolling settlement on T+2 basis *i.e.* the settlement of trades will be on the 2nd working day from the trade day. This will enable faster turnover of stock and more liquidity with the investor.
- Faster disbursement of non cash corporate benefits

like rights, bonus, etc. - NSDL provides for direct credit of non cash corporate entitlements to an investors account, thereby ensuring faster disbursement and avoiding risk of loss of certificates in transit.

- Reduction in brokerage by many brokers for trading in dematerialised securities Brokers provide this benefit to investors as dealing in dematerialised securities reduces their back office cost of handling paper and also eliminates the risk of being the introducing broker.
- Reduction in handling of huge volumes of paper
- periodic status reports to investors on their holdings and transactions, leading to better controls.
- Elimination of problems related to change of address of investor - In case of change of address, investors are saved from undergoing the entire change procedure with each company or registrar. Investors have to only inform their DP with all relevant documents and the required changes are effected in the database of all the companies, where the investor is a registered holder of securities.
- Elimination of problems related to transmission of demat shares - In case of dematerialised holdings, the process of transmission is more convenient as the transmission formalities for all securities held in a demat account can be completed by submitting documents to the DP whereas, in case of physical securities the surviving joint holder(s)/legal heirs/ nominee has to correspond independently with each company in which shares are held.
- Elimination of problems related to selling securities on behalf of a minor - A natural guardian is not required to take court approval for selling demat securities on behalf of a minor.
- Ease in portfolio monitoring since statement of account gives a consolidated position of investments in all instruments.

SAFETY IN DEPOSITORY SYSTEM

There are various checks and measures in the depository system to ensure safety of the investor holdings.

These include:

- A DP can be operational only after registration by SEBI, which is based on the recommendation from NSDL and their own independent evaluation. SEBI has prescribed criteria for becoming a DP in the regulations.
- DPs are allowed to effect any debit and credit to an account only on the basis of valid instruction from the client.
- Every day, there is a system driven mandatory reconciliation between DP and NSDL.
- All transactions are recorded at NSDL Central System and in the databases maintained by business partners.
- There are periodic inspections into the activities of both DP and R&T agent by NSDL. This also includes records based on which the debit/credit are effected.
- All investors have a right to receive their statement of accounts periodically from the DP.
- Every month NSDL forwards statement of account to a random sample of investors as a counter check.
- In the depository, the depository holds the investor accounts on trust. Therefore, if the DP goes bankrupt the creditors of the DP will have no access to the holdings in the name of the clients of the DP. These investors can transfer their holdings to an account held with another DP.
- The data interchange between NSDL and its business partners is protected by protection measures of international standards such as encryption hardware lock. The protection measures adopted by NSDL are more than what is prescribed in the SEBI Regulations.
- *Freeze Facility*: A depository account holder may freeze securities lying in the account for as long as

the account holder wants it. By freezing the account, account holder can prevent unexpected debits or credits or both, creeping into its account. The following types of freeze facility available in the NSDL system may be availed of by submitting freeze instruction to the DP in the prescribed form.

- Freeze for debits only
- Freeze for debits as well as credits
- Freeze a particular ISIN in the account
- Freeze a specific number of securities held under an ISIN in an account

- *Certification in Depository Operations:* NSDL has introduced a Certification Programme in Depository Operations, and it has been made compulsory for all DPs to appoint a person qualified in this certification in each of its branches. This way, NSDL wants to ensure that each branch of a DP that services investors has atleast one person who has thorough knowledge about depository system.
- *Insurance Cover*: NSDL has taken a comprehensive insurance policy to help DP to indemnifying investors for the loss accrued to them due to errors, omissions, commission or negligence of DP.
- *Computer and communication infrastructure*: NSDL and its business partners use hardware, software and communication systems, which conform to industry standards. Further, the systems are accepted by NSDL only after a rigorous testing procedure. NSDL's central system comprises an IBM mainframe system with a back-up facility and a remote disaster back-up site.
- *Machine level back-up*: The IBM mainframe in which the data is processed has adequate redundancy built into its configuration. There is a standby central processing unit to which processing can be switched over to in case of main system CPU failure. The disk has RAID implementation, which ensures that a failure of hard disk will not lead to loss in data.

System has spare disk configuration where data is automatically copied from the main disk upon encountering the first failure.All network components like router, communication controllers etc., have on-line redundancy and thus a failure does not result in loss of transaction. Disaster back up site: A disaster back up site equipped with a computer identical to the mainframe computer and computing resources has been set up at a distant location about 175 km away from Mumbai. The depository operations are often switched between the computing resources at Mumbai office and disaster back up site to ensure that the disaster site is always operational.Back-up in case of power failure: Continuity in power supply to the main systems is assured by providing for;

- Dual uninterrupted power supply for IBM-Mainframe and related components wherein the two UPSs are connected in tandem. In case of failure of primary UPS, the secondary UPS takes over instantaneously and thus, there is no interruption in operation, and
- Back-up diesel generator sets.

- *Periodic Review*: The NSDL hardware, software and communication systems are continuously reviewed in order to make them more secure and adequate for the size of business. These reviews are a part of an ongoing exercise wherein security considerations are given as much importance as operational efficiency.

DEPOSITORY SYSTEM IN INDIA

India has adopted the Depository System for securities trading in which book entry is done electronically and no paper is involved.

The physical form of securities is extinguished and shares or securities are held in an electronic form. Before the introduction of the depository system through the Depository

Act, 1996, the process of sale, purchase and transfer of securities was a huge problem, and there was no safety at all.

KEY FEATURES OF THE DEPOSITORY SYSTEM IN INDIA

- *Multi-Depository System*: The depository model adopted in India provides for a competitive multi-depository system. There can be various entities providing depository services. A depository should be a company formed under the Company Act, 1956 and should have been granted a certificate of registration under the Securities and Exchange Board of India Act, 1992. Presently, there are two depositories registered with SEBI, namely:
  - National Securities Depository Limited, and
  - Central Depository Service Limited.
- *Depository services through depository participants*: The depositories can provide their services to investors through their agents called depository participants. These agents are appointed subject to the conditions prescribed under Securities and Exchange Board of India Regulations, 1996 and other applicable conditions.
- *Dematerialisation*: The model adopted in India provides for dematerialisation of securities. This is a significant step in the direction of achieving a completely paper-free securities market. Dematerialization is a process by which physical certificates of an investor are converted into electronic form and credited to the account of the depository participant.
- *Fungibility*: The securities held in dematerialized form do not bear any notable feature like distinctive number, folio number or certificate number. Once shares get dematerialized, they lose their identity in terms of share certificate distinctive numbers and folio numbers. Thus all securities in the same class are identical and interchangeable. For example, all

equity shares in the class of fully paid up shares are interchangeable.

- *Registered Owner/ Beneficial Owner*: In the depository system, the ownership of securities dematerialized is bifurcated between Registered Owner and Beneficial Owner. The Depositories Act, 'Registered Owner' means a depository whose name is entered as such in the register of the issuer. A 'Beneficial Owner' means a person whose name is recorded as such with the depository. Though the securities are registered in the name of the depository actually holding them, the rights, benefits and liabilities in respect of the securities held by the depository remain with the beneficial owner. For the securities dematerialized, NSDL/CDSL is the Registered Owner in the books of the issuer; but ownership rights and liabilities rest with Beneficial Owner. All the rights, duties and liabilities underlying the security are on the beneficial owner of the security.
- *Free Transferability of shares*: Transfer of shares held in dematerialized form takes place freely through electronic book-entry system.

SEBI REGULATIONS

As in the case of FIIs, SEBI's primary role in the venture capital fund is envisaged as of a facilitator for growth rather than that of a regulator. SEBI Regulations should encourage more venture capital investments in a hassle free manner. The multiplicity of regulations, as far as possible, should be avoided and one set of regulatory guidelines may be issued under the aegis of one nodal agency for interface with the venture capital investors which could be SEBI.

SEBI Regulations should focus more on adequate disclosure as investors in venture capital activities are institutions or high networth individuals who are expected to have the capability of taking an informed decision based on the disclosures. The regulatory requirement of seeking approval of the placement memorandum from SEBI may be dispensed with by strengthening the disclosure requirements. The SEBI Regulations also provide in the case of a VCF incorporated as a trust for compulsory registration of instrument of trust under the Indian Registration Act. As per the provisions of Indian Registration Act, the registration of trust document is optional. There are operational problems in the case of existing VCFs to register the document of trust after lapse of four months period.

It should be left to the choice of the applicant whether to register the trust document and there should not be any compulsion for registration of documents under the Indian Registration Act under the SEBI Regulation. The venture capital activity is in nascent stage in India as of today and many dimensions of it are still to be unfolded. SEBI Regulations therefore should not curtail the flexibility of investment by a VCF.

The present regulatory framework permits the investment by VCF in sick industrial undertaking needs a review. There are various agencies who are engaged in restructuring, financing to sick industries and there is no acute necessity for venture capital funds to invest mainly in sick industrial undertakings.

The VCF should focus on investment in green shoe high technology oriented, knowledge based, research oriented industries, however, VCFs may also be provided flexibility to participate in the restructuring process of sick industries as and when required.

RECOMMENDATIONS

The following amendments are recommended under the existing SEBI Venture Capital Regulations:

- The definition of VCF should be amended to include any other structures and also the funds set up, scheme floated by a trust, company, body corporate or other legal entities.
- The Regulation should make provisions for registration of Foreign Venture Capital Investors.
- The investment criteria needs to be redefined to

permit investment by VCF primarily in equity or equity related instruments or securities convertible into equity of VCUs and also by way of subscription to IPO and preferential offer in case of companies to be listed or already listed. The limit of atleast 80% of the funds raised by the VCF may be dispensed with and new investment criteria as dealt under the heading Investment related issues may be incorporated.

- The relaxations for venture capital undertaking/funds under SEBI Takeover Code and SEBI guidelines as dealt under the heading of Exit related issues may also be incorporated.
- The provision for investment in sick companies and financial assistance in any other manner may be dispensed with.
- The existing provisions for approval of placement memorandum by SEBI may be dispensed with but the content of placement memorandum may be strengthened to include all the significant information necessary for an investor to arrive at a fair decision.
- SEBI regulations should be amended to dispense with the requirement of registration of the instrument of trust under the Indian Registration Act.

3

Mutual Funds

CONCEPT

A mutual fund is a professionally managed investment company that combines the money of many individuals and invests this "pooled" money in a wide variety of different securities. It is by pooling the money of many individuals that mutual funds are able to provide the diversification and money management that were once reserved only for the wealthy. Professional money managers take this pool of money and invest it in a wide variety of stocks, bonds, or other securities depending on the investment objective, or goal, of the particular fund. It is the investment objective of the fund that guides the manager in selecting the various securities for the fund.It is the investment objective of the mutual fund that also guides the investor on which funds to invest in.

Since different investors have different objectives, there are a number of different kinds of mutual funds, *i.e.,* some mutual funds may provide monthly income while others seek long-term capital appreciation. Mutual funds can be classified according to their investment objective. Some of the classifications include money market funds, growth funds, balanced funds, income funds, and many others. As suggested, discuss the many different types of funds and their characteristics elsewhere on this website.

HOW TO PROFIT WITH MUTUAL FUNDS

When you invest in a mutual fund you hope that the value will rise and you can eventually sell your shares for a profit.

This is one of the ways you can profit with mutual funds. Another way is through capital gains. When a mutual fund sells a security for a higher price than it originally paid for it, it is known as a capital gain.

Most mutual funds distribute their capital gains to shareholders at least annually, some more often. The last way to profit with mutual funds is with dividends or interest. If the fund has invested in bonds or dividend-paying stocks, it must pass the dividends or interest earned on to its shareholders. Like capital gains, this is done at least annually.

NET ASSET VALUE (NAV)

When you invest your money in a mutual fund, you buy shares in that fund. To determine the price of those shares, each day the fund adds up the total value of the securities held in its portfolio. This total is divided by the number of shares outstanding.

To find out the value of your holdings, you simply multiply the number of shares you own by the net asset value. The NAV of most funds is listed in most daily newspapers. The NAV will change daily depending on how well the underlying securities of the fund perform. If the securities held by the fund go up in value so will the value of your shares.

OPEN END AND CLOSED END MUTUAL FUNDS

Mutual funds are generally classified The investment objective of the fund. They are also classified just as to how they are bought and sold. There are open- or closed-end funds and there are load or no-load funds.

An open-end mutual fund is a mutual fund that continuously issues new shares as needed and buys them back when investors wish to sell. There is no limit to how many shares an open-end fund can sell. The buy and sell price is based on the net asset value of the fund. The majority of mutual funds on the market today are open-end fûnds and are the type we are concerned with in this tutorial. The characteristics of a closed-end mutual fund more closely resemble that of an individual stock. A closed-end fund is a mutual fund that issues a fixed number of shares which are then traded on a stock exchange or over the counter. Although the underlying value of the securities in a closed-end fund may be, for example, $10.00 per share, they may sell for more or less depending on investors outlook for the future value of the securities.

LOAD FUNDS VS NO-LOAD FUNDS

Load funds are simply mutual funds with a sales charge, or load. Load funds are generally sold by stockbrokers, financial planners, or other financial salespeople who charge you a commission every time you buy new shares. Under rules set by the National Association of Securities Dealers, the maximum charge or load allowed is 8.5% which is deducted from the amount of your investment.

On a $1,000 investment, for example, you are really beginning with just $915.00. The difference goes to the salesperson who sold you the shares. This is known as a front-end load. There may also be a fee charged when you redeem, or sell, your shares. This fee, known as a back-end load, may be the only charge or it may be in addition to the front-end load. No-load funds are mutual funds with no sales charge. They are generally bought directly from the fund.

100% of your money is invested in shares of the particular fund. Similar to no-load funds are funds known as low-load funds. These are funds with a load of between 1% and 3% and are bought either directly from the fund or through financial salespeople. One other fee to be aware of is the so-called 12b-1 fee. This regulation allows mutual funds to charge up to 1.25% of their net asset value to pay for such things as advertising and marketing expenses. If a fund charges 12b-1 fees it must be stated in the prospectus.

In this tutorial we are only concerned with open-end mutual funds. This author further suggests learning all you can about mutual funds and sticking with no-load or low-load mutual funds. There is no evidence that load funds perform better than no-load funds. Unless you need help in selecting a fund, go with a no-load fund and save the sales charge. Over time that "small" fee can mean many thousands of dollars to you. Let's look at an example:

Let's assume you invest $10,000 in each of two funds, one a no-load fund and the other a load fund with an 8.5% load. Let's further assume both funds earn an identical 15% average annual return. After 5 years, the no-load fund would outperform the load fund by $1,710; after 10 years, $3,439; and after 20 years the no-load fund would outperform the load fund by $13,911 – more than your original total investment!

$10,000 invested:

15% average annual total return:

	No-Load	Load	Difference
5 Years	20,114	18,404	1,710
10 Years	40,456	37,017	3,439
20 Years	163,665	149,754	13,911

It does pay to stay with no-load or low-load funds. In *Introduction to Mutual Funds,* we have described what a mutual fund is and how they are classified according to their investment objective. We have shown the three ways you can profit with mutual funds. We have also described the charges a mutual fund can levy and why it may be best to stick with no-load or low-load funds.

HISTORY OF MUTUAL FUNDS

The concept of mutual funds originated in England. British and Scottish investment companies helped finance the American economy after the Civil War. They did so by investing in farm mortgages, railroads, and other industrial companies. The first modern, open-end investment company was Massachusetts Investors Trust founded in 1924.

Many other funds followed until the stock market crash of 1929. Many of these first funds were highly leveraged and when the market crashed – they crashed hard. The Securites and Exchange Commission, the average dollar invested in these leveraged funds in July of 1929 was worth only $.05 by the end of 1937.

Because of the abuses that occurred in the stock market during the 1920s, several major legislative acts were enacted. Among them were the Securities Act of 1933, the Securities Exchange Act of 1934, the Investment Advisers Act of 1940, and the Investment Company Act of 1940. In addition to the federal statutes, most states have adopted their own regulations governing mutual funds.

These laws require, among other things, that a mutual fund be registered with the SEC and meet certain operating standards. Also, mutual funds must provide potential investors with a current prospectus. The prospectus must contain information regarding the fund's management, its investment objectives and policies, fees and other information. The laws also limit what a mutual fund can state in its advertisements. These laws, as well as more recently enacted legislation, serve to protect the individual investor.

The various laws also dictate how a mutual fund is structured: There must be a custodian whose functions include safeguarding the fund's assets. The custodian, which is usually a bank, will provide payment when securities are bought and receives payment when securities are sold.

The transfer agent, which may or may not be the same institution as the custodian, administers shareholders' account records, *i.e.*, issues new shares, cancels redeemed shares, and distributes dividends and capital gains to the shareholders. The investment adviser, which is usually the same as the management company, is in charge of the fund's portfolio. The investment adviser makes the buy and sell decisions of the fund and is usually paid based on a percentage of the fund's assets. The average fee is one half of one per cent annually.

In 1940, there were 68 mutual funds with combined net assets of almost 450 million dollars. By 1970, the figures increased to 361 mutual funds with net assets of over 47 billion dollars. By the end of 1994, there were over 95 million accounts in over 6,000 different mutual funds with 2.1 trillion dollars in assets. And by 2004, there were over 8.1 trillion dollars in assets in more than 8,300 U.S.-based mutual funds! What has accounted for this tremendous growth in mutual funds? One reason was the introduction, in the early 1970s, of the money market fund. The money market mutual fund allowed the small investor, for the first time, to receive the relatively high, short-term interest rates offered by the money market that was previously available only to institutions and wealthy individuals. 30% of all mutual fund investors got their start in mutual funds with a money market fund.

A second reason is the dramatic growth in the number of funds available. Since 1970 there has been an increase of almost 8,000 funds – a total of more than 8,300 at the end of 2004. These funds offer an investment objective to meet virtually any investor's needs.

Another reason is the popularity of using mutual funds for retirement assets. By the end of 2004, mutual funds accounted for $3.1 trillion – or 24 per cent – of the $12.9 trillion U.S. retirement market. Nearly two-thirds of households which have IRAs include mutual funds in their IRAs. In 2004, 92 million individuals in 54 million U.S. households owned mutual funds. This is up from just 6% in 1980.

The median age of mutual fund shareholders is 48. 71% are married and more than half are college graduates. Their median household income is $68,700. They have financial assets of $125,000 with mutual fund shares accounting for 47% of these assets. 70% bought their first mutual fund more than 10 years ago. The median number of funds owned is 4.

Because of their growth and popularity, mutual funds have become the nation's second largest type of financial institution – behind only commercial banks.

ADVANTAGES OF MUTUAL FUNDS

Mutual funds offer many advantages to the individual investor.

These advantages include:

- Diversification
- Professional Management
- Low Cost
- Ease of Recordkeeping
- Dollar-cost-averaging

- Liquidity
- Family of Funds
- Convenience

DIVERSIFICATION

"Don't put all your eggs in one basket." We have all heard these words many times. In investing this is certainly true. If you invest your nest egg in the stock of a single company and something unforeseen happens, *i.e.*, the company goes bankrupt, new technology makes the company's product obsolete, etc., you could wipe out your entire investment. A major attraction to mutual funds is the diversification they offer investors.

A typical fund will have dozens, or perhaps, hundreds of different securities in their portfolio. A poor performance by one of the companies in the portfolio will have much less of an effect on the total return and safety of your principal. Every dollar you have invested in a mutual fund has this diversification.

PROFESSIONAL MANAGEMENT

Professional management is another key attraction to mutual funds. The average investor just does not have the time or experience needed to make informed and profitable decisions.

Fund managers perform extensive economic and financial research. They may visit dozens or hundreds of companies and talk with hundreds of top business executives in a years time. They study balance sheets, trade publications, research reports, marketing reports and a myriad of other financial data. When you buy shares in a mutual fund you are getting this professional management for a relatively very low fee.

The typical management fee of a mutual fund is 1/2 of 1% of that funds assets on a yearly basis. On a $5,000 investment, this is a yearly fee of $25.00. Professional money management has always been available to institutions and wealthy individuals. Now it is available to everyone through mutual funds.

LOW COST

Even if you had the time, the experience, and the knowledge necessary to profitably select your own stocks and the wherewithal to properly diversify, you cannot do it as cheaply as a mutual fund can. Even using discount brokers you will pay up to two per cent or more in commissions – even more using a full service broker. You will pay again when you sell. Because they may buy millions of dollars worth of stock at a time, mutual funds are able to negotiate broker's fees to the bare minimum.

Using no-load mutual funds there are no sales charges – 100% of your money is being invested for you. There are even funds which have no minimum initial investment or minimum subsequent investment – you can start investing with as little as $100.00 or even less!

EASE OF RECORDKEEPING

Mutual funds handle all the paperwork and record keeping necessary to keep track of your investment transactions. They will mail your dividend checks promptly or reinvest them in additional shares. They will provide accurate year-end summaries of all your transactions for income tax purposes. If you have any questions many are available 24 hours a day via a toll-free phone call.

DOLLAR-COST-AVERAGING

If you fear you will invest in a mutual fund right before the market goes into a nose dive, you should consider dollar-cost-averaging. This is a technique of investing a set amount of money at regular intervals, monthly or quarterly, rather than a lump sum all at once. You invest the same amount of money regardless of whether the stock market is going up or down. In fact, this strategy will turn the ups and downs of the market into an advantage.

Let's Look at an Example

Suppose you will have $100.00 available to invest for each of the next four months. You are interested in a mutual fund whose shares are currently selling for $10.00 each. You invest your initial $100.00 and get 10 shares in return. The next month, despite the fact the market dropped – your shares are now trading at $5.00 – you again invest your $100.00 and this time you receive 20 shares.

Let's assume by the next month the market has recovered and the shares are again trading at $10.00. You invest your $100.00 and receive 10 shares.

The next month finds the market continuing its rise and your shares are now selling for $12.50. You invest your $100.00 and receive 8 shares.

Let's see how you have done:

Monthly Investment	Price	SharesPurchased
100	10.00	10
100	5.00	20
100	10	10
100	12.50	8
$400		48

Average share cost – $8.33

Ending share price – $12.50

You have invested a total of $400.00 and own 48 shares at an average price of $8.33 per share. Your 48 shares are worth a total of $600.00 – you have made a profit of $200.00 in a mixed market.

Investing A Lump Sum:

SingleInvestment	Price	SharesPurchased
400	10.00	40
$400		40

Average share cost – $10.00

Ending share price – $12.50

Had you invested the whole $400.00 in the first month you would have received 40 shares at the price of $10.00 each. Those shares would now be worth $500.00 for a gain of $100.00. Certainly a good return but only 50% as well as using dollar-cost-averaging. The stock market will always fluctuate. This is a way to take advantage of that fluctuation. Dollar-cost-averaging guarantees that you will always buy more shares when the price of the shares are lower and less shares when the price is higher. It doesn't take a lot of brilliance or hard work – just discipline. You must invest the same amount every month.

Liquidity

Mutual fund investors can cash in their shares at any time and receive the current value of their holdings. The fund is always ready to redeem its shares. Most funds will allow you to use a wire transfer to transfer the funds directly to your bank account.

Many funds also have a check writing privilege – if you need your money in a hurry, simply write a check. Many funds also provide for redemption via a toll-free phone call.

FAMILY OF FUNDS

Many mutual funds are part of a "family of funds". The advantage to this is an option known as an exchange privilege or fund switching. Fund switching has become quite popular as fund companies have made it easy to move your money from one fund to another, usually with only a toll-free telephone call.

Switching is an easy and convenient way to take advantage of changing market conditions. If the stock market began to decline, for instance, and your money was in a stock fund, you might consider switching your investment into a money market fund within the same family.

CONVENIENCE

Mutual fund shares are easy to buy. Generally, no-load funds have a toll-free number an investor can call for information. Some fund companies have even set up retail centres for investors. Many have payroll deduction plans and some funds, with proper authorization, will deduct and invest on a regular basis a specified amount from the shareholder's bank account. You can automatically reinvest all dividends and capital gains distributions allowing you to compound your earnings. Conversely, you have the option of automatic withdrawal – you may elect to have your earnings and/or part of your principal sent to you, or anyone you designate, on a regular basis.

Many funds offer checkwriting privileges. This can be very helpful when you need to have quick access to your money. Mutual funds are excellent vehicles for retirement investing. The generally long-term nature of mutual fund investing fits well with the long-term objectives of investing for retirement.

TYPES OF MUTUAL FUNDS

There are over 8,300 U.S.-based mutual funds in existence today. We have classified these funds into 21 major categories according to their investment objectives:

AGGRESSIVE GROWTH FUNDS

Seek maximum capital gains as their investment objective. Current income is not a significant factor. Some may invest in stocks of businesses that are somewhat out of the mainstream, such as fledgling companies, new industries, companies fallen on hard times, or industries temporarily out of favour. Some may also use specialized investment techniques such as option writing or short-term trading.

BALANCED FUNDS

Generally have a three-part investment objective: 1) to conserve the investors' initial principal, 2) to pay current income, and 3) to promote long-term growth of both principal and income. Balanced funds have a portfolio mix of bonds, preferred stocks, and common stocks.

CORPORATE BOND FUNDS

Like income funds, seek a high level of income. They do so by buying bonds of corporations for the majority of the fund's portfolio. The rest of the portfolio may be in U.S. Treasury bonds or bonds issued by a federal agency.

FLEXIBLE PORTFOLIO FUNDS

May be 100% invested in stocks OR bonds OR money market instruments, depending on market conditions. These funds give the money managers the greatest flexibility in anticipating or responding to economic changes.

GNMA OR GINNIE MAE FUNDS

Invest in mortgage securities backed by the Government National Mortgage Association. To qualify for this category, the majority of the portfolio must always be invested in mortgage-backed securities.

GLOBAL BOND FUNDS

Invest in the debt securities of companies and countries worldwide, including the United States.

GLOBAL EQUITY FUNDS

Invest in securities traded worldwide, including the U.S. Compared to direct investments, global funds offer investors an easier avenue to investing abroad. The funds' professional money managers handle the trading and recordkeeping details and deal with differences in currencies, languages, time zones, laws and regulations, and business customs and practices. In addition to another layer of diversification, global funds add another layer of risk – exchange-rate risk.

GROWTH FUNDS

Invest in the common stock of well-established companies. Their primary aim is to produce an increase in the value of their investments rather than a flow of dividends. Investors who buy a growth fund are more interested in seeing the fund's share price rise than in receiving income from dividends.

GROWTH AND INCOME FUNDS

Invest mainly in the common stock of companies that have had increasing share value but also a solid record of paying dividends. This type of fund attempts to combine long-term capital growth with a steady stream of income.

HIGH-YIELD BOND FUNDS

Maintain at least two-thirds of their portfolios in lower-rated corporate bonds. In return for a generally higher yield, investors must bear a greater degree of risk than for higher-rated bonds.

INCOME-BOND FUNDS

Seek a high level of current income for their shareholders by investing at all times in a mix of corporate and government bonds.

INCOME-EQUITY FUNDS

Seek a high level of current income for their shareholders by investing primarily in equity securities of companies with good dividend-paying records.

INCOME-MIXED FUNDS

Seek a high level of current income for their shareholders by investing in income-producing securities, including both equities and debt instruments.

INTERNATIONAL FUNDS

Invest in equity securities of companies located outside the U.S. Two thirds of their portfolios must be so invested at all times to be categorized here.

LONG-TERM MUNICIPAL BOND FUNDS

Invest in bonds issued by states and municipalities to finance schools, highways, hospitals, airports, bridges, water and sewer works, and other public projects. In most cases, income earned on these securities is not taxed by the federal government, but may be taxed under state and local laws. For some taxpayers, portions of income earned on these securities may be subject to the federal alternative minimum tax.

PRECIOUS METALS/GOLD FUNDS

Maintain two thirds of their portfolios invested in securities associated with gold, silver, and other precious metals.

STATE MUNICIPAL BOND FUNDS – LONG-TERM

Work just like other long-term municipal bond funds except their portfolios contain the issues of only one state. A resident of that state has the advantage of receiving income free of both federal and state tax.

For some taxpayers, portions of income from these securities may be subject to the federal alternative minimum tax.

STATE TAX-EXEMPT MONEY MARKET FUNDS

Work just like other tax-exempt money market funds except their portfolios contain the issues of only one state. A resident of that state has the advantage of receiving income free of both federal and state tax. For some taxpayers, portions of income from these securities may be subject to the federal alternative minimum tax.

TAXABLE MONEY MARKET FUNDS

Seek to maintain a stable net asset value by investing in the short-term, high-grade securities sold in the money market, such as treasury bills, bank certificates of deposit, and commercial paper. Money market funds limit the average maturity of their portfolio to 90 days or less.

TAX-EXEMPT MONEY MARKET FUNDS – NATIONAL

Invest in municipal securities with relatively short maturities. Investors who use these funds seek investments with minimum risks. For some taxpayers, portions of income from certain of these securities may be subject to the federal alternative minimum tax.

U.S. GOVERNMENT INCOME FUNDS

Invest in a variety of government securities. These include U.S. Treasury bonds, federally guaranteed mortgage-backed securities, and other government notes.

SELECTING A MUTUAL FUND

To decide which funds would be most appropriate for you to invest your hard earned money you must first decide on what you would like to accomplish with your investments. Where are you now? Are you in your twenties just starting out in your chosen career? Perhaps you're in your fifties approaching the peak of your career. Maybe you're preparing to send your oldest child off to their first day of school and you want to make sure he or she will be able to attend college. Maybe you want to save and invest for that house or vacation hideaway you've been dreaming about for years. What do you want to accomplish? What are your goals? These are the questions you must answer that are unique to your situation.

Investing in mutual funds is not some sort of get-rich-quick scheme. Investments in mutual funds are generally for the longer term – they should be measured in years, not weeks or months. You should not be investing money in mutual funds if you will need that money next month.

Generally your twenties and thirties are a time of beginnings: career, marriage, children, first home, etc. It is also a good time to begin investing in mutual funds. With time on your side, growth and aggressive growth funds may be a good choice to begin your mutual fund investing. These funds could be used for future college costs, a new home, or to get a head start on your retirement. Your forties and fifties are likely to be your peak earning years. Perhaps a time when you should have less of your mutual fund assets in growth funds and more in income and tax-free income funds.

In your sixties and beyond, most of your biggest expenses are behind you, *i.e.*, college expenses, housing, etc., and you have more time to enjoy yourself. Perhaps a time to shift more of your assets into fixed income funds to increase income for living expenses or leisure activities. Another factor to consider when choosing a mutual fund is your tolerance for risk. While all investments have some risk associated with them, no investment is worthwhile if you stay awake at night worrying about it. Your comfort level with risk is important in determining how aggressively or conservatively you choose to invest and must be balanced with your desire to achieve your financial goals. We suggest you call or write a few of the mutual fund companies and ask for some literature regarding their funds. Once you receive their literature, read it! One of the items you will receive is the prospectus. All funds will provide one. The prospectus will provide you with the investment objective of the fund – how it invests your money.

It will also contain a wealth of other information: how to buy and redeem shares, sales charges, initial and subsequent investment requirements, fund expenses, information on the funds investment advisor, and much more. In short, the prospectus contains most of the information you need to make an informed decision on whether to invest in that particular fund or not.

INVEST IN A MUTUAL FUND

Investing in a mutual fund is just an efficient way of pooling resources by various individuals with similar goals. This collectively increases buying power and allows for the employment of a professional manager to invest and monitor the group's resources.

A mutual fund is thus a manager of a portfolio of stocks, bonds, money market instruments, or a combination of securities.

There are three main benefits in putting your money in a fund rather than playing the markets by yourself:

1. One of the biggest benefits you derive is diversification. Since each mutual fund holds a number of securities, you are essentially spreading your money, and therefore your risk, over a number of investments. The advantage is rather obvious, as you do not stand the danger of your investment being wiped out at one stroke.
2. Also fund managers handle investments in a professional and transparent manner. They thus have the latest data on the companies and industry trend as well as well researched data on potential investments.

3. All it is far easier for you as a small investor to buy into a mutual fund than into the markets. Nearly all mutual funds have low investment minimums, making them accessible to nearly everyone.

But also bear in mind that your risks have not disappeared just because you invest in mutual fund. All funds are subject to risks and those that look primarily to stock markets run higher risks.

Of course the potential for higher returns is also higher here than in funds that look to debt markets or government securities in a bid to lower their risk profile and earn steady income.

CLASSIFICATION OF MUTUAL FUNDS

Mutual Funds can be segregated based on their functions. *They are classified as*:

- Equity Funds.
- Bond Funds.
- Balanced Funds.
- Gilt Funds.
- Money-Market Funds.
- Tax Saving funds.
- Equity Linked Savings Schemes, etc.

The implication is that these schemes will operate based on their specific classification. A pure equity fund will invest a majority of their funds in the equity market. Similarly a pure Bond Fund will invest the majority of their funds in the Bond Market. Hence it is important for the investor to identify his requirements and then select a mutual fund that best suits their preferences.

For instance, an individual with a reasonably high net worth will be more interested in investments which will help reduce his tax burden. Hence he may opt for the tax-saving schemes. However these schemes may generate comparatively lesser returns. If the person is a risk-taker and at the same time he wants to save on taxes, in such a situation he can invest in ELSS schemes.

MUTUAL FUNDS VS. OTHER INVESTMENTS

Mutual funds offer several advantages over investing in individual stocks. For example, the transaction costs are divided among all the mutual fund shareholders, which allows for cost-effective diversification. Investors may also benefit by having a third party apply expertise and dedicate time to manage and research investment options, although there is dispute over whether professional fund managers can, on average, outperform simple index funds that mimic public indexes.

Yet, the Wall Street Journal reported that separately managed accounts performed better than mutual funds in 22 of 25 categories from 2006 to 2008. This included beating mutual funds performance in 2008, a tough year in which the global stock market lost US$21 trillion in value. In the story, Morningstar, Inc said SMAs outperformed mutual funds in 25 of 36 stock and bond market categories. Whether actively managed or passively indexed, mutual funds are not immune to risks. They share the same risks associated with the investments made. If the fund invests primarily in stocks, it is usually subject to the same ups and downs and risks as the stock market.

SHARE CLASSES

Many mutual funds offer more than one class of shares. For example, you may have seen a fund that offers "Class A" and "Class B" shares. Each class will invest in the same pool of securities and will have the same investment objectives and policies. But each class will have different shareholder services and/or distribution arrangements with different fees and expenses.

These differences are supposed to reflect different costs involved in servicing investors in various classes; for example, one class may be sold through brokers with a front-end load, and another class may be sold direct to the public with no load but a "12b-1 fee" included in the class's expenses. Still a third class might have a minimum investment of $10,000,000 and be available only to financial institutions. In some cases, by aggregating regular investments made by many individuals, a retirement plan may qualify to purchase "institutional" shares even though no members of the plan would qualify individually. As a result, each class will likely have different performance results.

A multi-class structure offers investors the ability to select a fee and expense structure that is most appropriate for their investment goals.

LOAD AND EXPENSES

A front-end load or sales charge is a commission paid to a broker by a mutual fund when shares are purchased, taken as a percentage of funds invested. The value of the investment is reduced by the amount of the load. Some funds have a deferred sales charge or back-end load.

In this type of fund an investor pays no sales charge when purchasing shares, but will pay a commission out of the proceeds when shares are redeemed depending on how long they are held. Another derivative structure is a level-load fund, in which no sales charge is paid when buying the fund, but a back-end load may be charged if the shares purchased are sold within a year.

Load funds are sold through financial intermediaries such as brokers, financial planners, and other types of registered representatives who charge a commission for their services. Shares of front-end load funds are frequently eligible for breakpoints based on a number of variables. These include other accounts in the same fund family held by the investor or various family members, or committing to buy more of the fund within a set period of time in return for a lower commission "today".

It is possible to buy many mutual funds without paying a sales charge. These are called no-load funds. In addition to being available from the fund company itself, no-load funds may be sold by some discount brokers for a flat transaction fee or even no fee at all. No-load funds include both index funds and actively managed funds. The largest mutual fund families selling no-load index funds are Vanguard and Fidelity, though there are a number of smaller mutual fund families with no-load funds as well. Expense ratios in some no-load index funds are less than 0.2% per year versus the typical actively managed fund's expense ratio of about 1.5% per year. Load funds usually have even higher expense ratios when the load is considered.

The expense ratio is the anticipated annual cost to the investor of holding shares of the fund. For example, on a $100,000 investment, an expense ratio of 0.2% means $200 of annual expense, while a 1.5% expense ratio would result in $1,500 of annual expense.

These expenses are before any sales commissions paid to purchase the mutual fund. Many fee-only financial advisors strongly suggest no-load funds such as index funds. If the advisor is not of the fee-only type but is instead compensated by commissions, the advisor may have a conflict of interest in selling high-commission load funds.

CONSTITUTION AND MANAGEMENT OF MUTUAL FUND

TRUST DEED TO BE REGISTERED UNDER THE REGISTRATION ACT

A mutual fund shall be constituted in the form of a trust and the instrument of trust shall be in the form of a deed, duly registered under the provisions of the Indian Registration Act, 1908 (16 of 1908) executed by the sponsor in favour of the trustees named in such an instrument.

CONTENTS OF TRUST DEED

(1) The trust deed shall contain such clauses as are mentioned in the Third Schedule and such other clauses which are necessary for safeguarding the interests of the unit holders. (2) No trust deed shall contain a clause which has the effect of- (i) limiting or extinguishing the obligations and liabilities of the trust in relation to any mutual fund or the unit holders; or (ii) indemnifying the trustees or the asset management

company for loss or damage caused to the unit holders by their acts of negligence or acts of commissions or omissions.

DISQUALIFICATION FROM BEING APPOINTED AS TRUSTEES

(1) A mutual fund shall appoint trustees in accordance with these regulations.

(2) No person shall be eligible to be appointed as a trustee unless.
   - He is a person of ability, integrity and standing; and
   - Has not been found guilty of moral turpitude; and
   - Has not been convicted of any economic offence or violation of any securities laws; and
   - Has furnished particulars as specified in Form C.

(3) An asset management company or any of its officers or employees shall not be eligible to act as a trustee of any mutual fund.

(4) No person who is appointed as a trustee of a mutual fund can be appointed as a trustee of any other mutual fund unless.
   - Such a person is an independent trustee referred to in sub-regulation (5); and
   - Prior approval of the mutual fund of which he is a trustee has been obtained for such an appointment.

(5) Two thirds of the trustees shall be independent persons and shall not be associated with the sponsors or be associated with them in any manner whatsoever [original clause substituted]

(6) In case a company is appointed as a trustee then its directors can act as trustees of any other trust provided that the object of the trust is not in conflict with the object of the mutual fund.

APPROVAL OF THE BOARD FOR APPOINTMENT OF TRUSTEE

- No trustee shall initially or any time thereafter be appointed without prior approval of the Board.

- The existing trustees of any mutual fund may form a trustee company to act as a trustee with the prior approval of the Board.

RIGHTS AND OBLIGATIONS OF THE TRUSTEES

- The trustees and the asset management company shall with the prior approval of the Board enter into an investment management agreement.
- The investment management agreement shall contain such clauses as are mentioned in the Fourth Schedule and such other clauses as are necessary for the purpose of making investments.
- The trustees shall have a right to obtain from the asset management company such information as is considered necessary by the trustees.
- The trustees shall ensure before the launch of any scheme that the asset management company has;-
  - Systems in place for its back office, dealing room and accounting;
  - Appointed all key personnel including fund managers for the schemes and submitted their bio-data which shall contain the educational qualifications, past experience in the securities market with the trustees, within 15 days of their appointment;
  - Appointed auditors to audit its accounts;
  - Appointed a compliance officer to comply with regulatory requirement and to redress investor grievances;
  - Appointed registrars and laid down parameters for their supervision;
  - Prepared a compliance manual and designed internal control mechanisms including internal audit systems;
  - Specified norms for empanelment of brokers and marketing agents.
- The trustees shall ensure that an asset management company has been diligent in empanelling the

brokers, in monitoring securities transactions with brokers and avoiding undue concentration of business with any broker.

- The trustees shall ensure that the asset management company has not given any undue or unfair advantage to any associates or dealt with any of the associates of the asset management company in any manner detrimental to interest of the unitholders.
- The trustees shall ensure that the transactions entered into by the asset management company are in accordance with these regulations and the scheme.
- The trustees shall ensure that the asset management company has been managing the mutual fund schemes independently of other activities and have taken adequate steps to ensure that the interest of investors of one scheme are not being compromised with those of any other scheme or of other activities of the asset management company.
- The trustees shall ensure that all the activities of the asset management company are in accordance with the provisions of these regulations.
- Where the trustees have reason to believe that the conduct of business of the mutual fund is not in accordance with these regulations and the scheme they shall forthwith take such remedial steps as are necessary by them and shall immediately inform the Board of the violation and the action taken by them.
- Each trustee shall file the details of his transactions of dealing in securities with the Mutual Fund on a quarterly basis.
- The trustees shall be accountable for, and be the custodian of, the funds and property of the respective schemes and shall hold the same in trust for the benefit of the unit holders in accordance with these regulations and the provisions of trust deed.
- The trustees shall take steps to ensure that the transactions of the mutual fund are in accordance with the provisions of the trust deed.

- The trustees shall be responsible for the calculation of any income due to be paid to the mutual fund and also of any income received in the mutual fund for the holders of the units of any scheme in accordance with these regulations and the trust deed.
- The trustees shall obtain the consent of the unitholders
  - Whenever required to do so by the Board in the interest of the unit-holders; or
  - Whenever required to do so on the requisition made by three-fourths of the unit holders of any scheme; or
  - When the majority of the trustees decide to wind up or prematurely redeem the units; or
  - When any change in the fundamental attributes of any scheme or the trust or fees and expenses payable or any other change which would modify the scheme or affect the interest of the unitholders is proposed to be carried out unless the consent of not less than three-fourths of the unit holders is obtained:

Provided that no such change shall be carried out unless three fourths of the unit holders have given their consent and the unit holders who do not give their consent are allowed to redeem their holdings in the scheme.

[Provided further that in case of an open ended scheme, the consent of the unitholders shall not be necessary if:

- The change in fundamental attribute is carried out after one year from the date of allotment of units.
- The unitholders are informed about the proposed change in fundamental attribute by sending individual communication and an advertisement is given in English daily newspaper having nationwide circulation and in a newspaper published in the language of the region where the head office of the mutual fund is situated.
- The unitholders are given an option to exit at the prevailing Net Asset Value without any exit load.]

Explanation: For the purposes of this clause "fundamental attributes" means the investment objective and terms of a scheme.

- The trustees shall call for the details of transactions in securities by the key personnel of the asset management company in his own name or on behalf of the asset management company and shall report to the Board, as and when required.
- The trustees shall quarterly review all transactions carried out between the mutual funds, asset management company and its associates.
- The trustees shall quarterly review the networth of the asset management company and in case of any shortfall, ensure that the asset management company make up for the shortfall as per clause (f) of sub-regulation (1) of regulation 21.
- The trustees shall periodically review all service contracts such as custody arrangements, transfer agency of the securities and satisfy itself that such contracts are executed in the interest of the unitholders.
- The trustees shall ensure that there is no conflict of interest between the manner of deployment of its networth by the asset management company and the interest of the unitholders.
- The trustees shall periodically review the investor complaints received and the redressal of the same by the asset management company.
- The trustees shall abide by the Code of Conduct as specified in the Fifth Schedule.
- The trustees shall furnish to the Board on a half yearly basis, -
  - A report on the activities of the mutual fund;
  - A certificate stating that the trustees have satisfied themselves that there have been no instances of self dealing or front running by any of the trustees, directors and key personnel of the asset management company;

- A certificate to the effect that the asset management company has been managing the schemes independently of any other activities and in case any activities of the nature referred to in sub-regulation (2) of regulation 24 have been undertaken by the asset management company and has taken adequate steps to ensure that the interest of the unitholders are protected.

- The independent trustees referred to in sub-regulation (5) of regulation 16 shall give their comments on the report received from the asset management company regarding the investments by the mutual fund in the securities of group companies of the sponsor.
- Trustees shall exercise due diligence as under:

GENERAL DUE DILIGENCE

- The Trustees shall be discerning in the appointment of the directors on the Board of the asset management company.
- Trustees shall review the desirability of continuance of the asset management company if substantial irregularities are observed in any of the schemes and shall not allow the asset management company to float new schemes.
- The trustee shall ensure that the trust property is properly protected, held and administered by proper persons and by a proper number of such persons.
- The trustee shall ensure that all service providers are holding appropriate registrations from the Board or concerned regulatory authority.
- The Trustees shall arrange for test checks of service contracts.
- Trustees shall immediately report to Board of any special developments in the mutual fund.

SPECIFIC DUE DILIGENCE

The Trustees shall:

- Obtain internal audit reports at regular intervals from independent auditors appointed by the Trustees.

- Obtain compliance certificates at regular intervals from the asset management company.
- Hold meeting of trustees more frequently.
- Consider the reports of the independent auditor and compliance reports of asset management company at the meetings of trustees for appropriate action.
- Maintain records of the decisions of the Trustees at their meetings and of the minutes of the meetings.
- Prescribe and adhere to a code of ethics by the Trustees, asset management company and its personnel.
- Communicate in writing to the asset management company of the deficiencies and checking on the rectification of deficiencies.
- Notwithstanding anything contained in sub-regulations (1) to (25), the trustees shall not be held liable for acts done in good faith if they have exercised adequate due diligence honestly.
- The independent directors of the trustees or asset management company shall pay specific attention to the following, as may be applicable, namely:
  - The Investment Management Agreement and the compensation paid under the agreement.
  - Service contracts with affiliates - whether the asset management company has charged higher fees than outside contractors for the same services.
  - Selection of the asset management company's independent directors
  - Securities transactions involving affiliates to the extent such transactions are permitted.
  - Selecting and nominating individuals to fill independent directors vacancies.
  - Code of ethics must be designed to prevent fraudulent, deceptive or manipulative practices by insiders in connection with personal securities transactions.
  - The reasonableness of fees paid to sponsors, asset management company and any others for services provided.

- Principal underwriting contracts and their renewals.
- Any service contract with the associates of the asset management company.

MUTUAL FUNDS IN INDIA

A Mutual Fund is a trust that pools the savings of a number of investors who share a common financial goal. The money collected and invested by the fund manager in different types of securities depending upon the objective of the scheme. These could range from shares to debentures to money market instruments. The income earned through these investments and its unit holders in proportion to the number of units owned by them shares the capital appreciation realised by the scheme. Thus, a Mutual Fund is the most suitable investment for the common person as it offers an opportunity to invest in a diversified, professionally managed portfolio at a relatively low cost. Anybody with an investible surplus of as little as a few thousand rupees can invest in Mutual Funds.

Each Mutual Fund scheme has a defined investment objective and strategy A mutual fund is the answer to all these situations. It appoints professionally qualified and experienced staff that manages each of these functions on a full time basis. The large pool of money collected in the fund allows it to hire such staff at a very low cost to each investor. In effect, the mutual fund vehicle exploits economies of scale in all three areas - research, investments and transaction processing. While the concept of individuals coming together to invest money collectively is not new, the mutual fund in its present form is a 20th century phenomenon.

In fact, mutual funds gained popularity only after the Second World War. Globally, there are thousands of firms offering tens of thousands of mutual funds with different investment objectives. Today, mutual funds collectively manage almost as much as or more money as compared to banks. A Mutual Fund is a trust that pools the savings of a number of investors who share a common financial goal. The money thus collected is then invested in capital market instruments such as shares, debentures and other securities. The income earned through these investments and the capital appreciation realised is shared by its unit holders in proportion to the number of units owned by them. Thus, a Mutual Fund is the most suitable investment for the common person as it offers an opportunity to invest in a diversified, professionally managed basket of securities at a relatively low cost.

THE SECURITY AND EXCHANGE BOARD OF INDIA

Regulations,1996 defines a mutual fund as a " a fund establishment in the form of a trust to raise money through the sale of units to the public or a part of the public under one or more schemes for investing in securities, including money market instruments." Mutual Funds have been a significant source of investment in both government and corporate securities. It has been for the decades the monopoly of the state with UTI being the key player with invested funds exceeding Rs. 300 bn.. The state owned insurance companies also hold a portfolio of stocks. Presently, numerous mutual funds exist, including private and foreign companies. Banks - mainly state owned too have established Mutual Funds. Foreign participation in mutual funds and asset management companies permitted on a case-by-case basis.

STRUCTURE OF THE INDIAN MUTUAL FUND INDUSTRY

The Indian mutual fund industry is dominated by the Unit Trust of India, which has a total corpus of Rs700bn collected from more than 20 million investors. The UTI has many funds/ schemes in all categories *i.e.* equity, balanced, income etc with some being open-ended and some being closed-ended. The Unit Scheme 1964 commonly referred to as US 64, which is a balanced fund, is the biggest scheme with a corpus of about Rs200bn. Most of its investors believe that the UTI is government owned and controlled, which, while legally incorrect, is true for all practical purposes. The second largest category of mutual funds is the ones floated by nationalized banks. Can bank Asset Management floated by Canara Bank and SBI Funds Management floated by the State Bank of India are the largest of these. GIC AMC floated by General Insurance Corporation and Jeevan Bima Sahayog AMC floated by the LIC are some of the other prominent ones.

Some of the AMCs operating currently are:

Name of the AMC	Nature of ownership
Alliance Capital Asset Management (I) Private Limited	Private foreign
Birla Sun Life Asset Management Company Limited	Private Indian
Bank of Baroda Asset Management Company Limited	Banks
Bank of India Asset Management Company Limited	Banks
Canbank Investment Management Services Limited	Banks
Cholamandalam Cazenove Asset Management Company Limited	Private foreign
Dundee Asset Management Company Limited	Private foreign
DSP Merrill Lynch Asset Management Company Limited	Private foreign
Escorts Asset Management Limited	Private Indian
First India Asset Management Limited	Private Indian
GIC Asset Management Company Limited	Institutions
IDBI Investment Management Company Limited	Institutions
Indfund Management Limited	Banks
ING Investment Asset Management Company Private Limited	Private foreign
J M Capital Management Limited	Private Indian
Jardine Fleming (I) Asset Management Limited	Private foreign
Kotak Mahindra Asset Management Company Limited	Private Indian
Kothari Pioneer Asset Management Company Limited	Private Indian
Jeevan Bima Sahayog Asset Management Company Limited	Institutions
Morgan Stanley Asset Management Company Private Limited	Private foreign
Punjab National Bank Asset Management Company Limited	Banks
Reliance Capital Asset Management Company Limited	Private Indian
State Bank of India Funds Management Limited	Banks
Shriram Asset Management Company Limited	Private Indian
Sun F and C Asset Management (I) Private Limited	Private foreign
Sundaram Newton Asset Management Company Limited	Private foreign
Tata Asset Management Company Limited	Private Indian
Credit Capital Asset Management Company Limited	Private Indian
Templeton Asset Management (India) Private Limited	Private foreign
Unit Trust of India	Institutions
Zurich Asset Management Company (I) Limited	Private foreign

The most important trend in the mutual fund industry is the aggressive expansion of the foreign owned mutual fund companies and the decline of the companies floated by nationalized banks and smaller private sector players. Many nationalized banks got into the mutual fund business in the early nineties and got off to a good start due to the stock market boom prevailing then.

These banks did not really understand the mutual fund business and they just viewed it as another kind of banking activity. Few hired specialized staff and generally chose to transfer staff from the parent organizations. The performance of most of the schemes floated by these funds was not good. Some schemes had offered guaranteed returns and their parent organizations had to bail out these AMCs by paying large amounts of money as the difference between the guaranteed and actual returns. The service levels were also very bad. Most of these AMCs have not been able to retain staff, float new schemes etc. and it is doubtful whether, barring a few exceptions, they have serious plans of continuing the activity in a major way.

The experience of some of the AMCs floated by private sector Indian companies was also very similar. They quickly realised that the AMC business is a business, which makes money in the long term and requires deep-pocketed support in the intermediate years. Some have sold out to foreign owned companies, some have merged with others and there is general restructuring going on. They can be credited with introducing many new practices such as new product innovation, sharp improvement in service standards and disclosure, usage of technology, broker education and support etc. In fact, they have forced the industry to upgrade itself and service levels of organizations like UTI have improved dramatically in the last few years in response to the competition provided by these.

PERFORMANCE OF MUTUAL FUNDS IN INDIA

Let us start the discussion of the performance of mutual

funds in India from the day the concept of mutual fund took birth in India. The year was 1963. Unit Trust of India invited investors or rather to those who believed in savings, to park their money in UTI Mutual Fund. The performance of mutual funds in India in the initial phase was not even closer to satisfactory level.

People rarely understood, and of course investing was out of question. But yes, some 24 million shareholders were accustomed with guaranteed high returns by the beginning of liberalization of the industry in 1992. This good record of UTI became marketing tool for new entrants. The expectations of investors touched the sky in profitability factor. However, people were miles away from the preparedness of risks factor after the liberalization.

The Assets under Management of UTI was Rs. 67bn. by the end of 1987. Let me concentrate about the performance of mutual funds in India through figures. From Rs. 67bn. the Assets Under Management rose to Rs. 470 bn. in March 1993 and the figure had a three times higher performance by April 2004. It rose as high as Rs. 1,540bn.

The net asset value of mutual funds in India declined when stock prices started falling in the year 1992. Those days, the market regulations did not allow portfolio shifts into alternative investments. There was rather no choice apart from holding the cash or to further continue investing in shares. One more thing to be noted, since only closed-end funds were floated in the market, the investors disinvested by selling at a loss in the secondary market.

The performance of mutual funds in India suffered qualitatively. The 1992 stock market scandal, the losses by disinvestments and of course the lack of transparent rules in the whereabouts rocked confidence among the investors. Partly owing to a relatively weak stock market performance, mutual funds have not yet recovered, with funds trading at an average discount of 1020 per cent of their net asset value.

The measure was taken to make mutual funds the key instrument for long-term saving. The more the variety offered, the quantitative will be investors. At last to mention, as long as mutual fund companies are performing with lower risks and higher profitability within a short span of time, more and more people will be inclined to invest until and unless they are fully educated with the dos and don'ts of mutual funds.

MARKET TRENDS

Comparision of Mutual Funds with Other Instrument

A lone UTI with just one scheme in 1964 now competes with as many as 400 odd products and 34 players in the market. In spite of the stiff competition and losing market share, Last six years have been the most turbulent as well as exiting ones for the industry. New players have come in, while others have decided to close shop by either selling off or merging with others. Product innovation is now passé with the game shifting to performance delivery in fund management as well as service. Those directly associated with the fund management industry like distributors, registrars and transfer agents, and even the regulators have become more mature and responsible.

The industry is also having a profound impact on financial markets. While UTI has always been a dominant player on the bourses as well as the debt markets, the new generations of private funds, which have gained substantial mass, are now flexing their muscles.

Fund managers, by their selection criteria for stocks have forced corporate governance on the industry. Rewarding honest and transparent management with higher valuations has created a system of risk-reward created where the corporate sector is more transparent then before.

Funds have shifted their focus to the recession free sectors like pharmaceuticals, FMCG and technology sector. Funds performances are improving. Funds collection, which averaged at less than Rs100bn per annum over five-year period spanning 1993-98 doubled to Rs210bn in 1998-99. In the current year mobilization till now have exceeded Rs300bn. Total collection for the current financial year ending March 2000 is expected to reach Rs450bn. What is particularly noteworthy is that bulk of the mobilization has been by the private sector mutual funds rather than public sector mutual funds. Indeed private MFs saw a net inflow of Rs. 7819.34 Crore during the first nine months of the year as against a net inflow of Rs.604.40 Crore in the case of public sector funds.

Mutual funds advantages: The benefits on offer are many with good post-tax returns and reasonable safety being the hallmark that we normally associate with them. Some of the other major benefits of investing in them are:

NUMBER OF AVAILABLE OPTIONS

Mutual funds invest according to the underlying investment objective as specified at the time of launching a scheme. So, we have equity funds, debt funds, gilt funds and many others that cater to the different needs of the investor. The availability of these options makes them a good option. While equity funds can be as risky as the stock markets themselves, debt funds offer the kind of security that aimed at the time of making investments.

Money market funds offer the liquidity that desired by big investors who wish to park surplus funds for very short-term periods. The only pertinent factor here is that the fund has to selected keeping the risk profile of the investor in mind because the products have different risks associated with them. So, while equity funds are a good bet for a long term, they may not find favour with corporate or High Net worth Individuals who have short-term needs.

DIVERSIFICATION

Investments spread across a wide cross-section of industries and sectors and so the risk is reduced. Diversification reduces the risk because not all stocks move in the same direction at the same time. One can achieve this diversification through a Mutual Fund with far less money than one can on his own.

PROFESSIONAL MANAGEMENT

Mutual Funds employ the services of skilled professionals

who have years of experience to back them up. They use intensive research techniques to analyse each investment option for the potential of returns along with their risk levels to come up with the figures for performance that determine the suitability of any potential investment.

POTENTIAL OF RETURNS

Returns in the mutual funds are generally better than any other option in any other avenue over a reasonable period. People can pick their investment horizon and stay put in the chosen fund for the duration. Equity funds can outperform most other investments over long periods by placing long-term calls on fundamentally good stocks.

The debt funds too will outperform other options such as banks. Though they are affected by the interest rate risk in general, the returns generated are more as they pick securities with different duration that have different yields and so are able to increase the overall returns.

4

Insurance Services

INTRODUCTION

Insurance is a mechanism that helps to reduce the effects of adverse situations in the economical way. It promises to pay to the owner or beneficiary of the asset, a certain sum if the loss occurs. The business of insurance is related to the protection of the economic values of assets. The asset would have been created through the efforts of the owner. The asset is valuable to the owner, because he expects to get some benefits from it because it meets some of his needs. This benefit may be an income or in some other form.

In the case of a factory or a cow, the product generated by it is sold and income is generated. In the case of a motor car, it provides comfort and convenience in transportation, there is no direct income. Both are assets and provide benefits. Every asset is expected to last for a certain period of time during which it will provide the benefits, after that, the benefit may not be available. There is a life-time for a machine in a factory or a cow or a motor car. None of them will last for ever. The owner is aware of this and he can so manage his affairs that by the end of that period or life-time, a substitute is made available. Thus, he makes sure that the benefit is not lost. However, the asset may get lost earlier.

An accident or some other unfortunate event may destroy it or make it incapable of giving the benefits. An epidemic may kill the cow suddenly. In that case, the owner and those enjoying the benefits therefrom, would be deprived of the benefits. The planned substitute would not have been ready.

There is an adverse or unpleasant situation. Here, insurance helps to reduce the effects of such adverse situations.

PURPOSE AND NEED OF INSURANCE

The risk only means that there is a possibility of loss or damage. The damage may or may not happen. Insurance is done against the possibility that the damage may happen. There has to be an uncertainty about the risk. The earthquake may occur, but the building may not have been affected at all. The word 'possibility' implies uncertainty. Insurance is relevant only if there are uncertainties.

In case of a human being, death is certain, but it's time is uncertain. The person is insured, because of the uncertainty about the time of his death. In the case of a person who is ill,the time of death is not uncertain, though not exactly known. It would be 'soon'. He can't be insured.

HOW INSURANCE WORKS

The mechanism of insurance is very simple. People who are exposed to the same risks come together and agree that, if any one of them suffers a loss, the others will share the loss and make good to the person who lost. The manner in which the loss is to be shared can be determined beforehand. It can be equal among all. It can also be proportional to the risk that each person is exposed to.

PRINCIPLES OF INSURANCE

UTMOST GOOD FAITH (UBERRIMAE FIDES)

As a client it is your duty to disclose all material facts to the risk being covered. A material fact is a fact which would influence the mind of a prudent underwriter in deciding whether to accept a risk for insurance and on what terms. The duty to disclose operates at the time of inception, at renewal and at any point mid term.

INDEMNITY

On the happening of an event insured against, the Insured

will be placed in the same monetary position that he/she occupied immediately before the event taking place.

In the event of a claim the insured must:

- Prove that the event occurred
- Prove that a monetary loss has occurred
- Transfer any rights which he/she may have for recovery from another source to the Insurer, if he/she has been fully indemnified.

SUBROGATION

The right of an insurer which has paid a claim under a policy to step into the shoes of the insured so as to exercise in his name all rights he might have with regard to the recovery of the loss which was the subject of the relevant claim paid under the policy up to the amount of that paid claim. The insurer's subrogation rights may be qualified in the policy.

In the context of insurance subrogation is a feature of the principle of indemnity and therefore only applies to contracts of indemnity so that it does not apply to life assurance or personal accident policies. It is intended to prevent an insured recovering more than the indemnity he receives under his insurance and enables his insurer to recover or reduce its loss.

CONTRIBUTION

The right of an insurer to call on other insurers similarly, but not necessarily equally, liable to the same insured to share the loss of an indemnity payment *i.e.* a travel policy may have overlapping cover with the contents part of a household policy. The principle of contribution allows the insured to make a claim against one insurer who then has the right to call on any other insurers liable for the loss to share the claim payment.

INSURABLE INTEREST

If an insured wishes to enforce a contract of insurance before the Courts he must have an insurable interest in the subject matter of the insurance, which is to say that he stands to benefit from its preservation and will suffer from its loss. In non-marine insurances, the insured must have insurable interest when the policy is taken out and also at the date of loss giving rise to a claim under the policy.

PROXIMATE CAUSE

An insurer will only be liable to pay a claim under an insurance contract if the loss that gives rise to the claim was proximately caused by an insured peril. This means that the loss must be directly attributed to an insured peril without any break in the chain of causation.

TYPES OF INSURANCE

Any risk that can be quantified can potentially be insured. Specific kinds of risk that may give rise to claims are known as "perils". An insurance policy will set out in detail which perils are covered by the policy and which are not. A single policy may cover risks in one or more of the categories. For example, auto insurance would typically cover both property risk and liability risk. A homeowner's insurance policy in the U.S. typically includes property insurance covering damage to the home and the owner's belongings, liability insurance covering certain legal claims against the owner, and even a small amount of coverage for medical expenses of guests who are injured on the owner's property.

Business insurance can be any kind of insurance that protects businesses against risks.

Some principal subtypes of business insurance are:

- The various kinds of professional liability insurance, also called professional indemnity insurance; and
- The business owner's policy, which bundles into one policy many of the kinds of coverage that a business owner needs, in a way analogous to how homeowners insurance bundles the coverages that a homeowner needs.

AUTO INSURANCE

Auto insurance protects you against financial loss if you have an accident. It is a contract between the insured and the insurance company. You agree to pay the premium and the insurance company agrees to pay losses as defined in the policy.

Auto insurance provides property, liability and medical coverage:

- Property coverage pays for damage to or theft of the car.
- Liability coverage pays for the legal responsibility to others for bodily injury or property damage.
- Medical coverage pays for the cost of treating injuries, rehabilitation and sometimes lost wages and funeral expenses.

An auto insurance policy comprises six kinds of coverage. Most countries require you to buy some, but not all, of these coverages. If you're financing a car, the lender may also have requirements. Most auto policies are for six months to a year. In the United States, the insurance company should notify you by mail when it's time to renew the policy and to pay the premium.

HOME INSURANCE

Home insurance provides compensation for damage or destruction of a home from disasters. In some geographical areas, the standard insurances exclude certain types of disasters, such as flood and earthquakes, that require additional coverage. Maintenance-related problems are the homeowners' responsibility.

The policy may include inventory, or this can be bought as a separate policy, especially for people who rent housing. In some countries, insurers offer a package which may include liability and legal responsibility for injuries and property damage caused by members of the household, including pets.

HEALTH

Health insurance policies by the National Health Service in the United Kingdom or other publicly-funded health programmes will cover the cost of medical treatments. Dental insurance, like medical insurance, is coverage for individuals to protect them against dental costs. In the U.S., dental insurance is often part of an employer's benefits package, along with health insurance.

ACCIDENT, SICKNESS AND UNEMPLOYMENT INSURANCE

- Disability insurance policies provide financial support in the event the policyholder is unable to work because of disabling illness or injury. It provides monthly support to help pay such obligations as mortgage loans and credit cards.
- Disability overhead insurance allows business owners to cover the overhead expenses of their business while they are unable to work.
- Total permanent disability insurance provides benefits when a person is permanently disabled and can no longer work in their profession, often taken as an adjunct to life insurance.
- Workers' compensation insurance replaces all or part of a worker's wages lost and accompanying medical expenses incurred because of a job-related injury.

CASUALTY

Casualty insurance insures against accidents, not necessarily tied to any specific property:

- Crime insurance is a form of casualty insurance that covers the policyholder against losses arising from the criminal acts of third parties. For example, a company can obtain crime insurance to cover losses arising from theft or embezzlement.
- Political risk insurance is a form of casualty insurance that can be taken out by businesses with operations in countries in which there is a risk that revolution or other political conditions will result in a loss.

LIFE

Life insurance provides a monetary benefit to a decedent's family or other designated beneficiary, and may specifically provide for income to an insured person's family, burial, funeral and other final expenses. Life insurance policies often allow the option of having the proceeds paid to the beneficiary either in a lump sum cash payment or an annuity. Annuities provide a stream of payments and are generally classified as insurance because they are issued by insurance companies and regulated as insurance and require the same kinds of actuarial and investment management expertise that life insurance requires.

Annuities and pensions that pay a benefit for life are sometimes regarded as insurance against the possibility that a retiree will outlive his or her financial resources. In that sense, they are the complement of life insurance and, from an underwriting perspective, are the mirror image of life insurance. Certain life insurance contracts accumulate cash values, which may be taken by the insured if the policy is surrendered or which may be borrowed against. Some policies, such as annuities and endowment policies, are financial instruments to accumulate or liquidate wealth when it is needed. In many countries, such as the U.S. and the UK, the tax law provides that the interest on this cash value is not taxable under certain circumstances. This leads to widespread use of life insurance as a tax-efficient method of saving as well as protection in the event of early death.

In U.S., the tax on interest income on life insurance policies and annuities is generally deferred. However, in some cases the benefit derived from tax deferral may be offset by a low return. This depends upon the insuring company, the type of policy and other variables. Moreover, other income tax saving vehicles may be better alternatives for value accumulation.

PROPERTY

Property insurance provides protection against risks to property, such as fire, theft or weather damage. This includes specialized forms of insurance such as fire insurance, flood insurance, earthquake insurance, home insurance, inland marine insurance or boiler insurance.

- Automobile insurance, known in the UK as motor insurance, is probably the most common form of insurance and may cover both legal liability claims against the driver and loss of or damage to the insured's vehicle itself. Throughout the United States an auto insurance policy is required to legally operate a motor vehicle on public roads. In some jurisdictions, bodily injury compensation for automobile accident victims has been changed to a no-fault system, which reduces or eliminates the ability to sue for compensation but provides automatic eligibility for benefits. Credit card companies insure against damage on rented cars.

  - Driving School Insurance provides cover for any authorized driver whilst undergoing tuition, cover also unlike other motor policies provides cover for instructor liability where both the pupil and driving instructor are equally liable in the event of a claim.

- Aviation insurance insures against hull, spares, deductibles, hull wear and liability risks.
- Boiler insurance insures against accidental physical damage to equipment or machinery.
- Builder's risk insurance insures against the risk of physical loss or damage to property during construction. Builder's risk insurance is typically written on an "all risk" basis covering damage due to any cause not otherwise expressly excluded. Builder's risk insurance is coverage that protects a person's or organization's insurable interest in materials, fixtures and/or equipment being used in the construction or renovation of a building or structure should those items sustain physical loss or damage from a covered cause.
- Crop insurance "Farmers use crop insurance to reduce or manage various risks associated with growing crops. Such risks include crop loss or damage caused by weather, hail, drought, frost damage, insects, or disease, for instance."
- Earthquake insurance is a form of property insurance that pays the policyholder in the event of an earthquake that causes damage to the property. Most

ordinary homeowners insurance policies do not cover earthquake damage. Most earthquake insurance policies feature a high deductible. Rates depend on location and the probability of an earthquake, as well as the construction of the home.

- A fidelity bond is a form of casualty insurance that covers policyholders for losses that they incur as a result of fraudulent acts by specified individuals. It usually insures a business for losses caused by the dishonest acts of its employees.
- Flood insurance protects against property loss due to flooding. Many insurers in the U.S. do not provide flood insurance in some portions of the country. In response to this, the federal government created the National Flood Insurance Programme which serves as the insurer of last resort.
- Home insurance, also commonly called hazard insurance or homeowners insurance, is the type of property insurance that covers private homes.
- Landlord insurance covers residential and commercial properties which are rented to others. Most homeowner's insurance covers only owner-occupied homes.
- Marine insurance and marine cargo insurance cover the loss or damage of ships at sea or on inland waterways, and of cargo in transit, regardless of the method of transit. When the owner of the cargo and the carrier are separate corporations, marine cargo insurance typically compensates the owner of cargo for losses sustained from fire, shipwreck, etc., but excludes losses that can be recovered from the carrier or the carrier's insurance. Many marine insurance underwriters will include "time element" coverage in such policies, which extends the indemnity to cover loss of profit and other business expenses attributable to the delay caused by a covered loss.
- Surety bond insurance is a three party insurance guaranteeing the performance of the principal.

- Terrorism insurance provides protection against any loss or damage caused by terrorist activities.
- Volcano insurance is an insurance that covers volcano damage in Hawaii.
- Windstorm insurance is an insurance covering the damage that can be caused by hurricanes and tropical cyclones.

LIABILITY

Liability insurance is a very broad superset that covers legal claims against the insured. Many types of insurance include an aspect of liability coverage. For example, a homeowner's insurance policy will normally include liability coverage which protects the insured in the event of a claim brought by someone who slips and falls on the property; automobile insurance also includes an aspect of liability insurance that indemnifies against the harm that a crashing car can cause to others' lives, health, or property.

The protection offered by a liability insurance policy is twofold: a legal defence in the event of a lawsuit commenced against the policyholder and indemnification with respect to a settlement or court verdict.

Liability policies typically cover only the negligence of the insured, and will not apply to results of wilful or intentional acts by the insured:

- Public liability insurance covers a business against claims should its operations injure a member of the public or damage their property in some way.
- Directors and officers liability insurance protects an organization from costs associated with litigation resulting from mistakes made by directors and officers for which they are liable. In the industry, it is usually called "D&O" for short.
- Environmental liability insurance protects the insured from bodily injury, property damage and cleanup costs as a result of the dispersal, release or escape of pollutants.
- Errors and omissions insurance.

- Prize indemnity insurance protects the insured from giving away a large prize at a specific event. Examples would include offering prizes to contestants who can make a half-court shot at a basketball game, or a hole-in-one at a golf tournament.
- Professional liability insurance, also called professional indemnity insurance, protects insured professionals such as architectural corporation and medical practice against potential negligence claims made by their patients/clients. Professional liability insurance may take on different names depending on the profession. For example, professional liability insurance in reference to the medical profession may be called malpractice insurance. Notaries public may take out errors and omissions insurance. Other potential E&O policyholders include, for example, real estate brokers, Insurance agents, home inspectors, appraisers, and website developers.

CREDIT

Credit insurance repays some or all of a loan when certain things happen to the borrower such as unemployment, disability, or death:

- Mortgage insurance insures the lender against default by the borrower. Mortgage insurance is a form of credit insurance, although the name credit insurance more often is used to refer to policies that cover other kinds of debt.
- Many credit cards offer payment protection plans which are a form of credit insurance.

OTHER TYPES

- All-risk insurance is an insurance that covers a wide-range of incidents and perils, except those noted in the policy. All-risk insurance is different from peril-specific insurance that cover losses from only those perils listed in the policy. In car insurance, all-risk policy includes also the damages caused by the own driver.

- Collateral protection insurance or CPI, insures property held as collateral for loans made by lending institutions.
- Defence Base Act Workers' compensation or DBA Insurance provides coverage for civilian workers hired by the government to perform contracts outside the U.S. and Canada. DBA is required for all U.S. citizens, U.S. residents, U.S. Green Card holders, and all employees or subcontractors hired on overseas government contracts. Depending on the country, Foreign Nationals must also be covered under DBA. This coverage typically includes expenses related to medical treatment and loss of wages, as well as disability and death benefits.
- Expatriate insurance provides individuals and organizations operating outside of their home country with protection for automobiles, property, health, liability and business pursuits.
- Financial loss insurance or Business Interruption Insurance protects individuals and companies against various financial risks. For example, a business might purchase coverage to protect it from loss of sales if a fire in a factory prevented it from carrying out its business for a time. Insurance might also cover the failure of a creditor to pay money it owes to the insured. This type of insurance is frequently referred to as "business interruption insurance." Fidelity bonds and surety bonds are included in this category, although these products provide a benefit to a third party in the event the insured party fails to perform its obligations under a contract with the obligee.
- Kidnap and ransom insurance
- Legal Expenses Insurance covers policyholders against the potential costs of legal action against an institution or an individual.
- Locked funds insurance is a little-known hybrid insurance policy jointly issued by governments and banks. It is used to protect public funds from tamper

by unauthorized parties. In special cases, a government may authorize its use in protecting semi-private funds which are liable to tamper. The terms of this type of insurance are usually very strict. Therefore it is used only in extreme cases where maximum security of funds is required.

- Media Insurance is designed to cover professionals that engage in film, video and TV production.
- Nuclear incident insurance covers damages resulting from an incident involving radioactive materials and is generally arranged at the national level.
- Pet insurance insures pets against accidents and illnesses - some companies cover routine/wellness care and burial, as well.
- Pollution Insurance which consists of first-party coverage for contamination of insured property either by external or on-site sources. Coverage for liability to third parties arising from contamination of air, water, or land due to the sudden and accidental release of hazardous materials from the insured site. The policy usually covers the costs of cleanup and may include coverage for releases from underground storage tanks. Intentional acts are specifically excluded.
- Purchase insurance is aimed at providing protection on the products people purchase. Purchase insurance can cover individual purchase protection, warranties, guarantees, care plans and even mobile phone insurance. Such insurance is normally very limited in the scope of problems that are covered by the policy.
- Title insurance provides a guarantee that title to real property is vested in the purchaser and/or mortgagee, free and clear of liens or encumbrances. It is usually issued in conjunction with a search of the public records performed at the time of a real estate transaction.
- Travel insurance is an insurance cover taken by those

who travel abroad, which covers certain losses such as medical expenses, loss of personal belongings, travel delay, personal liabilities, etc.

INSURANCE FINANCING VEHICLES

- Fraternal insurance is provided on a cooperative basis by fraternal benefit societies or other social organizations.
- No-fault insurance is a type of insurance policy where insureds are indemnified by their own insurer regardless of fault in the incident.
- Protected Self-Insurance is an alternative risk financing mechanism in which an organization retains the mathematically calculated cost of risk within the organization and transfers the catastrophic risk with specific and aggregate limits to an insurer so the maximum total cost of the programme is known. A properly designed and underwritten Protected Self-Insurance Programme reduces and stabilizes the cost of insurance and provides valuable risk management information.
- Retrospectively Rated Insurance is a method of establishing a premium on large commercial accounts. The final premium is based on the insured's actual loss experience during the policy term, sometimes subject to a minimum and maximum premium, with the final premium determined by a formula. Under this plan, the current year's premium is based partially on the current year's losses, although the premium adjustments may take months or years beyond the current year's expiration date. The rating formula is guaranteed in the insurance contract. Formula: retrospective premium = converted loss + basic premium × tax multiplier. Numerous variations of this formula have been developed and are in use.
- Formal self insurance is the deliberate decision to pay for otherwise insurable losses out of one's own

money. This can be done on a formal basis by establishing a separate fund into which funds are deposited on a periodic basis, or by simply forgoing the purchase of available insurance and paying out-of-pocket. Self insurance is usually used to pay for high-frequency, low-severity losses. Such losses, if covered by conventional insurance, mean having to pay a premium that includes loadings for the company's general expenses, cost of putting the policy on the books, acquisition expenses, premium taxes, and contingencies. While this is true for all insurance, for small, frequent losses the transaction costs may exceed the benefit of volatility reduction that insurance otherwise affords.

- Reinsurance is a type of insurance purchased by insurance companies or self-insured employers to protect against unexpected losses. Financial reinsurance is a form of reinsurance that is primarily used for capital management rather than to transfer insurance risk.
- Social insurance can be many things to many people in many countries. But a summary of its essence is that it is a collection of insurance coverages, plus retirement savings, that requires participation by all citizens. By forcing everyone in society to be a policyholder and pay premiums, it ensures that everyone can become a claimant when or if he/she needs to. Along the way this inevitably becomes related to other concepts such as the justice system and the welfare state. This is a large, complicated topic that engenders tremendous debate:
    - National Insurance
    - Social safety net
    - Social security
    - Social Security debate
    - Social Security
    - Social welfare provision
- Stop-loss insurance provides protection against

catastrophic or unpredictable losses. It is purchased by organizations who do not want to assume 100% of the liability for losses arising from the plans. Under a stop-loss policy, the insurance company becomes liable for losses that exceed certain limits called deductibles.

CLOSED COMMUNITY SELF-INSURANCE

Some communities prefer to create virtual insurance amongst themselves by other means than contractual risk transfer, which assigns explicit numerical values to risk. A number of religious groups, including the Amish and some Muslim groups, depend on support provided by their communities when disasters strike. The risk presented by any given person is assumed collectively by the community who all bear the cost of rebuilding lost property and supporting people whose needs are suddenly greater after a loss of some kind. In supportive communities where others can be trusted to follow community leaders, this tacit form of insurance can work. In this manner the community can even out the extreme differences in insurability that exist among its members. Some further justification is also provided by invoking the moral hazard of explicit insurance contracts.

In the United Kingdom, The Crown did not insure property such as government buildings. If a government building was damaged, the cost of repair would be met from public funds because, in the long run, this was cheaper than paying insurance premiums. Since many UK government buildings have been sold to property companies, and rented back, this arrangement is now less common and may have disappeared altogether.

LIFE INSURANCE PRODUCTS

TERM ASSURANCE

Based on the benefit patterns the traditional Life Insurance products can be categorised into the following types:

- Term Insurance

- Whole Life Insurance
- Endowment Insurance
- Annuities

Term Insurance provides for life insurance protection for the selected term only. In case the person dies during the term, the benefits are payable under the policy and in case of his survival till the end of the selected term the policy normally expires without any benefit becoming payable.

Term insurance may be regarded as temporary insurance and is more nearly comparable with "Property and Casualty insurance" contracts than the other forms of Life insurance contracts.

WHOLE OF LIFE ASSURANCE

As the name suggests, the whole life insurance policies are intended to provide Life Insurance protection over one's lifetime. The essence of whole life insurance is that it provides for payment of the assured amount upon the insured's death regardless of when it occurs. Under these policies, the payment of the assured sum is a certainty in contrast to the term insurance contracts. Only the time of payment of the assured sum is an uncertainty.

Whole life policies can be either participating type or non-participating type. Participating type policies are those which are entitled to a share in the distributable surplus of the Life Insurance company, whereby the cash value of the policy can go up, with the announcement of bonus/ dividend. Non-participating policies have the same benefit throughout the life of the policy.

There can be the following types of whole life policies:

- Ordinary Whole Life Insurance
- Limited Payment Whole Life Insurance
- Convertible Whole Life Insurance

ENDOWMENT ASSURANCE

These are the most commonly sold policies. These policies assure that the benefits under the policy will be paid on the death of the life insured during the selected term or on his survival to the end of the term. Hence the assured benefits are payable either on the date of maturity or on death of the life insured, if earlier.

Endowment policies assist in providing for the payment of a lump sum amount for a specific purpose, say, provision for retirement, meeting the needs of the child etc. The money required for the purpose will be built up whether the person is alive till that date or not. Like whole life insurance policies, endowment policies can also be of participating and non-participating types.

ANNUITIES

An annuity is a series of periodic payments. An annuity contract is an insurance policy, under which the annuity provider agrees to pay the purchaser of annuity a series of regular periodical payments for a fixed period or during someone's life time.

Classification of Annuities:

- The number of lives covered
  - Single
  - Joint
- The beginning of the payment of annuity
  - Immediate annuity
  - Deferred annuity
- Method of premium payment
  - Single premium
  - Regular instalment

NON TRADITIONAL COVERS

Universal Life Insurance is another non-traditional type of Life Insurance introduced in the United States in the year 1979, which had an adjustable face value, floating interest rates based on market conditions and unbundling of savings and protection elements of Life Insurance.

After paying an initial minimum premium, policy owners may thereafter pay whatever amount and at whatever times they wish, or even skip premium payments, provided the cash value will cover policy charges. Similarly they had the option to raise or reduce the face value of the Insurance policy. For increasing the insurance coverage proof of continued insurability was insisted.

Under this type of policy, the policyholder pays an initial premium, which should not be less than a minimum for the given face value and the attained age of the Life to be Insured. From this premium payment, the mortality charge for the first period and the expenses charges will be deducted and the balance will be the policy's cash value. To this cash value a certain interest will be credited at the end of the period.

ULIPS

Most importantly, what are ULIPs? Here, you will find all the information you need to set your mind at ease about how to invest in ULIPs, and which ULIP is right for you. ULIPs are a category of goal-based financial solutions that combine the safety of insurance protection with wealth creation opportunities.

In ULIPs, a part of the investment goes towards providing you life cover. The residual portion of the ULIP is invested in a fund which in turn invests in stocks or bonds; the value of investments alters with the performance of the underlying fund opted by you. Simply put, ULIPs are structured in such that the protection element and the savings element are distinguishable, and hence managed according to your specific needs. In this way, the ULIP plan offers unprecedented flexibility and transparency.

WORKING OF ULIPS

It is critical that you understand how your money gets invested once you purchase a ULIP: When you decide the amount of premium to be paid and the amount of life cover you want from the ULIP, the insurer deducts some portion of the ULIP premium upfront.

This portion is known as the Premium Allocation charge, and varies from product to product. The rest of the premium is invested in the fund or mixture of funds chosen by you. Mortality charges and ULIP administration charges are thereafter deducted on a periodic basis by cancellation of units, whereas the ULIP fund management charges are adjusted from NAV on a daily basis.

Since the fund of your choice has an underlying investment – either in equity or debt or a combination of the two – your fund value will reflect the performance of the underlying asset classes. At the time of maturity of your plan, you are entitled to receive the fund value as at the time of maturity. The pie-chart the split of your ULIP premium:

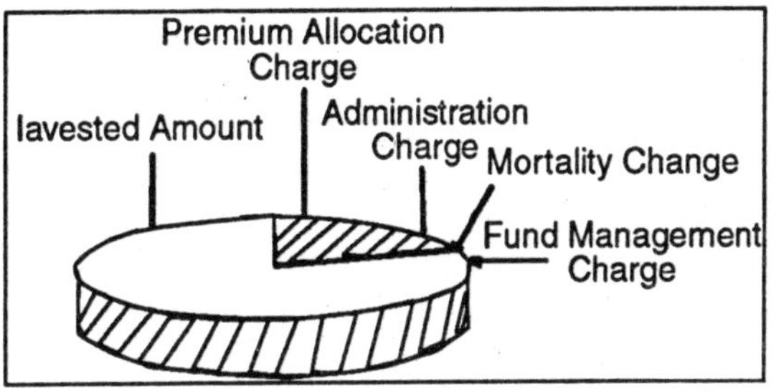

Fig. Premium Break Up

TYPES OF ULIPS

One of the big advantages that a ULIP offers is that whatever be your specific financial objective, chances are that there is a ULIP which is just right for you.

Retirement Planning

Retirement is the end of active employment and brings with it the cessation of regular income.

Today an increasing number of people have stated planning for their retirement:

- Almost 96% of the working population has no formal provisions for retirement
- With the growing nuclearisation of family structure, traditional support system of the younger earning members – is no longer available
- Developments in the healthcare space has lead to an increase in life expectancy
- Cost of living is increasing at an alarming rate

Pension plans from insurance companies ensure that regular, disciplined savings in such plans can accumulate over a period of time to provide a steady income post-retirement.

Usually all retirement plans have two distinctive phases:

1. The accumulation phase when you are saving and investing during your earning years to build up a retirement corpus and
2. The withdrawal phase when you actually reap the benefits of your investment as your annuity payouts begin

In a typical pension plan you have the flexibility to make a lump sum payment or a regular contribution every year during your earning years. Your money is then invested in funds of your choice.

You can opt to receive the annuity at any time after vesting age. Most of the Unit linked pension plans also come with a wide range of annuity options which gives you choice in structuring the post-retirement benefit pay-outs. Also at the time of vesting you can make a lump sum tax-exempted withdrawal of up to 33 per cent of the accumulated corpus.

In a retirement plan, the earlier you begin the greater you gain post retirement due to the power of compounding. Let us take an example of Gaurav and Hari. Both of them want to retire at the age of 60. Gaurav starts investing Rs. 10,000 every year from the age of 25 till the time that he retires. In all, he would have invested Rs. 350,000. If his investments were to earn 7% return every year, at the time of his retirement, Gaurav will have a retirement corpus of Rs. 13, 82,368.

Now, Hari starts investing 10 years later and in order to make up for the lost time, invests Rs.15,000 every year. So, by the time of his retirement, he would have invested Rs. 3,75,000. And assuming the same annual return of 7%, he will end up with a retirement corpus of Rs 9, 48,735.

So, you see how despite setting aside more than 50% of Gaurav's annual contribution, Hari ends up with a retirement corpus which is almost a third lesser than Gaurav's. That is the power of compounding. Which is why, it is never too early to invest in a ULIP for retirement planning.

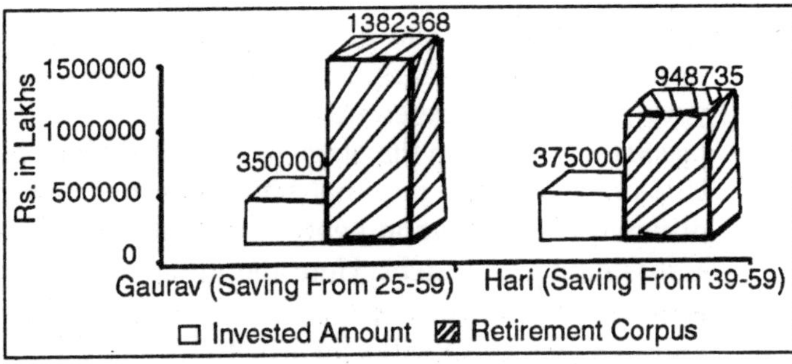

Fig. Retirement Corpus at Age of 60 @ 7% Annual

Long Term Wealth Creation

ULIPs are the right insurance solutions for you if you are looking for a strong wealth creation proposition allied to a core insurance benefit. Such plans are ideal for people who are in their late 20s and early 30s and by investing in such a plan get the flexibility of using it to fund any of their long-term financial goals such as purchase of a house or funding their children's education. The added element of life cover serves to make these plans a wholesome financial investment option.

Wealth Creation ULIPs can be primarily classified as:

- *Single premium*: Regular premium plan: Depending upon you needs and premium paying capacity you can either opt for a single premium plan where you need to pay premium only once during the term of entire policy or regular premium plans where you can premium at a frequency chosen by you depending upon your convenience
- *Guarantee plans*: Non guarantee plans: Today there are wealth creation ULIPS which also offer guaranteed benefit. These plans are ideal insurance-cum-investment option for customers who want to enjoy the potentially higher returns of a market linked instrument, but without taking any market risk. On the other hand non guarantee plans comes with an in - built range of fund options to choose from –ranging from aggressive funds to conservative

funds so that you can decide to invest your money in line with your market outlook, time horizon and your investment preferences and needs.

- *Life Stage based*: Non life Stage based: Life Stage based Ulips factor in the fact that your priorities differ at different life stages and hence distribute your money across equity and debt. Here the initial allocation is decided as per your age since age is a significant indicator of risk appetite. Such a strategy ensures that the asset allocation at all times is in sync with your age and changing financial needs.

Children's Education

One of the most important responsibilities you have as a parent is to ensure that your child gets the best possible education that can be provided. Apart from conventional schooling, it becomes important to expose your child to different activities such as dance, painting and sports training for holistic development. As a parent, you want to ensure that their development is not hampered either due to rising costs or unforeseen circumstances. Today there are ULIPs that offer money at key milestones of your child's education thus ensuring that your child's education continues unhampered even if something unfortunate happens to you. While, the death of a parent is an irreparable emotional loss, child education plans safeguard the child against the financial ramifications of the death of a parent.

Apart from benefit, child plans also offers features.

- Flexibility of adding on various riders like Income benefit rider, disability rider etc to get additional benefits.For e.g. In case of income benefit rider, In the event of the death of the parent, the child will receive a regular pre-determined amount every year to meet the educational expenses.
- In case of unfortunate incidence of the death of a parent, not only will the child receive the sum assured immediately but will also continue to receive money at the key educational milestones.

Health Solutions

When you are young and working you save for various goals like marriage, education, retirement etc. but saving for health care is never considered or left for later. During these years we have various sources of income or savings on which we can rely for health emergencies.

But with increasing cost of healthcare, proportion of this spend is increasing at an alarming pace. This is forcing families to borrow or sell assets to meet expenses during medical emergencies. And during old age health care expenses increase due to health deterioration because of age and higher incidence of chronic illness. Thus it is important for you to invest in health insurance today so that tomorrow you are fully prepared to meet rising healthcare expenses, which would be incurred during old age, with the right health insurance plan.

Health ULIP is a recent innovation from the health insurance industry. In a health ULIP part of your premiums are allocated for investment designed specifically to build a health fund to meet future health related expenses. It aims to create a health savings kitty by investing in a long term flexible savings plan with multiple fund options. The health fund thus created allows you to claim for health related expenses of any kind and also fund your future health insurance charges. You can also avail of tax benefit on premium paid u/s 80D.

WHEN ULIP WORK BEST?

Whether you are in the process of deciding which ULIP to invest in; or whether you already have a unit linked insurance policy to secure your important financial goals there are some key principles which should govern any decision related to ULIPs.

Adhering to these key principles will allow you to make optimum utilization of your ULIP:

- Appropriate Life Cover
- Right Fund Option
- Long Term Investment
- Know the Charges
- Know the Features

CREDIT TRADING

INVESTMENT GRADE CORPORATES

The Investment Grade Corporates business unit originates, syndicates, underwrites and trades investment grade domestic corporate and sovereign debt. In addition, the group trades short-term securities such as floating rate notes, both US and European commercial paper and non-convertible preferred stock.

Local offices for this product group reside in New York, London, Zurich and Tokyo. The products traded include Agencies, Medium Term Notes, Bank and Finance, Preferred Stocks, Commercial Paper, Projects/Slobs, Floaters, Utilities, Industrials, Yankees, and Eurobonds.

CREDIT DERIVATIVES

The Developed Market Credit Derivatives Group trades and structures credit derivatives on Investment Grade and High Yield credits. The group is a leading dealer in both flow and structured products, helping to provide credit-hedging solutions to our clients.

The group has an active and broad flow business which trades single-name credit default swaps on over 800 individual credits, credit linked notes and index swaps. The structured business includes portfolio transactions, synthetic CDOs, structured notes and repackaged credit assets. The group has also been a leader in working with other parts of the credit cluster to provide derivative solutions, including several synthetic asset securitizations. The main trading centres are New York, London, Zurich and Hong Kong.

5

Lease Financing

In order to start and sustain a business one needs finance. In the unit one on feasibility study, you have already seen the process of estimating financial requirements.

The process involved:

- Making a list of all the assets
- Identifying the sources of supply
- Estimating the cost of acquisition when the assets are to be acquired on outright basis.

Then investment requirements as well as entrepreneur's fear will increase. To scare away the entrepreneur's fear, the emphasis should be given to resources and not to the ownership. In this unit we intend to familiarize you with some important financial innovations *i.e.*, leasing, hire purchase and ctoring.

OBJECTIVES

After going through this unit you should be able to:

- Describe the meaning of leasing
- Explain the role and importance of lease financing in economic development of a country
- Distinguish between the various types of leases
- Describe the meaning of hire purchase
- Distinguish between leasing and hire purchase
- Describe the meaning of factoring

CONCEPT 0F LEASE FINANCING

Lease financing denotes procurement of assets through lease. The subject of leasing falls in the category of finance.

Leasing has grown as a big industry in the USA and UK and spread to other countries during the present century. In India, the concept was pioneered in 1973 when the First Leasing Company was set up in Madras and the eighties have seen a rapid growth of this business.

Lease as a concept involves a contract whereby the ownership, financing and risk taking of any equipment or asset are separated and shared by two or more parties. Thus, the lessor may finance and lessee may accept the risk through the use of it while a third party may own it.

Alternatively the lessor may finance and own it while the lessee enjoys the use of it and bears the risk. There are various combinations in which the characteristics are shared by the lessor and lessee.

MEANING OF LEASE FINANCING

A lease transaction is a commercial arrangement whereby an equipment owner or Manufacturer conveys to the equipment user the right to use the equipment in return for a rental. In other words, lease is a contract between the owner of an asset and its user for the right to use the asset during a specified period in return for a mutually agreed periodic payment.

The important feature of a lease contract is separation of the ownership of the asset from its usage. Lease financing is based on the observation made by Donald B. Grant: "Why own a cow when the milk is so cheap? All you really need is milk and not the cow."

IMPORTANCE OF LEASE FINANCING

Leasing industry plays an important role in the economic development of a country by providing money incentives to lessee. The lessee does not have to pay the cost of asset at the time of signing the contract of leases.

Leasing contracts are more flexible so lessees can structure the leasing contracts according to their needs for finance. The lessee can also pass on the risk of obsolescence to the lessor by acquiring those appliances, which have high technological obsolescence. To day, most of us are familiar with leases of houses, apartments, offices, etc.

TYPES OF LEASE AGREEMENTS

Lease agreements are basically of two types.

They are:

1. Financial lease and
2. Operating lease.

The other variations in lease agreements are:

- Sale and lease back
- Leveraged leasing and
- Direct leasing.

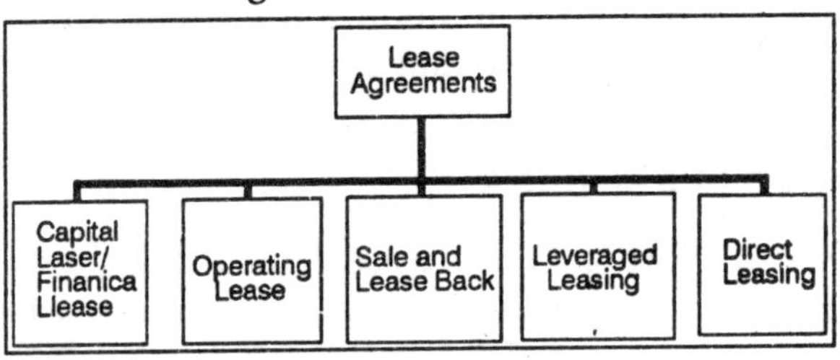

Fig. Types of Leases

FINANCIAL LEASE

Long-term, non-cancellable lease contracts are known as financial leases. The essential point of financial lease agreement is that it contains a condition whereby the lessor agrees to transfer the title for the asset at the end of the lease period at a nominal cost.

At lease it must give an option to the lessee to purchase the asset he has used at the expiry of the lease. Under this lease the lessor recovers 90% of the fair value of the asset as lease rentals and the lease period is 75% of the economic life of the asset.

The lease agreement is irrevocable. All the risks incidental to the asset ownership and all the benefits arising there from are transferred to the lessee who bears the cost of maintenance, insurance and repairs. Only title deeds remain with the lessor. Financial lease is also known as 'capital lease'. In India, financial leases are very popular with high-cost and high technology equipment.

OPERATING LEASE

An operating lease stands in contrast to the financial lease in almost all aspects. This lease agreement gives to the lessee only a limited right to use the asset. The lessor is responsible for the upkeep and maintenance of the asset. The lessee is not given any uplift to purchase the asset at the end of the lease period.

Normally the lease is for a short period and even otherwise is revocable at a short notice. Mines, Computers hardware, trucks and automobiles are found suitable for operating lease because the rate of obsolescence is very high in this kind of assets.

SALE AND LEASE BACK

It is a sub-part of finance lease. Under this, the owner of an asset sells the asset to a party, who in turn leases back the same asset to the owner in consideration of lease rentals. However, under this arrangement, the assets are not physically exchanged but it all happens in records only. This is nothing but a paper transaction.

Sale and lease back transaction is suitable for those assets, which are not subjected depreciation but appreciation, say land. The advantage of this method is that the lessee can satisfy himself completely regarding the quality of the asset and after possession of the asset convert the sale into a lease arrangement.

The sale and lease back transaction can be expressed with the help of the following figure.

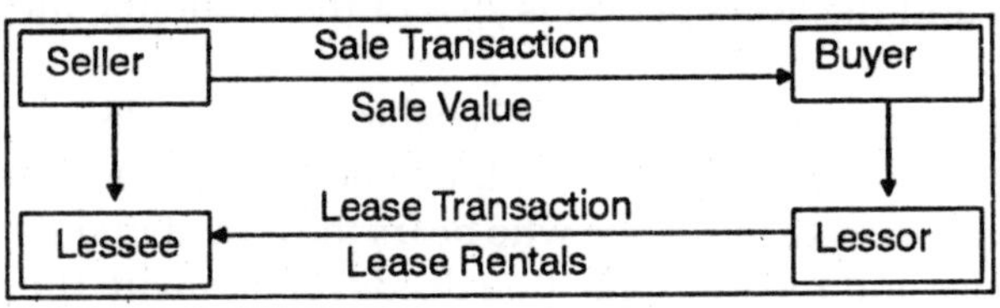

Fig. Structure of a sale and Leaseback Deal

Under this transaction, the seller assumes the role of a lessee and the buyer assumes the role of a lessor. The seller gets the agreed selling price and the buyer gets the lease rentals. It is possible to structure the sale at agreed value and to adjust difference in the lease rentals. Thus the effect of profit/ loss on sale of assets can be deferred.

LEVERAGED LEASING

Under leveraged leasing arrangement, a third party is involved beside lessor and lessee. The lessor borrows a part of the purchase cost of the asset from the third party *i.e.*, lender and the asset so purchased is held as security against the loan. The lender is paid off from the lease rentals directly by the lessee and the surplus after meeting the claims of the lender goes to the lessor. The lessor, the owner of the asset is entitled to depreciation allowance associated with the asset.

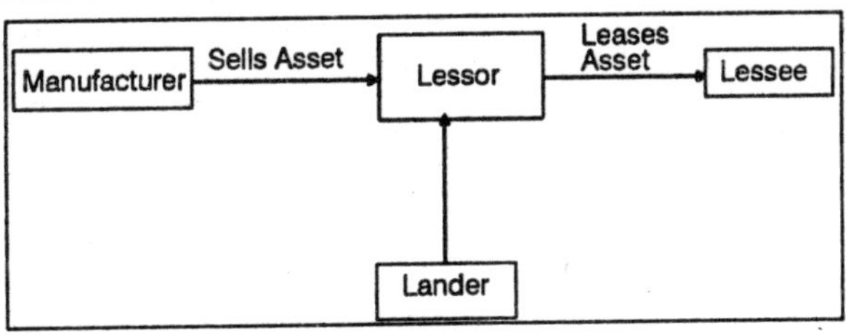

Fig. Leveraged Lease

DIRECT LEASING

Under direct leasing, a firm acquires the right to use an asset from the manufacturer directly. The ownership of the asset leased out remains with the manufacturer itself. The major types of direct lessor include manufacturers, finance companies, independent lease companies, special purpose leasing companies etc

LEASING IN INDIA

Leasing has grown by leaps and bounds in the eighties but it is estimated that hardly 1% of the industrial investment in India is covered by the lease finance, as against 40% in USA and 30% in UK and 10% in Japan.

The prospects of leasing in India are good due to growing investment needs and scarcity of funds with public financial institutions.

This type of lease finances is particularly suitable in India where a large number of small companies have emerged more recently. Leasing in the sphere of land and building has been in existence in India for a long time, while equipment leasing has become very common in the recent times.

CONCEPT AND MEANING OF HIRE PURCHASE

Hire purchase is a type of instalment credit under which the hire purchaser, called the hirer, agrees to take the goods on hire at a stated rental, which is inclusive of the repayment of principal as well as interest, with an option to purchase. Under this transaction, the hire purchaser acquires the property immediately on signing the hire purchase agreement but the ownership or title of the same is transferred only when the last instalment is paid.

The hire purchase system is regulated by the Hire Purchase Act 1972. This Act defines a hire purchase as"an agreement under which goods are let on hire and under which the hirer has an option to purchase them in accordance with the terms of the agreement and includes an agreement under which:

- The owner delivers possession of goods thereof to a person on condition that such person pays the agreed amount in periodic instalments.
- The property in the goods is to pass to such person on the payment of the last of such instalments, and
- Such person has a right to terminate the agreement at any time before the property so passes".

Hire purchase should be distinguished from instalment sale wherein property passes to the purchaser with the payment of the first instalment. But in case of HP buyer gets ownership after paying the last instalment. HP also differs form leasing.

Table. Defference between Lease Financing and Hire Purchase

Basis	Lease Financing	Hire Purchase
Meaning	A lease transaction is a commercial arrangement whereby an equipment owner or manufacturer conveys to the equipment user the right to use the equipment in return for a rental.	Hire purchase is a type of instalment credit under which the hire purchaser agrees to take the goods on hire at a stated rental, which is inclusive of the repayment of principal as well as interest, with an option to purchase.
Option to user	No option is provided to the lessee (user) to purchase the goods.	Option is provided to the hirer (user).
Nature of expenditure	Lease rentals paid by the lessee are entirely revenue ependiture of the lesses.	Only Interest element included in the HP instalments is revenue expenditure by nature.
Components	Lease rentals comprise of 2 elements 1. finance charge and 2. Capital recovery.	HP instalments compriseof 3 elements 1. Normal trading profit 2. Finance charge and 3. Recovery of cost of goods/assest.

NSIC AND HIRE PURCHASE

Small scale firms can acquire industrial machinery, office equipment, vehicles, etc., without making full payment through hire purchase. With the help of assets acquired through hire purchase they can produce and sell.

From the earning payments can easily be made in instalments. Ultimately the ownership of assets can be acquired. Now several agencies like National Small Industries Corporation provide machinery and equipment to small scale units on hire purchase basis and on lease basis. NSIC follows the following Hire Purchase procedure and Hire Purchase Plan for financing plant and machinery to small scale units.

FACTORING

Factoring is another type of financial service provided by the specialist organizations. When small scale firms sell on credit basis, collection of receivable poses a problem. In that case factoring organizations play an important role in collection of debtors.

Factoring involves sale of receivables to specialized firm, called factors. Factors collect receivables and also advance cash against receivables to solve the client firm's liquidity problem. For providing their services, they charge interest on advance and commission for other services. In other words, factoring is an arrangement under which a financial institution undertakes the task of collecting the book debts of its client in return for a service charge in the form of discount or rebate. The factoring institution eliminates the client's risk of bad debts by taking over the responsibility of book debts due to the client.

The factoring institution advances a proportion of the value of book debts of the client immediately and the balance on maturity of book debts.

FACTORING PROCEDURE

The agreement between the supplier and the factor specifies the factoring procedure. Usually the firm sends the customer's order to the factor for evaluating the customer's creditworthiness and approval. Once the factor is satisfied about the customer's credit worthiness and agrees to buy receivables, the firm dispatches goods to the customer.

The customer will be informed that his account has been sold to the factor, and he is instructed to make payment directly to the factor. To perform his functions of credit evaluation and collection for a large number of clients, a factor may maintain a credit department with specialized staff. Once the factor has purchased a firm's receivables and if he agrees to own them, he will have to provide protection against any bad-debt losses to the firm.

MERITS

- As a result of factoring services, the enterprise can concentrate on manufacturing and selling.
- The risk of bad debts is eliminated.
- The factoring institution also provides advice on business trends and other related matters. In India, subsidiaries of four Indian banks-State Bank of India, Canara Bank, Punjab National Bank and Allahabad Bank are providing factoring services.

ADVANTAGES OF LEASING

Equipment leasing offers a number of important advantages.

LEASING PROVIDES 100 PER CENT FINANCING

Most leases simply require first and last payments paid in advance and a small documentation fee. No security deposits or up-front money is required. Enterprise Financial Solutions, Inc. pays your vendor in full including installation, delivery and taxes unless state law prohibits.

LEASING PRESERVES CREDIT LINES

Credit lines with banks and other depository institutions are precious and hard to establish. Conserve those lines for inventory, A/R or other uses and emergencies. EFSI will take care of the financing for your capital equipment so that your lines of credit remain free.

LEASING INCREASES PURCHASING POWER

Your needs may be for a $50,000 machine but your available cash/credit only allows for $30,000, hence you settle for a smaller piece of machinery that only meets your needs half-way. EFSI can increase your purchasing power by allowing you to finance the needed equipment for the job. That way you get the equipment you need to meet demand and promote growth.

LEASING BALANCES USAGE AND COST

Leasing makes sense when the equipment you use creates a return that exceeds its cost. In other words, leasing allows you to set a fixed monthly payment for the use of equipment that creates an anticipated return exceeding that payment. That way you are certain that your operation is profitable and the equipment serves its purpose.

LEASING PROVIDES FIXED RATE FINANCING

Leasing is not subject to market fluctuations and interest rate increases. You can negotiate the monthly payments up front and secure a fixed rate for the life of the lease. This makes it much easier to project cash flow and budgets for planning purposes.

LEASING CONSERVES WORKING CAPITAL

Keep your hard-earned cash on hand or invested. Enterprise Financial Solutions, Inc. enables you to enjoy the working capital your company receives since it covers all costs associated with capital equipment purchases. This ability to grow and keep your cash ultimately puts you ahead of your competition and ensures long-term profitability.

LEASING IS CONVENIENT

Unlike dealing with bank loans and other alternative types of financing, leasing is an easy and convenient process. Typically, all we require is a one-page application for any request up to $50,000.

LEASING IS TAX-ADVANTAGED

When structured properly, a lease agreement may allow you to receive tax benefits. These benefits and their availability are subject to an array of factors and we suggest you talk with your accountant about these benefits. Similarly, any tax benefit received from the ownership of the equipment by EFSI is passed on to the lessee through competitive rates and lower fees.

LEASING IS A HEDGE AGAINST INFLATION

Since your payments apply to the use of the equipment you do not pay for ownership on equipment that consistently depreciates.

Furthermore, your cash savings can yield a return that fights inflationary pressures.

LEASING PROVIDES FLEXIBLE PAYMENTS

Lease payments can be structured to meet your needs. This adjustment is possible by correcting the residual value of the equipment due at lease end. By changing your end of lease balloon payment from $10,000 to $25,000 for example, you can lower your monthly payment significantly.

LEASING PROVIDES OPTIONS

Leasing provides flexible end of lease options. Equipment at the end of the lease term can returned, extended or purchased.

DISADVANTAGES OF LEASING

Leasing is a preferred means of financing for certain businesses. However it is not for everyone. The type of industry and type of equipment required also need to be considered.

Tax implications also need to be compared between leasing and purchasing equipment:

- You have an obligation to continue making payments. Typically, leases may not be terminated before the original term is completed. Therefore, the renter is responsible for paying off the lease. This can pose a major financial problem for the owners of a business experiences a downturn.

- You have no equity until you decide to purchase the equipment at the end of the lease term, at which point the equipment has depreciated significantly.
- Although you are not the owner, you are still responsible for maintaining the equipment as specified by the terms of the lease. Failure to do so can prove costly.

EVALUATION OF LEASE AGREEMENT

A Lease Agreement is a written document that sets down terms, rules and obligations that exist between the owner of the property and the person or entity that desires to lease the space. Rent or lease payments are the consideration paid by the renter to the owner in exchange for the renter's exclusive use of the property. Each and every term of a commercial lease agreement is negotiable - that is, the terms of the lease are contractually agreed-upon by the renter and the owner. Residential leases have certain statutory protections in so much as the State may require the owner to cap security deposits or follow rules protecting a tenant's privacy.

6

Venture Capital

INTRODUCTION

Capital is the lifeblood of businesses. While no amount of money will make a bad business successful, no business can survive without enough money to develop products, hire employees, establish markets and attract customers. For many businesses, particularly in the early stages before profits become predictable, traditional sources of capital such as banks and credit unions are simply unavailable. For those businesses, venture capital may be the best hope to raise the money needed to succeed.

Today, there are more Maine-based venture capital firms than ever before. But while there is no shortage of capital, not every business can get the money it needs or wants. Venture capital is not the answer for all businesses in need of capital. But for those businesses that offer the potential of rapid growth and the potential for considerable profit, informed investors are ready to open their checkbooks.

These high growth businesses not only offer the prospect of substantial returns to owners and investors, they also create new jobs and strengthen the economy. The technology focus of many venture capital stage companies means that the jobs created tend to be relatively high quality jobs. Maine State Government has recognized the importance of supporting these next generation companies and has provided substantial resources to assist entrepreneurs in raising capital. Maine entrepreneurs want to know whether venture capital is right for them, where to find it, and how to get it. This Primer on

Venture Capital in Maine is designed to answer those questions. It explains what venture capital is, how venture capital investors work, what they are looking for, how to approach them, and what to expect when it comes time to structure an investment.

A explains many of the terms that are used in the venture capital world. Finally, the Additional Resources provides some additional sources of capital and more in-depth information.

Venture capital typically comes from four generic sources:

1. Private venture capital firms
2. Individual investors generally referred to as "angel investors"
3. Corporations making strategic investments
4. Governmental sources.

Angel investors have been making investments in Maine for many years without any formal tracking of their activity. The first formal venture capital firm in Maine, the Maine Capital Corporation, began operations in 1980. Maine Capital Corporation raised $2,000,000, of which $1,000,000 came from Maine investors with an incentive from the State Legislature in the form of a tax credit. From the groundwork laid by Maine Capital Corporation, successor North Atlantic Capital Corporation has raised two additional funds focused on later-stage businesses.

Other funds have also been created to serve businesses in Maine. These formal venture capital funds have not only invested their own capital in Maine businesses, they have attracted out-of-state capital to Maine as well. The result has been a steady increase in the amount of venture capital raised by Maine businesses, although the recession and "dot.com bust" that began in 2001 has at least temporarily halted the upward trend.

While the formal venture capital funds may get the bulk of the attention, angel investors likely fund the most businesses. Angel investors are typically individuals with a business background who invest relatively small amounts of money in small business ventures in or near their communities. They usually make their investments with an expectation of a significant return. But they may also be motivated by a desire to be helpful to a struggling entrepreneur and may provide management, financial, and marketing assistance along with their cash investment.

To the frustration of entrepreneurs, angel investors are difficult to find, preferring a degree of anonymity to protect their privacy. Yet angel investment plays a key role in supporting early stage Maine businesses. Corporate venture capital, or investments by corporations into smaller companies, grew exponentially in the United States during the latter half of the 1990s.

This activity has slowed considerably since early 2001. While some corporate venture capital has undoubtedly been invested in Maine businesses, there is no easy way to track or measure it. It does not appear to be a significant source of capital for most Maine entrepreneurs.

Maine Government resources range from the technical advice and business development assistance provided by the Department of Economic and Community Development and Small Business Development Centres, to the competitive grants awarded by the Maine Technology Institute, to venture money for selected companies from the Small Enterprise Growth Fund, to the many financing programmes of the Finance Authority of Maine. Every Maine entrepreneur should become familiar with these resources.

The Finance Authority of Maine has published this Primer as a service and resource for the many entrepreneurs in Maine who are collectively striving to build Maine's economic future. This Primer is consistent with FAME's primary goal of providing targeted financing tools, information and solutions that enable Maine citizens to take advantage of opportunities that may be available to them.

This is the third major publication relating to venture capital published by FAME, following *A Study of the Availability and Sources of Venture Capital in Maine* issued in 1995, and *Capital Availability for High-Technology Businesses in Maine,* which was issued in 2000. The Finance Authority of Maine is charged by Maine law with finding ways to help businesses get access to the capital they need to start-up, prosper and create jobs. As part of this effort, FAME has supported entrepreneurs and their efforts through a number of programmes and services, ranging from early-stage patient capital programmes to loan guarantee and tax-exempt bond programmes for established businesses.

Programmes and services targeted at early-stage businesses include:

- *Maine Seed Capital Tax Credit Programme*: This valuable incentive allows entrepreneurs to attract investor capital by offering the investor a credit against Maine income taxes of up to 40% of an eligible investment in a Maine business, and 60% in areas of high unemployment.
- *Small Enterprise Growth Fund*: A State-funded venture capital fund that can invest up to $500,000 in patient capital in promising companies that demonstrate a potential for high growth and public benefit.
- *Maine Economic Development Venture Capital Revolving Investment Programme*: This programme allows FAME to invest as an equal partner in eligible private venture capital funds that agree to support emerging and early-growth businesses in Maine. It leverages private capital and encourages experienced professional venture capital fund managers to invest in Maine businesses.
- *Small Business Loan Insurance Programmes*: FAME is able to use its loan insurance programmes in conjunction with a bank loan to assist small businesses that demonstrate the ability to repay a loan.
- *Economic Recovery Loan Programme*: FAME can also provide direct loans, generally subordinate to loans from other sources, to help businesses that have exhausted other sources of financing but demonstrate a reasonable likelihood of being able to repay a loan.
- *Venture capital forums*: FAME has hosted a number of venture capital forums designed to bring

entrepreneurs and investors together to share information about venture investing in Maine, and to discuss policy issues and improvements to available programmes.

WHAT VENTURE CAPITAL IS (AND IS NOT)

The range of business investment opportunities that interest venture investors is quite broad and hard to precisely define. Simply stated, venture capital is money provided by individual investors or entities seeking a high return on their investment in privately owned business ventures. In order to get those high returns, venture investors are willing to accept a relatively high degree of risk of loss of their investment. Generally speaking, the financial risk posed by a business venture corresponds with its stage of development, as shown in Figure. Certainly there are mature businesses that are struggling and may present a high level of risk, but Figure summarizes the risk spectrum as it applies to most businesses:

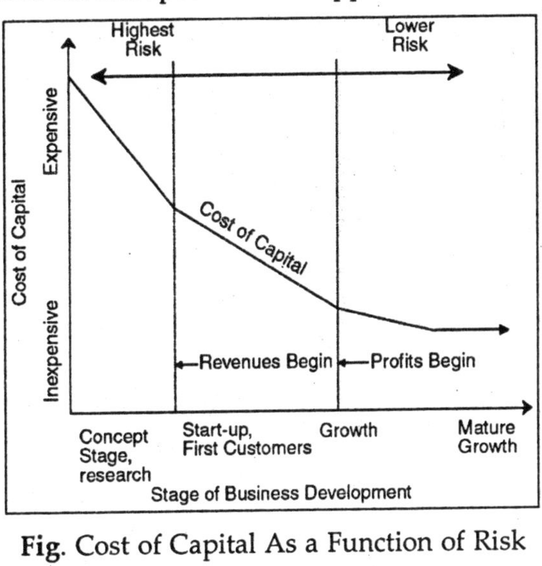

Fig. Cost of Capital As a Function of Risk

The highest risk level for a business is at its earliest stages before it has begun to generate much revenue. As businesses begin to sell products or services, expand, achieve breakeven cash flow and profitability, the level of risk of an investment in that business drops, moving to the right of Figure.

As the risk declines, the cost of raising capital for the business declines also, as shown by Figure. The cost of raising capital is the price the business must pay to get the capital it needs. It pays that price either in the form of a share of ownership in the business or through payments of interest, dividends, royalties, or other payments. Raising capital also gets easier as the risk level declines, especially once the business progresses to the point that banks become interested in lending it money.

Given a choice, entrepreneurs looking for money for their business will try to raise that capital at the lowest cost possible. Usually, the least cost option for a business is a loan from a bank or other commercial lender.

These lenders look for an annual return that is typically in the range of about 5% to 12%, varying with changes in the Prime Rate of interest. Venture investors, on the other hand, look for annualized returns more in the range of 25% and up. So entrepreneurs looking for money will usually look for venture capital only if they do not have the choice of lower cost capital.

Banks and other lenders can offer comparatively low rates because they lend to companies that have a low risk of defaulting on their loans. Companies that present a low risk of default would be placed on the right side of Figure. Some entrepreneurs complain that banks will only lend to businesses that do not need the money.

The truth is that banks earn a comparatively small profit on the funds they lend; therefore, they cannot afford to make many bad loans. One bad loan may cost a bank more than the profit it makes on 25 good loans.

Banks strive to keep their losses on bad loans to significantly less than 1% of their portfolios, so they lend to businesses that demonstrate the ability to repay the loan. Also, banks are looking for current income, and expect payments of interest, and usually principal as well, on a monthly basis.

Venture capital investors, on one hand, are willing to make investments in businesses that are too risky for banks; that is, companies which would be placed towards the left side of Figure.

Because higher risk means a greater ratio of bad investments to good ones, venture investors expect a much higher return on their successful investments to make up for the losses on their investments in companies that are not successful.

Most venture investors do not expect to get regular payments, at least until the company is established and profitable. They look to make their profit down the road when the company is sold or when it issues stock to the public in an Initial Public Offering.

Stated another way, venture investors look to participate in the increased value of a successful business venture, while banks and other lenders look to lend money for a fee and expect to receive regular payments regardless of changes in corporate value. Figure is a simplified way of looking at the respective risk-reward tradeoffs applicable to venture capital investors and bank lenders:

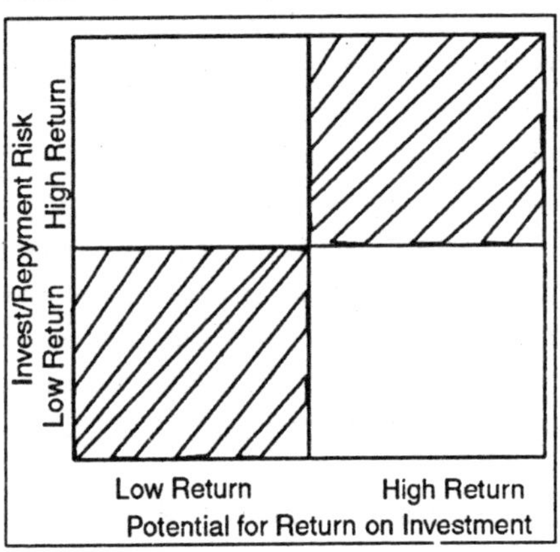

Fig. The Risk/reward Matrix

Note that while venture capital investors invest in a high risk, high return environment and banks lend in a low risk, low return environment, there are no capital sources in the high risk, low return quadrant. Venture capital is not the answer for all businesses that are unable to get a bank loan. Venture investors are not interested in taking a high degree of risk for a low return and entrepreneurs are usually not willing to offer a high return on an investment with low risk when they can probably get the money they need from a bank at a lower cost.

Businesses in the centre of the diagram or in the high risk, low return quadrant can sometimes find funds from friends and family. Or they may seek public sector sources of equity investments, "near equity" loans and loan guarantees provided by state and local governmental and nonprofit entities. However, these sources, while often weighing public benefit in their investment decision process, are still required to make prudent risk/return decisions in order to remain viable over the long term.

The fundamental question each entrepreneur should consider before pursuing venture capital is whether the potential for return to the investors is high enough to attract the investors' attention. For companies that have not yet generated any revenues or are less than a year or two old, most venture investors are not likely to be interested unless they see a potential to make at least five to ten times their investment over a five to seven year period.

Producing that kind of return to investors usually requires two things: the company has to grow rapidly, and it has to successfully execute an "exit" or "liquidity event" to produce the cash the investors are looking for. To raise venture capital, an entrepreneur has to address these two issues and be able to show both the growth potential and the likelihood that the investment can be converted to cash within a reasonable time frame.

Most investors are not interested in funding a "lifestyle" company, which to a venture capitalist means a company that can provide a decent living for the entrepreneur and his or her employees, but cannot produce an attractive return to the investor within a reasonable time frame. Figure further describes what venture capitalists can and cannot do when making investments. There are three main types of "liquidity events" allowing investors to get the value of their investment out of the company. A public offering of stock through an Initial Public Offering is the most visible exit and often the most remunerative.

The second and more common exit is a sale or merger of the company, which may well mean that the entrepreneur has to be willing to give up his or her ownership and involvement in the company. A third way to pay off investors is to "redeem" the stock: *i.e.,* buy it back. The money to buy the stock back can come from other investors, from a bank or other lender, or perhaps even from profits.

A business typically seeks venture capital when it is at a stage that requires a significant change in the way it operates to achieve the growth goals of its managers. Whether the change is bringing a new product to market, a substantial ramp-up in sales activities or the acquisition of new machinery and equipment, the choice of pursuing venture capital brings with it some important decisions for the entrepreneur. To help make those decisions.

Table. What Venture Capital...

Is:	Is Not:
A source of capital for high risk businesses for growth	Right for "lifestyle" businesses or those without strong potential
A source of "patient" capital	Money without strings or cost
An investment in the business related debts and expenses	Money to repay nonbusiness-
Money to drive business growth and development indefinitely	An inexhaustible supply of money that will continue
A validation of the business by outsiders investors	Free from restrictions and conditions imposed by the
A way to get access to the investors' contacts and resources	A loan that you can prepay at a low cost if things go well

A source of strategic planning, management and recruiting assistance	An end in itself; rather it is just the beginning of the relationship
A way to get help raising funds future and investors	A guarantee that the free in the market will reward the business
Money that does not have to paid back by the entrepreneur if the business fails	Available unless the investors be can see a way to liquidate their investment in 5-7 years.
Investment looking for a "liquidity event" so investors can cash out	Right for entrepreneurs who want to keep ownership and control indefinitely

HOW VENTURE CAPITAL INVESTORS WORK

In order to understand how to approach venture capital investors successfully, it is important for entrepreneurs to understand how they work, what they are looking for, and what is important to them. While there are different types of venture capital investors with different goals, they all share a desire for a good return on their investment.

Success in raising money depends first and foremost on how well the entrepreneur makes the case that the business will be successful and produce an attractive return on investment.There are four main categories of venture capital investors: venture capital firms, angel investors, corporate venture capital investors, and governmental investors. This Chapter will focus first on venture capital firms, which make up the traditional venture capital industry, outlining the general principles and business considerations that guide their investment strategies. It will then outline the other three categories of investors and how their goals and approaches may differ.

VENTURE CAPITAL FIRMS

Venture capital firms are entities, usually limited partnerships or limited liability companies, that raise funds from high net worth individuals and institutional investors to invest in a portfolio of business ventures with an expectation of a high return on investment. They are managed by experienced venture investors who have the credentials to entice sophisticated institutional and high net worth investors to place large amounts of money under their management. Of the four main categories of venture investors, venture capital firms are the most focused on generating the highest possible return on investment, because that is what their investors are paying them to do.

There are many different types of venture capital firms with different styles, investment targets, and return expectations. Some focus on early stage companies; others target later stage businesses with proven track records. Some seek a balanced portfolio with some early and some later stage investments. Still others specialize in specific industries, such as information technology or energy.

Many focus on a limited geographic area, although some larger funds may invest nationally or internationally. And some, like Coastal Ventures and CEI Community Ventures, Inc. in Portland, invest with social goals as well as expectations of return on investment. Figure shows a breakdown of generic types of venture capital firms and their average returns through the third quarter of 2002:

Table. Average Annualized Rates of Return on Venture Capital Funds by Type of Fund

Fund Type	1 Year	5 Years	10 Years	20 Years
Seed/Early Stage	–28.6%	44.1%	34.2%	20.7%
Balanced	–19.2%	22%	22.1%	14.7%
Later Stage	–16.4%	13.3%	23.7%	16.1%
Buyout	–8.2%	1.4%	8.8%	12.4%
Mezzanine	–1.6%	7.7%	10.9%	11%
Average of All Funds	–12.3%	8.3%	15.1%	14.5%

The venture capital fund types in Figure are listed in declining order of the amount of risk they are typically willing to take. Seed and early stage funds take the most risk, investing in businesses that have not proven themselves in the market. Over time, seed and early stage funds have achieved the highest average annual rate of return.

Balanced funds invest in a range from seed to later stage companies to spread risk. Later stage funds target companies that have proven their business plan in the marketplace and are striving for continued expansion. Buyout funds focus on mature companies that are recapitalizing or restructuring, usually leveraging equity investment with bank debt.

And mezzanine funds tend to target proven performers that are close to a public stock offering or sale to a larger industry player. Their risk of having one of their investments fail is much lower than for seed and early stage funds, but their return potential is also lower on the investments that are successful.

It is important for entrepreneurs to understand that in order to raise capital from venture capital firms, they will have to offer a reasonable prospect of paying *much higher returns* to the investors than these portfolio averages. In fact, seed and early stage venture firms target returns of 50% or more per year on each investment.

The reasons for this are grounded in three realities of venture capital firm economics:

1. The first reality of venture capital firm economics is that the returns shown in Figure reflect the entire portfolios of the venture capital funds, both the winners and the write-offs. Obviously, no one can predict which investments will be successful. The managers naturally hope and expect that each of their investments will succeed or they would not invest. But given the inevitability that some investments will fail and some will ultimately pay disappointing returns, all venture firms try to structure their investments so that the returns on successful investments are far higher than the averages. That way, the successful investments more than make up for the losers.

2. The second reality of venture firm economics is that the expenses of running each fund are deducted from the fund, and the fund averages shown in Figure are returns *after* all payments due to the managers. The managers have to target higher returns on each investment to be able to both get paid for their investment acumen and to beat the industry averages in Figure. The typical arrangement between the managers and the investors in a venture capital fund is that the managers get 2.5% of funds under management each year for the administrative expenses of operating the fund. In addition, as a reward and incentive to the managers, they are entitled to a "carried interest", which is a share of the profits of about 20%.
3. The third reality of venture firm economics is that they strive to exceed the industry averages so that they can show future investors a track record that will encourage those investors to invest in the venture firm's next fund. It is harder for venture firms to raise money if their historical returns have been at industry averages. Preferably "top quartile" returns: that is, returns that are better than three quarters of all comparable venture capital firms. And, of course, all venture firms want to perform significantly better than publicly traded stocks, since investors will not accept the risks of illiquid, private securities if they do not expect substantially higher returns.

There are two common ways of quantifying returns to investors. The more accurate way is to view the returns as an annualized rate of return over the period between investment and final return. This is referred to as the "Internal Rate of Return", or "IRR", and is expressed as a percentage as in Figure. The other view is a simple cash-on-cash return: how much was the ultimate return compared to the amount invested, expressed as a percentage or a multiple. For example, if a fund invests $1,000,000 and receives back $5,000,000, their cash-on-cash return is 500% or "5x".

Figure shows the relationship between the Internal Rate of Return calculation and the cash-on-cash return. For the venture capital investor, it answers the question "What multiple of my investment do we need to get back so that we are at least achieving an average return on my investment?"

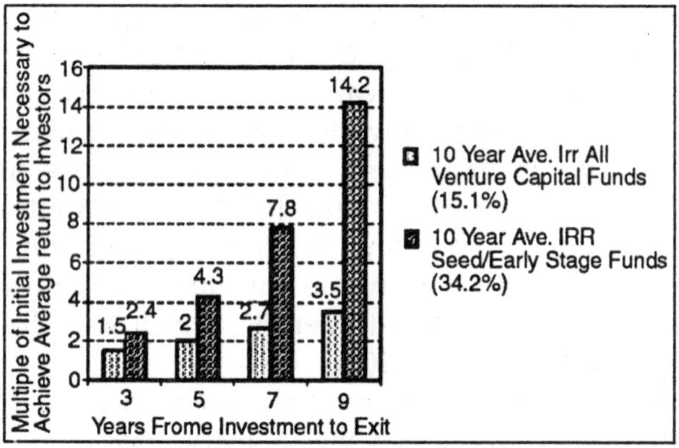

Fig. Multiple of Initial Investment Needed to Produce Industry Average Return

The bottom axis shows the number of years between the original investment and the return of the investment to the fund, ranging from three to nine years. The bars show the multiple of the original investment needed to achieve just an average net return to the fund as compared to the 10-year averages shown in Figure for all venture capital funds, and for just seed and early stage funds.

For example, if a venture capital fund invests $1,000,000 in a business and the business is sold after seven years, the fund needs to recoup $2,700,000, or 2.7 times its investment on a cash-on-cash return basis, just to hit the 15.1% industry average Internal Rate of Return for all venture capital funds over the last 10 years, including the relatively low risk buyout and mezzanine funds.

If that fund were instead a seed and early stage investment fund, its return would need to be $7,800,000, or 7.8 times its investment, to hit the 34.2% average Internal Rate of Return for seed and early stage funds. Naturally, most fund managers hope to get substantially higher returns to balance their portfolios and address the three venture firm economic realities. It is also emphasizes the importance of time in the venture capital equation. The longer the time between investment and return, the greater the return needs to be to provide the targeted annualized return on investment. That is why venture capital firms push companies hard to grow as quickly as possible to the point where the company can be sold for an attractive return.

So how do venture capital firms select investments to produce the high returns they are looking for? Each firm has its own strategy.

However, the following investment principles guide most firms:

- Be highly selective. The reality is that venture firms may look at and reject 100 or more investment opportunities for each one they fund. Sometimes they pass over great investment opportunities that are outside that particular firm's area of interest or specialty, or that are potential competitors of companies they have already invested in, or that would cause too much portfolio exposure to a particular industry, or simply because the deal is not referred to them by a trusted source. Many are quickly passed over because the Executive Summary does not convey the exciting potential of the business in a compelling way. Others do not meet the firm's exacting selection criteria. Most successful venture firms have a "deal flow pipeline" that brings in hundreds of qualified business plans each year. The managers can afford to be extremely selective about where to invest their time and money.
- Seek companies with innovative products and "unfair" advantages in large, ripe markets. In order to grow at the rate necessary to produce venture capital-type returns, companies generally need to have unique or innovative technologies or services that put them well ahead of the competition, or that can make significant changes in their industries. This generally requires both a technical or product

advantage, and a market that is ready to reward that advantage: that is, the customers are anxious for the product. Also, the market has to be big enough to offer the necessary growth potential and attractive exit opportunities.

- Back outstanding management teams. Many venture investors believe that a strong management team will be successful even if the product is mediocre, while a poor management team will not get the job done no matter how good the product is. Some venture firms will only back teams that have shown the ability to manage a business successfully in the same or a similar industry. Other venture investors will help to assemble the right management team around the right product or idea. In either case, venture investors want to back managers who are capable, determined, and persistent, but who are willing to step aside if and when necessary for the good of the company and its investors.
- Invest in companies with a clear and realistic exit strategy. Venture capital firms want to be close and effective partners with their portfolio companies, but only for as short a time as necessary to prepare the company for a profitable exit opportunity. Making an investment is only the beginning for a venture investor: getting the investment back with a maximized return is the end game. That means investors will look for companies that have the potential for a liquidation event such as the sale of the company or issuance of stock to the public through an Initial Public Offering within a few years. In some cases, it may be possible for the company to buy the stock back from the investors, usually by borrowing the capital or finding new equity investors. Without an exit, an investment becomes one of the "walking dead" in a venture firm portfolio: too good to shut down, but not good enough to attract a buyer.

- Add value to the development of the business and play a significant role in the ongoing management of the company. Particularly for early stage venture firms, the ideal investment is one where the venture firm has the experience, contacts, and strategic relationships to add significant value to the venture beyond the money invested. Generally, investors like to be actively involved by taking a seat on the Board of Directors and talking to the management team on a regular basis. Entrepreneurs should view venture firms not just as sources of capital, but also as invaluable resources for day-to-day management assistance, strategic planning, assistance in hiring the right management team, contacts with critical suppliers and customers, and help in raising additional capital.
- Make sure that companies have access to enough cash to get to cash flow breakeven. The harsh investment climate of recent years has reminded venture investors of this rule. Many companies have foundered because they were unable to raise more money when their venture capital ran out and the existing venture investors were not willing to continue to fund ongoing losses. Investors pay close attention to the "burn rate", which is the amount by which spending is outpacing revenues each month. When the money runs out, the venture investor either has to put more in, hope the company can raise more, or write off the investment. There is no longer an inexhaustible supply of capital to support struggling companies and bail out prior investors, as there seemed to be during the venture industry "feeding frenzy" that ended in mid-2001.
- Build a diverse investment portfolio. Particularly for seed and early stage investments, seasoned venture investors know that it is very difficult to predict which investments will succeed. When this risk is spread over a portfolio of 10 to 20 investments or

more, the overall level of risk to the investors is greatly reduced. In a typical early stage portfolio, of every ten investments, perhaps four will be complete losses and three will become "walking dead": viable but not easy to liquidate. The lion's share of the returns to investors will come from the other three investments, which are the portfolio winners. Many funds also seek to diversify their portfolio so it is not too heavily weighted towards one industry or technology, where the entire portfolio could be dragged down by a single mistake.

Once a venture firm has identified a company that seems promising, it begins what is usually an exhaustive review and analysis process referred to as "due diligence". This review begins with extensive discussions with the members of the management team to assess their understanding of the product and the market, to test the business plan they have assembled, and to evaluate their ability to carry it out.

The prospective investors will then draw upon their own experience and contacts to make independent inquiries about the product or service and the market the company is focusing on. They will perform background checks on the management and talk to customers, suppliers, and competitors.

They may employ experts on the technology, the production and distribution capabilities of the company, and the size and growth potential in the market to evaluate the investment proposal and to assess the possibilities for an exit.

They will review the legal documents that created the business and that outline the ownership and control process, as well as employment contracts, stock option agreements, and personnel policies. They will closely investigate the company's claims of protection of intellectual property, such as patents, copyrights, trademarks, and determine whether the company owns or has the rights to the assets necessary to its operations.

Successful investors strive to know the business almost as well as the founder or chief executive officer. This intensive due diligence process allows the potential investors to make an informed judgment about whether the risk of the venture is outweighed by the potential for return on investment. The process involves a significant investment of time and money by the venture firm. At the point in the due diligence process where the venture firm determines that it is seriously interested in making an investment, common practice is to issue a "term sheet" outlining the terms and conditions on which it is willing to make an investment. A discussion of the typical terms and conditions contained in term sheets issued by venture capital firms and other sophisticated investors.

Once an investment is made, venture firms tend to be active investors, closely following the progress of the company and looking for ways to help management achieve its objectives. They are likely to ask for a seat on the Board of Directors, and certain to insist on regular financial reporting. Initially, their efforts are focused on helping the business grow.

This can include everything from help in filling key management positions to introductions to potential customers, suppliers, and sources of follow-on capital. As the business prospers, venture firms begin to encourage the company to find an exit opportunity that the investor can convert its investment into cash.

In this phase, venture investors can be helpful in attracting potential acquirers or developing other exit strategies. Many of the legal terms and conditions imposed by venture investors when they make an investment are designed to push the company towards a profitable exit event.

ANGEL INVESTORS

Angel investors are high net worth individuals who invest in as few as one, or as many as a dozen or so businesses, usually located near their home. They invest with an expectation of an attractive return, using many of the same criteria for weighing investment risk and return potential that a venture firm would use.

Angels are attractive sources of capital for businesses for several reasons. First, they tend to be somewhat more accommodating to entrepreneurs than venture capital firms because they are investing their own money and have greater flexibility in making investment decisions. Second, they are willing to invest smaller amounts of money than venture firms and may be interested in investment prospects that are too small to interest venture capital firms. Third, many angels have valuable experience and contacts from running their own businesses that can be useful to entrepreneurs, and they may have more time to invest than a venture firm does.

Finally, angel investors may be interested in making an investment for reasons other than purely financial ones, such as a desire to share their experience with a local business, help out friends, or strengthen their community.

The nature of angel investors makes them particularly appropriate for early stage companies, helping bridge the financing gap until a company is ready to approach venture capital firms. In many cases, this role in bridging the financing gap is reflected in the way the angel investment is structured. For example, rather than developing an elaborate term sheet and arguing about valuation, an angel may invest through a "bridge note" that is designed to convert to equity on the same or similar terms and valuation as the next financing round.

In effect, the angel leaves the structuring and valuation decisions to the venture firms who arrive later. If there is never another financing round, the investor hopes to get his or her money back through payments on the note, or the note may convert to stock. The greatest drawback to angel capital is the difficulty in finding the right angel.

Most angel investors do not advertise their investment interest, leaving it up to the entrepreneur to find them. The best way to find an angel investor is through the entrepreneur's existing network of friends, relatives and business contacts. Other options include angel networks like the CommonAngels in Boston or forums like the Maine Investment Exchange or CapitalVenue that bring entrepreneurs and angels together.

CORPORATE VENTURE INVESTORS

Corporate venture investors are companies that have their own business operations but that also make venture capital investments in smaller businesses. Like venture capital firms, corporate venture investors invest with the goal of an attractive return, using many of the same investment parameters. The primary difference between a corporate venture investor and a venture capital firm is that corporate investors usually invest in businesses that offer a strategic benefit to the investor's business or that might be potential acquisition candidates in the future.

Strategic benefits might include access to cutting-edge technology, insight into new business opportunities, or the ability to provide input into the development of an attractive product or service that the corporate investor needs. Finding corporate investors is usually a matter of determining which companies might have a strategic reason to be supportive of the entrepreneur's business. To date, corporate venture capital activity has been limited in Maine.

GOVERNMENTAL FUNDING

State and federal governments play a significant role in providing financial assistance to growing businesses, often on better terms than can be obtained from private investors. Financial assistance programmes target job creation, rural development, research, and other public benefits, and are described further in Chapter 7. In Maine, the Small Enterprise Growth Fund is a state-funded venture capital fund that currently can invest up to $500,000 in eligible Maine-based businesses.

With statutory authority for the Fund vested in an 11-member, Governor-appointed Small Enterprise Growth Board, the Small Enterprise Growth Fund considers investments based on substantially the same criteria as a private venture capital fund. However, investment decisions are also based in part on public benefit criteria, including job creation.

Maine also provides capital for early stage technology-based ventures through the Maine Technology Institute, which provides grants or repayable investments for research and development leading to commercialization. Grants of up to $500,000 are awarded on a competitive basis, with applications reviewed by peer review panels.

The primary applicable programme of the Federal Government is the Small Business Innovation Research Programme. Administered by the U.S. Small Business Administration, the SBIR programme is a grant programme designed to support research and development activities by small businesses. Each year, ten federal agencies accept proposals for research and development in designated fields. Funding is competitive and is based on whether the application meets the qualifications of the agency requests for proposals, technical merit, the degree of innovation involved, and the potential for commercialization.

SBIR grants are up to $100,000 for an initial six month Phase 1 project to investigate feasibility, and up to $750,000 in Phase 2 for expansion of the work done in a successful initial project. The SBA also administers the Small Business Investment Company Programme, which provides investment capital to licensed venture capital companies that meet SBA criteria and observe SBA rules and regulations.

HOW TO APPROACH VENTURE INVESTORS

The best way to be successful in approaching venture investors is to offer them a well-constructed investment opportunity that meets their goals and objectives. The easier it is for the investor to see how attractive the opportunity is, the more likely he or she is to invest.

The first step is to develop an executive summary describing the business opportunity in one to two pages, backed up by a business plan that outlines the business, the need for financing, and the opportunity for investors. While there are legendary deals cut over drinks and outlined on a cocktail napkin, the vast majority of investment decisions are made in a more deliberative fashion.

The executive summary is very important because it is often the key to getting an investor to read the business plan. It is a brief summary of the business plan, drafted in such a way that it communicates the excitement of the investment opportunity to the investor and whets his or her appetite to read the business plan. In verbal form, it is often called an "elevator pitch", which is an explanation that is both compelling and brief enough to be delivered in the time it takes an elevator to get from one floor to another. The business plan should be clear enough that the investor understands it and believes it.

The plan should be designed to convey to a prospective investor a fairly complete description of the business and the investment opportunity. It should convince the reader that the author of the business plan has thought through the need for the capital, how it will be used, and what the impact on the business will be. A sloppy, incomplete, or superficial business plan gives a bad impression of the investment opportunity and the entrepreneur. There are many business plan guides and tools available on the Internet and in the business parts of larger bookstores.

While there is no required form, the business plan presented to a venture capitalist should cover certain basic points:

- The mission of the business and the objectives of the management team;
- A description of the product or service, its history, and an explanation of what problem it solves or what is unique or exciting about it;
- Objectives of any ongoing research and development activities;
- The ownership structure and capitalization;
- The amount of investment needed and what it will be used for;
- A description of the market and the competition, and where the company fits into the market;
- Whether the product or service has any proprietary advantage or other protection from competition;
- A description of the industry, its growth trends, prospects, and its major challenges;
- The operations plan with an explanation of challenges, solutions, and strategic relationships;
- The marketing and sales strategy, with the names and size of principal customers;

- The organizational chart, with track records, compensation packages, and resumes of key management and board members, and hiring plans for unfilled positions;
- The historical financial data, along with financial objectives and projections, with assumptions, showing cash flow needs of the business and how they will be met; and
- A discussion of exit opportunities and strategies.

The business plan should be clear in conveying the excitement about the opportunity, but should also be frank in assessing the major challenges and risks. Failing to disclose and address major problems will only call into question the rest of the business plan and the integrity of the author.

Once the executive summary and business plan are put together, the challenge is getting them in front of investors. For privacy reasons, most angel investors do not want to be deluged with business plans from entrepreneurs seeking capital. Entrepreneurs usually find them through a referral from a mutual acquaintance.

In some areas, there are angels who band together to review and discuss investment opportunities. These groups, like the Maine Investment Exchange based in Portland or the CommonAngels based in Boston, offer entrepreneurs a relatively quick and easy way to gain the attention of potential angel investors.

The entrepreneur should make every effort to set up a meeting with prospective venture firm investors to explain the opportunity and the business plan in person. This is not always easy, since venture firms cannot invest the time to meet with everyone who submits a business plan. Because of the fact that most venture firms see hundreds of investment opportunities each year, companies seeking capital should try to differentiate themselves to get attention.

The best way to get attention and a meeting is to get an introduction to the venture firm from someone that the firm respects, such as a lawyer, an accountant, a scientist, a customer, a company in their investment portfolio, an investor in the fund, or an investor in the company. An introduction combined with a positive recommen-dation will often get an applicant priority attention. Alternatively, the entrepreneur should try to find a way to meet someone from the venture firm at a venture capital conference or a function designed to introduce investors to prospects, such as the periodic events sponsored by the Maine Investment Exchange or CapitalVenue.

If the only available approach is to deliver an executive summary and business plan to the venture firm, it should be followed up with a telephone call and a request for a meeting. In approaching venture firms, entrepreneurs should remember that these firms typically turn down 99 out of 100 applicants. Because venture firms target so few investments for each portfolio, the fact that they say "no" is not necessarily an adverse reflection on the entrepreneur.

Venture firms pass over many potentially worthy investments for reasons unrelated to the merits of the proposal. For example, they may be targeting different technologies or industries, they may already have enough exposure to similar businesses, or they may be between funds and not actively investing.

If the answer is "no," the entrepreneur should try to find out as much as the venture firm will offer about why it was not interested. This information can be valuable in approaching other venture firms. It also may reveal a misunderstanding about the business plan that can be corrected or an obstacle that can be overcome. Entrepreneurs should try to distinguish between a "no" that can be turned into a "yes" and a "no" that is final.

If the "no" is final, the entrepreneur can still ask for suggestions of other investors that might be interested in the business. Entrepreneurs should take care not to burn any bridges, but to learn from each "no" and look for ways to improve the business plan. If the venture firm or angel expresses further interest, the investor usually determines the next steps. In this stage, it is critical that the company be responsive to the questions and concerns of the investor. Even a signed term sheet does not mean that the cash is in hand; the investor can still balk at anything that comes up during the due diligence process. When the investor makes an investment, the relationship is only beginning.

It is important that the company keeps the investor well informed and avoids unhappy surprises. The investor can be a key to the success of the business by providing wise counsel, contacts to important strategic partners, and more money when needed.

Most businesses, particularly early stage ones, will have to go back to their investors for more money at some point, so it is important to continue to treat investors as well or better after they invest as they were treated before the investment. And in the long run, an entrepreneur who makes money for an investor has an advocate and supporter for life.

INVESTMENT STRUCTURE AND VALUATION

You have found a venture investor who wants to provide you with the capital you need to move your business to the next level. You have received a term sheet from the investor that outlines the amount of money that will be invested in your company, the percentage of ownership or rights to ownership the investor is expecting, and the significant terms and conditions of the financing.

You are ready to agree to it and anxious to get a check. But before you sign the term sheet, you need to make sure you understand what all the fine print means. Ideally, you should have your attorney review any term sheet, as well any documents that are necessary for the closing of the investment. If you have not already started working with an attorney, this is the time to retain one, or you may regret it and pay a price later. You should select someone who is familiar with venture capital financing, understands accepted practices in the industry, and which provisions in the term sheet and closing documents can and should be negotiated. An inexperience attorney can do your relationship with the investors more harm than good and cost you needless time and money.

The first thing to be aware of is that usually the term sheet will specifically say that it is nonbinding and an expression of intent, not a firm commitment. Because the term sheet is nonbinding, in fact have money in the bank. Investors can and do change their minds and decide not to make investments for which they have issued term sheets, usually because they learn something while making further investigation that makes the investment less attractive, or possibly because they find out that something you told them is not true.

To the extent any provisions are intended to be binding, they are specifically stated in the term sheet. Binding provisions might include an obligation to pay the investor's closing expenses and attorney's fees, even if the investment does not take place, or a requirement that the business not talk to other prospective investors for some designated period of time. A major issue, and one that tends to be hotly debated between the company and the investor, is the valuation of the company.

The valuation is important because it determines the per cent of the ownership of the company that the investor is buying. The entrepreneur argues for a higher valuation so his or her percentage of ownership stays as high as possible. The investor argues for a lower valuation in order to maximize its return on investment. The determination of what the valuation should be is more art than science, particularly for early stage companies that do not have a track record of revenues and earnings.

Venture investors are primarily concerned with arriving at a valuation that can provide them with their targeted return on investment. Valuation requires an estimation of the company's potential for growth and its likelihood of achieving that growth. Further, prospective investors will make an assessment of how similar companies are being valued in the market today, and a prediction of how attractive the company will be in the marketplace after three to five years of successful operations. From the perspective of investors, the amount of time, effort and money previously invested in the company is not very relevant to its valuation, nor is the valuation that might have been placed on the company by earlier investors. One common method of establishing a valuation is to project what the revenues or profits of the company will be in five years and multiply those revenues or profits by the projected ratio of price to revenues or price to earnings that might be applicable to companies in that industry at that time. The result, the valuation at the five-year mark, is then discounted back to the present using a discount rate equal to the hoped-for internal rate of return on the investment.

To the investor, the resulting number represents the valuation today that will allow them to achieve their desired return on investment at some point in the future. Venture investors are naturally likely to take a more conservative view of future revenues and profits than you do for purposes of determining what your company's value is, to provide some cushion if things do not go as well as you expect.

You should not take this as an adverse reflection on your credibility or honesty. Rather, it is a reflection of the investor's experience that businesses do not always progress according to projections. Ideally, you would like to have several venture capital firms or investors competing to invest in your company. Then you can truly test what valuation the market will bear. The fewer term sheets you have, and the more you need the money, the less negotiating leverage you will have.

Also, the advice, experience and connections an investor can bring to the company may be of great value. In the long run, how well the company performs and the price it is ultimately worth in the future is more important than getting the highest possible valuation today. If the venture investor brings needed expertise or connections to potential customers, strategic partners and future sources of capital, that contribution can be more valuable than the investment they are making. Equity investors talk about valuations either "pre-money" or "post-money", and it is important to understand the difference.

"Pre-money" valuation is what the investor is valuing your company at before he or she makes an investment, while "post-money" is the "pre-money" valuation plus the amount of the new investment in the company. For example, if an investor invests $1,000,000 at a pre-money valuation of $3,000,000, the post-money valuation on the date the investment occurs is $4,000,000 and the investor owns, or has the right to own, 25% of the company.

If, however, the investor puts in $1,000,000 at a post-money valuation of $3,000,000, the investor will own 33% of the company. You should be prepared to generate a table outlining the capitalization of your company. Commonly referred to as a "cap table", this is an important tool for both you and your investors to understand the ownership of the company today and on the day after the investment takes place. The new investment results in "dilution" of the ownership of any existing shareholders.

For example, if you are the only owner today, you own 100% of the company. If an investor puts in $1,000,000 at a $3,000,000 pre-money valuation, you will own 75% of a company now worth $4,000,000. *Note that the value of your ownership interest has not changed even though you no longer own 100%.* Investors will want to know what your plans are for issuing stock options, and may place limitations on them because of their potential impact on dilution.

Stock options are a right to purchase stock in the company at a designated price at the election of the holder of the option. Options are generally used to provide an incentive to employees or other key people to support the growth of the company.

The difference between the "strike price" and the value of the stock on the day the option is exercised can provide a significant financial benefit to the option holder when the stock becomes marketable. Stock options having a strike price less than the value of the stock are referred to as "in the money".

On the other hand, when the stock price is less than the option strike price, the options are "under water". Stock options, if any are issued or reserved for issue, need to be factored into the cap table on a fully diluted basis: *i.e.*, assuming they are exercised, so everyone can understand what their fully diluted ownership position is.

The same is true of any warrants issued or to be issued by the company. Like stock options, warrants are rights to purchase stock in the future at a designated "strike price", and exercise of those warrants dilutes the ownership of all existing shareholders. Commonly granted to investors or entities that have loaned money to the company, warrants differ from options in that they are, or may, be separately tradable, whereas options are usually only for the benefit of the initial recipient.

Some investors, particularly in later stage companies, may structure their investment as a loan with an "equity kicker" in the form of warrants. Those investors get their return on investment through payments of principal and interest, plus they share in the increased value of the company through the warrants to buy stock in the future should it increase their strike price. An important consideration is the extent to which the investor expects to have control of the company.

While the investor will in most cases have voting stock equal to its percentage ownership, it is also likely to require one or more positions on the company's board of directors. Since the board of directors control key business decisions, not the least of which is the employment and compensation of key personnel, the composition of the board is important both to the entrepreneurs and the investors.

While it is typical for investors to have less than a majority on the board, it is not unusual to have provisions that give the investors the right to appoint additional board members under certain conditions, such as failure to meet agreed benchmarks. Also common are provisions that require supermajorities for certain major decisions, such as taking on additional investors or selling the company or its assets.

The term sheet will also outline what form the investor's equity interest will take and what rights will be required. From the entrepreneur's point of view, you would like it if the investor purchases common stock, the same security you probably own. Common stock is the basic unit of equity ownership. Investors, however, usually expect to be granted "preferred stock", giving them some priorities and other advantages over common stockholders, and reflecting the fact that they are paying cash for their stock while the majority owners may have gotten their shares in exchange for "sweat equity". Later rounds of investors may additionally expect preference over prior preferred investors. The term sheet outlines what the investor expects its preferred stock will look like:

DIVIDEND PREFERENCE

Some preferred stock investments will require that a dividend of some specified per cent be accrued on the preferred stock and paid before any dividend can be paid to holders of common stock.

Others may not specifically provide for a dividend payment, but almost certainly will require that no dividend be paid to the common holders unless the preferred holders are also paid. In cases where there is more than one "series" of preferred stock, the later investors may demand dividend preference over holders of earlier series.

LIQUIDATION PREFERENCE

What if your $4,000,000 post-money company has to be liquidated in a year for $1,000,000? You as the holder of common stock would like to split the proceeds on a pro rata basis with all of your investors, but holders of preferred stock are going to insist that they get paid first.

In this example, the preferred holders would get their money back and you and the other common holders would get nothing. In fact, preferred holders will probably not be happy just to get their money back first in the event of a distress sale of the company. Most will expect all of their accrued but unpaid dividends to be paid as well.

It has also become increasingly common for investors to ask for dividends plus a multiple of two or three times their investment. That increases the chances that the investors will achieve a decent return if the company is sold at a distress price, but it also increases the likelihood that the holders of common stock will receive nothing.

CONVERSION RIGHTS

Preferred stock typically comes with the right to convert to common stock at the option of the holder. For example, if the company is successful and able to go to the public stock markets with an Initial Public Offering, preferred holders will usually convert to common stock right before the IPO. The common stock can then be sold at the price of publicly traded stock, although such sale is often subject to a restriction on sale for a period of time after the IPO.

If the company is being sold to another company at a significantly higher price than the post-money valuation at the time the preferred stock was issued, the preferred holders will likely convert and be paid their pro rata share of the profitable sale.

PARTICIPATING PREFERRED STOCK

Traditionally, preferred stock holders could hold their preferred stock and be paid their investment amount plus any accrued dividends, or they could convert to common stock and share in the bounty of an IPO or favourable sale. Since the bursting of the technology bubble and the decline in private equity investment activity, however, it has become common for preferred holders to get the benefits of both.

In the case of "participating preferred stock", the holders are entitled to have their investment repaid along with any accrued dividends and any multiple of their investment they may have negotiated, and then still retain the right to convert to common stock and "participate" along with all other common stockholders in the remaining proceeds of a favourable sale or IPO.

REDEMPTION RIGHTS

Investors usually have the right to require the company to "redeem" or repurchase the investors' shares at or after a designated period of time and at a specified price. While not often exercised, this right provides the investors with another potential exit opportunity. Investors would consider using a redemption provision in the case of a company that was doing well enough to be able to raise the capital to pay the redemption price, but not well enough to attract a buyer at a favourable price. It is also a tool to prod the managers of the company to look for a buyer when they might prefer not to.

ANTIDILUTION PROTECTION

Antidilution provisions protect the investors' pro rata ownership of the company in the case of events such as stock splits or the issuance of dividends in the form of stock. In addition, antidilution provisions generally address what happens if the company sells additional stock to investors. In its simplest form, an antidilution provision will require that if the number of common shares increases due to a stock split or stock dividend, then the number of shares into which the preferred stock can convert must increase accordingly.

For example, if the company issues each holder of common stock a new share of stock for each share already owned, the number of shares of common stock doubles and the value of each share is cut in half. In that case, preferred holders want to be able to convert their stock into double the number of common shares to protect their percentage ownership of the company.

More complicated issues arise when the company wants to issue new shares of stock to new investors. The issuance of stock to new investors dilutes the ownership of each existing investor. For example, if you own 60% of the company you founded and you have sold 40% to Investor A, and later you want to sell 25% to Investor B, your percentage ownership and Investor A's percentage ownership would have to drop since the total ownership cannot exceed 100%.

In this example, Investor A would now own 30% of the company, while you would own 45%. Investor A can avoid this by exercising a "pre-emptive right" to purchase the stock offered to Investor B. Or, if Investor B is paying a price per share higher than Investor A paid, Investor A may be satisfied that even though its percentage ownership has declined, the value of its investment has actually risen. The problem arises when the stock offered to Investor B is at a lower price per share. In that case, Investor A's antidilution protection kicks in. If Investor A has a right to "full ratchet" antidilution protection, and assuming the price to Investor B is half the price per share paid by Investor A, Investor A is entitled to convert into twice as many shares.

That right to additional shares comes at the expense of the common stockholders, who are diluted twice: once by the addition of Investor B and then by the increased number of shares that Investor A's investment can be converted into. This result can be quite draconian if Investor B is only buying a small number of shares for a relatively small amount of money.

From the founder's point of view, so-called "weighted average" antidilution protection is much more tolerable. Instead of recalculating Investor A's right to convert at the lower price paid by Investor B, a formula is used to prorate the adjustment based on how much stock is being sold to Investor B, a result that is more favourable to common shareholders than "full ratchet" antidilution.

REGISTRATION RIGHTS

In the happy event that the company is successful and becomes attractive to the public equity markets, investors may have registration rights: that is, the right to require the company to register some percentage of the common stock of the company for offering to the public. This is not often exercised, but it is a tool investors can use to push the company towards an exit event.

While many of the terms and conditions are clearly designed to protect and benefit the investors, most sophisticated investors will not demand overly burdensome preferential provisions because they want the managers of the company to have the financial incentive to make the company as successful as possible.

That usually requires an alignment of interest between the management team and the investors: everyone is in the same boat and all oars are pulling in the same direction. If the terms are so onerous that the entrepreneur and management team no longer have the incentive to see the business grow, the terms are self-defeating for the investor. The entrepreneur has every right to negotiate provisions he or she is comfortable with, and the more anxious the investor is to make the investment, the more flexible the terms will be.

On the other hand, entrepreneurs need to be careful about sending a message to the prospective investor that their respective interests are not aligned. A rocky courtship does not bode well for a strong marriage.

7

Plastic Money

CONCEPT AND DIFFERENT FORM OF PLASTIC MONEY

There has been a growth on electronic payment due to the shift in technology, growing access to internet among the customers and convenient modes of delivery and payment. Plastic money also known as Plastic cards acts as a vital tool for every day transaction of people today.

The various Plastic cards include ATM cards,Debit Card,ATM cum Debit Card,Credit Cards, Smart Card, Charge Cards, Co-branded cards, add on cards and so on.

ATM CARDS

Automated Teller machine (ATM) cards is capable of doing variety of functions.It can perform both cash and non-cash transactions in secured environment.

- ATM Cash Transactions includes deposits and withdrawals
- Non cash transactions incude
  - Providing Mini Statement of last five transactions.In some banks upto last ten transactions
  - Balance enquiry
  - Stop Payment instructions
  - Transfer of funds between acounts
  - Requisition of Cheque books,drafts etc.
  - Bill payments

DEBIT CARD

The bank issues debit card only if the person has an account in the bank.This card is useful to make payment from Member Establishments who have arrangements with the card issuing bank or agency.

They check the balance and deduct the amount from the bank balance online. When a debit card is issued to make the payment,the total amount charged is instantly reduced from the bank balance of the account holder.

All credit and debit cards are affiliated to two major issuers-VISA and Master Card.Master Card and VISA are global non-profit organizations who promote the growth of the card business throughout the world.They have built vast network of Member Establishments so that customers can use the cards worldwide for their debit and credit purchases.

DEBIT CUM ATM CARD

This is most common nowadays.The same debit card can be used to draw cash from the ATM and also make payment to the shops for purchases.This is two in one card.

CREDIT CARDS

This card enables the client to obtain goods or services from the various shops having arrangement with the issuing agency even if there is no balance in his/her savings or current account.The bank assumes that the loan will be repaid by the customers at later date.

The credit card holder has to make payment for the dues before the due date. Otherwise late payment fee is levied in the next billing statement. Normally,a limit of the credit will be fixed by the bank for the amount of purchases to be made by the customer based on the net worth of the customer.

CHARGE CARDS

A Charge card has all features of credit card.But, after using the charge card the entire payments of the bills has to be made by the due date.If it is failed to be done,then the client is likely to be considered as a defaulter and he has to pay a steep late payment charges. But in case of Credit cards, the client is not declared as a defaulter if he misses to pay by due date..In such case,a late fee is levied in the next billing statements of the credit card holder.

AMEX and Diners Club card are well known branded charge cards.They have their own merchant establishments and tie ups/and does not depend on the network of Master card or VISA. These care are typically meant for the high income group categories and companies. These cards are not acceptable at many outlets. But wide variety of special privileges are enjoyed by the AMEX card holders and Diners Club Cardholders.

SMART CARDS

A smart Card contains an electronic chip which is used to store Cash. This is most useful to pay for small purchases for example in Fairs,coffee shops etc. No identification, signature or payment authorization is required for using this card. The exact amount of purchase is deducted from smart card during payment.Currently, this product is available in very developed countries like US.

AFFINITY CARD

The card issuer has a tie up with popular organizations and institutions which are often non-profit organizations like Stanchart Cricket Cards or City WWF card.When a card is used, a certain percentage is contributed to the organization or institution by the card issuer.

PHOTO CARD

When a Photo is imprinted on the card,it helps to identify the user of the credit card and is considered to be safer. In many cases,Photo card can also be used as identity card.

GLOBAL CARD

Global cards can be used as credit cards instead of cash and traveller cheques while traveling abroad to foreign countries for business or personal reasons.

ADD ON CARDS

It is a privilege offered to the spouse, parents, Children or other family members of the original card holder.Normally, an issuing bank permits two add on cards per credit card. All expenses incurred on add on card are billed to the primary card holder.

PETRO CARD

Some Petroleum companies allow customers to pay for the fuel through electronic medium.It offers a scheme of gifting the points to the customers,when they pay for the fuel using petro card.It is convenient, secured and speedy mode of transaction. Co-branded credit cards like IOC-Citi bank and HPCL-ICICI bank are the co-branded petro cards avaiable in the market.

Today,the Indian mode of payment has shifted from currency to electronic mode.This is due to the high money valued transactions and more risk involvement.The new electronic payment and settlement should follow the strict norms for banks and merchants to make secure payments and prevent money laundering as the transactions through plastic money will be increasing and increasing in the near future..

CREDIT AND DEBIT CARD

CREDIT CARD

A credit card is a small plastic card issued to users as a system of payment. It allows its holder to buy goods and services based on the holder's promise to pay for these goods and services. The issuer of the card grants a line of credit to the consumer from which the user can borrow money for payment to a merchant or as a cash advance to the user. Usage of the term "credit card" to imply a credit card account is a metonym.

A credit card is different from a charge card: a charge card requires the balance to be paid in full each month. In contrast, credit cards allow the consumers a continuing balance of debt, subject to interest being charged. Most credit cards are issued by banks or credit unions, and are the shape and size specified by the ISO/IEC 7810 standard as ID-1. This is defined as 85.60 × 53.98 mm in size.

How Credit Cards Work

Credit cards are issued after an account has been approved by the credit provider, after which cardholders can use it to make purchases at merchants accepting that card.

When a purchase is made, the credit card user agrees to pay the card issuer. The cardholder indicates consent to pay by signing a receipt with a record of the card details and indicating the amount to be paid or by entering a personal identification number. Also, many merchants now accept verbal authorizations via telephone and electronic authorization using the Internet, known as a 'Card/Cardholder Not Present' transaction.

Electronic verification systems allow merchants to verify in a few seconds that the card is valid and the credit card customer has sufficient credit to cover the purchase, allowing the verification to happen at time of purchase. The verification is performed using a credit card payment terminal or Point of Sale system with a communications link to the merchant's acquiring bank. Data from the card is obtained from a magnetic stripe or chip on the card; the latter system is called Chip and PIN in the United Kingdom and Ireland, and is implemented as an EMV card.

For transactions at which the buyer is not present and the card not shown, merchants additionally verify that the customer is in physical possession of the card and is the authorised user by asking for additional information such as the security code printed on the back of the card, date of expiry, and billing address.

Each month, the credit card user is sent a statement indicating the purchases undertaken with the card, any outstanding fees, and the total amount owed. After receiving the statement, the cardholder may dispute any charges that he or she thinks are incorrect. Otherwise, the cardholder must pay a defined minimum proportion of the bill by a due date, or may choose to pay a higher amount up to the entire amount owed. The credit issuer charges interest on the amount owed if the balance is not paid in full.

Some financial institutions can arrange for automatic payments to be deducted from the user's bank accounts, thus avoiding late payment altogether as long as the cardholder has sufficient funds.

Advertising, Solicitation, Application and Approval

Credit card advertising regulations include the Schumer box disclosure requirements. A large fraction of junk mail consists of credit card offers created from lists provided by the major credit reporting agencies. In the United States, the three major US credit bureaus allow consumers to opt out from related credit card solicitation offers via its Opt Out Pre Screen programme.

Interest Charges

Credit card issuers usually waive interest charges if the balance is paid in full each month, but typically will charge full interest on the entire outstanding balance from the date of each purchase if the total balance is not paid. For example, if a user had a $1,000 transaction and repaid it in full within this grace period, there would be no interest charged. If, however, even $1.00 of the total amount remained unpaid, interest would be charged on the $1,000 from the date of purchase until the payment is received.

The precise manner in which interest is charged is usually detailed in a cardholder agreement which may be summarized on the back of the monthly statement. The general calculation formula most financial institutions use to determine the amount of interest to be charged is APR/100 x ADB/365 x number of days revolved. Take the Annual percentage rate and divide by 100 then multiply to the amount of the average daily balance divided by 365 and then take this total and multiply by the total number of days the amount revolved before payment was made on the account.

Financial institutions refer to interest charged back to the original time of the transaction and up to the time a payment was made, if not in full, as RRFC or residual retail finance charge. Thus after an amount has revolved and a payment has been made, the user of the card will still receive interest charges on their statement after paying the next statement in full.

The credit card may simply serve as a form of revolving credit, or it may become a complicated financial instrument with multiple balance segments each at a different interest rate, possibly with a single umbrella credit limit, or with separate credit limits applicable to the various balance segments. Usually this compartmentalization is the result of special incentive offers from the issuing bank, to encourage balance transfers from cards of other issuers.

In the event that several interest rates apply to various balance segments, payment allocation is generally at the discretion of the issuing bank, and payments will therefore usually be allocated towards the lowest rate balances until paid in full before any money is paid towards higher rate balances. Interest rates can vary considerably from card to card, and the interest rate on a particular card may jump dramatically if the card user is late with a payment on that card or any other credit instrument, or even if the issuing bank decides to raise its revenue.

Benefits to Customers

The main benefit to each customer is convenience. Compared to debit cards and checks, a credit card allows small short-term loans to be quickly made to a customer who need not calculate a balance remaining before every transaction, provided the total charges do not exceed the maximum credit line for the card.

Credit cards also provide more fraud protection than debit cards. In the UK for example, the bank is jointly liable with the merchant for purchases of defective products over £100. Many credit cards offer rewards and benefits packages, such as offering enhanced product warranties at no cost, free loss/

damage coverage on new purchases, and points which may be redeemed for cash, products, or airline tickets. Additionally, carrying a credit card may be a convenience to some customers as it eliminates the need to carry any cash for most purposes.

Detriments to Customers

High interest and Bankruptcy

Low introductory credit card rates are limited to a fixed term, usually between 6 and 12 months, after which a higher rate is charged.

As all credit cards charge fees and interest, some customers become so indebted to their credit card provider that they are driven to bankruptcy. Some credit cards often levy a rate of 20 to 30 per cent after a payment is missed; in other cases a fixed charge is levied without change to the interest rate.

In some cases universal default may apply: the high default rate is applied to a card in good standing by missing a payment on an unrelated account from the same provider. This can lead to a snowball effect in which the consumer is drowned by unexpectedly high interest rates. Further most card holder agreements enable the issuer to arbitrarily raise the interest rate for any reason they see fit.

Inflated Pricing for all Consumers

Merchants that accept credit cards must pay interchange fees and discount fees on all credit-card transactions. In some cases merchants are barred by their credit agreements from passing these fees directly to credit card customers, or from setting a minimum transaction amount.

The result, at least in the United States, is that merchants may charge all customers higher prices to cover the fees on credit card transactions.

In the United States in 2008 credit card companies collected a total of $48 billion in interchange fees, or an average of $427 per family, with an average fee rate of about 2% per transaction.

Grace Period

A credit card's grace period is the time the customer has to pay the balance before interest is assessed on the outstanding balance. Grace periods vary, but usually range from 20 to 50 days depending on the type of credit card and the issuing bank. Some policies allow for reinstatement after certain conditions are met.

Usually, if a customer is late paying the balance, finance charges will be calculated and the grace period does not apply. Finance charges incurred depend on the grace period and balance; with most credit cards there is no grace period if there is any outstanding balance from the previous billing cycle or statement.

However, there are some credit cards that will only apply finance charge on the previous or old balance, excluding new transactions.

Benefits to Merchants

For merchants, a credit card transaction is often more secure than other forms of payment, such as checks, because the issuing bank commits to pay the merchant the moment the transaction is authorized, regardless of whether the consumer defaults on the credit card payment. In most cases, cards are even more secure than cash, because they discourage theft by the merchant's employees and reduce the amount of cash on the premises.

Prior to credit cards, each merchant had to evaluate each customer's credit history before extending credit. That task is now performed by the banks which assume the credit risk. Credit cards can also aid in securing a sale, especially if the customer does not have enough cash on his or her person or checking account.

Extra turnover is generated by the fact that the customer can purchase goods and/or services immediately and is less inhibited by the amount of cash in his or her pocket and the immediate state of his or her bank balance. Much of merchants' marketing is based on this immediacy. For each purchase, the bank charges the merchant a commission for this service and there may be a certain delay before the agreed payment is received by the merchant. The commission is often a percentage of the transaction amount, plus a fixed fee.

In addition, a merchant may be penalized or have their ability to receive payment using that credit card restricted if there are too many cancellations or reversals of charges as a result of disputes. Some small merchants require credit purchases to have a minimum amount to compensate for the transaction costs.

In some countries, for example the Nordic countries, banks guarantee payment on stolen cards only if an ID card is checked and the ID card number/civic registration number is written down on the receipt together with the signature. In these countries merchants therefore usually ask for ID.

Non-Nordic citizens, who are unlikely to possess a Nordic ID card or driving license, will instead have to show their passport, and the passport number will be written down on the receipt, sometimes together with other information. Some shops use the card's PIN for identification, and in that case showing an ID card is not necessary.

Costs to Merchants

Merchants are charged several fees for the privilege of accepting credit cards. The merchant is usually charged a commission of 1%-3%+ of the value of each transaction paid for by credit card.

The merchant may also pay a variable charge, called an interchange rate, for each transaction. In some instances of very low-value transactions, use of credit cards will significantly reduce the profit margin or cause the merchant to lose money on the transaction.

Merchants must accept these transactions as part of their costs to retain the right to accept credit card transactions. Merchants with very low average transaction prices or very high average transaction prices are more averse to accepting credit cards. In some cases merchants may charge users a "credit card supplement", either a fixed amount or a percentage, for payment by credit card. In certain countries, merchants are required to pay the acquiring banks a monthly terminal rental fee if the terminals are provided by the acquiring banks. Merchants can apply to the acquiring banks for waivers of the fees, which the banks usually agree to for merchants with a high volume of sales, but not for smaller ones.

Parties Involved

- *Cardholder*: The holder of the card used to make a purchase; the consumer.
- *Card-issuing bank*: The financial institution or other organization that issued the credit card to the cardholder. This bank bills the consumer for repayment and bears the risk that the card is used fraudulently. American Express and Discover were previously the only card-issuing banks for their respective brands, but as of 2007, this is no longer the case. Cards issued by banks to cardholders in a different country are known as offshore credit cards.
- *Merchant*: The individual or business accepting credit card payments for products or services sold to the cardholder.
- *Acquiring bank*: The financial institution accepting payment for the products or services on behalf of the merchant.
- *Independent sales organization*: Resellers of the services of the acquiring bank.
- *Merchant account*: This could refer to the acquiring bank or the independent sales organization, but in general is the organization that the merchant deals with.
- *Credit Card association*: An association of card-issuing banks such as Visa, MasterCard, Discover, American Express, etc. that set transaction terms for merchants, card-issuing banks, and acquiring banks.
- *Transaction network*: The system that implements the mechanics of the electronic transactions. May be operated by an independent company, and one company may operate multiple networks.

- *Affinity partner*: Some institutions lend their names to an issuer to attract customers that have a strong relationship with that institution, and get paid a fee or a percentage of the balance for each card issued using their name. Examples of typical affinity partners are sports teams, universities, charities, professional organizations, and major retailers.

The flow of information and money between these parties – always through the card associations – is known as the interchange, and it consists of a few steps.

Transaction Steps

- *Authorization*: The cardholder pays for the purchase and the merchant submits the transaction to the acquirer. The acquirer verifies the credit card number, the transaction type and the amount with the issuer and reserves that amount of the cardholder's credit limit for the merchant. An authorization will generate an approval code, which the merchant stores with the transaction.
- *Batching*: Authorized transactions are stored in "batches", which are sent to the acquirer. Batches are typically submitted once per day at the end of the business day. If a transaction is not submitted in the batch, the authorization will stay valid for a period determined by the issuer, after which the held amount will be returned back to the cardholder's available credit. Some transactions may be submitted in the batch without prior authorizations; these are either transactions falling under the merchant's floor limit or ones where the authorization was unsuccessful but the merchant still attempts to force the transaction through.
- *Clearing and Settlement*: The acquirer sends the batch transactions through the credit card association, which debits the issuers for payment and credits the acquirer. Essentially, the issuer pays the acquirer for the transaction.

- *Funding*: Once the acquirer has been paid, the acquirer pays the merchant. The merchant receives the amount totaling the funds in the batch minus either the "discount rate," "mid-qualified rate", or "non-qualified rate" which are tiers of fees the merchant pays the acquirer for processing the transactions.
- *Chargebacks*: A chargeback is an event in which money in a merchant account is held due to a dispute relating to the transaction. Chargebacks are typically initiated by the cardholder. In the event of a chargeback, the issuer returns the transaction to the acquirer for resolution. The acquirer then forwards the chargeback to the merchant, who must either accept the chargeback or contest it. A merchant is responsible for the chargeback only if she has violated the card acceptance procedures as per the merchant agreement with card acquirers.

Secured Credit Cards

A secured credit card is a type of credit card secured by a deposit account owned by the cardholder. Typically, the cardholder must deposit between 100% and 200% of the total amount of credit desired. Thus if the cardholder puts down $1000, they will be given credit in the range of $500–$1000. In some cases, credit card issuers will offer incentives even on their secured card portfolios.

In these cases, the deposit required may be significantly less than the required credit limit, and can be as low as 10% of the desired credit limit. This deposit is held in a special savings account. Credit card issuers offer this because they have noticed that delinquencies were notably reduced when the customer perceives something to lose if the balance is not repaid.

The cardholder of a secured credit card is still expected to make regular payments, as with a regular credit card, but should they default on a payment, the card issuer has the option of recovering the cost of the purchases paid to the merchants out of the deposit. The advantage of the secured card for an individual with negative or no credit history is that most companies report regularly to the major credit bureaus. This allows for building of positive credit history.

Although the deposit is in the hands of the credit card issuer as security in the event of default by the consumer, the deposit will not be debited simply for missing one or two payments. Usually the deposit is only used as an offset when the account is closed, either at the request of the customer or due to severe delinquency.

This means that an account which is less than 150 days delinquent will continue to accrue interest and fees, and could result in a balance which is much higher than the actual credit limit on the card. In these cases the total debt may far exceed the original deposit and the cardholder not only forfeits their deposit but is left with an additional debt.

Most of these conditions are usually described in a cardholder agreement which the cardholder signs when their account is opened. Secured credit cards are an option to allow a person with a poor credit history or no credit history to have a credit card which might not otherwise be available.

They are often offered as a means of rebuilding one's credit. Fees and service charges for secured credit cards often exceed those charged for ordinary non-secured credit cards, however, for people in certain situations, secured cards can often be less expensive in total cost than unsecured credit cards, even including the security deposit. Sometimes a credit card will be secured by the equity in the borrower's home.

Prepaid "Credit" Cards

A prepaid credit card is not a true credit card, since no credit is offered by the card issuer: the card-holder spends money which has been "stored" via a prior deposit by the card-holder or someone else, such as a parent or employer. However, it carries a credit-card brand and can be used in similar ways just as though it were a regular credit card. Unlike debit cards, prepaid credit cards do not require a PIN. After purchasing the card, the cardholder loads the account with any amount of money, up to the predetermined card limit and then uses the card to make purchases the same way as a typical credit card. Prepaid cards can be issued to minors since there is no credit line involved.

The main advantage over secured credit cards is that you are not required to come up with $500 or more to open an account. With prepaid credit cards you are not charged any interest but you are often charged a purchasing fee plus monthly fees after an arbitrary time period. Many other fees also usually apply to a prepaid card.

Prepaid credit cards are sometimes marketed to teenagers for shopping online without having their parents complete the transaction. Because of the many fees that apply to obtaining and using credit-card-branded prepaid cards, the Financial Consumer Agency of Canada describes them as "an expensive way to spend your own money". The agency publishes a booklet, "Pre-paid cards", which explains the advantages and disadvantages of this type of prepaid card.

Features

As well as convenient, accessible credit, credit cards offer consumers an easy way to track expenses, which is necessary for both monitoring personal expenditures and the tracking of work-related expenses for taxation and reimbursement purposes. Credit cards are accepted worldwide, and are available with a large variety of credit limits, repayment arrangement, and other perks.

Some countries, such as the United States, the United Kingdom, and France, limit the amount for which a consumer can be held liable due to fraudulent transactions as a result of a consumer's credit card being lost or stolen.

Security Problems and Solutions

Credit card security relies on the physical security of the plastic card as well as the privacy of the credit card number. Therefore, whenever a person other than the card owner has access to the card or its number, security is potentially compromised. Once, merchants would often accept credit card numbers without additional verification for mail order purchases. It's now common practice to only ship to confirmed addresses as a security measure to minimise fraudulent purchases.

Some merchants will accept a credit card number for in-store purchases, whereupon access to the number allows easy fraud, but many require the card itself to be present, and require a signature. A lost or stolen card can be cancelled, and if this is done quickly, will greatly limit the fraud that can take place in this way.

For internet purchases, there is sometimes the same level of security as for mail order hence requiring only that the fraudster take care about collecting the goods, but often there are additional measures. European banks can require a cardholder's security PIN be entered for in-person purchases with the card.

The PCI DSS is the security standard issued by The PCI SSC. This data security standard is used by acquiring banks to impose cardholder data security measures upon their merchants. The low security of the credit card system presents countless opportunities for fraud. This opportunity has created a huge [specify] black market in stolen credit card numbers, which are generally used quickly before the cards are reported stolen.

The goal of the credit card companies is not to eliminate fraud, but to "reduce it to manageable levels". This implies that high-cost low-return fraud prevention measures will not be used if their cost exceeds the potential gains from fraud reduction - as would be expected from organisations whose goal is profit maximisation.

Internet fraud may be by claiming a chargeback which is not justified, or carried out by the use of credit card information which can be stolen in many ways, the simplest being copying information from retailers, either online or offline. Despite efforts to improve security for remote purchases using credit cards, security breaches are usually the result of poor practice by merchants. For example, a website that safely uses SSL to encrypt card data from a client may then email the data, unencrypted, from the webserver to the merchant; or the merchant may store unencrypted details in a way that allows them to be accessed over the Internet or by a rogue employee; unencrypted card details are always a security risk. Even encryption data may be cracked.

Controlled Payment Numbers which are used by various banks such as Citibank, Discover (Secure Online Account Numbers, Bank of America (Shop Safe), 5 banks using eCarte Bleue and CMB's Virtualis in France, and Swedbank of Sweden's eKort product are another option for protecting against credit card fraud.

These are generally one-time use numbers that front one's actual account (debit/credit) number, and are generated as one shops on-line. They can be valid for a relatively short time, for the actual amount of the purchase, or for a price limit set by the user. Their use can be limited to one merchant. If the number given to the merchant is compromised, it will be rejected if an attempt is made to use it again.

A similar system of controls can be used on physical cards. For example if a consumer has a Chip and PIN enabled card the card can be limited so that it be used only at point of sale locations and only in a given territory. This technology provides the option for banks to support many other controls too that can be turned on and off and varied by the credit card owner in real time as circumstances change.

Apart from the obvious benefits of such controls: from a security perspective this means that a customer can have a Chip and PIN card secured for the real world, and limited for use in the home country.

In this eventuality a thief stealing the details will be prevented from using these overseas in non chip and pin countries. Similarly the real card can be restricted from use on-line so that stolen details will be declined if this tried. Then when card users shop online they can use virtual account numbers. In both circumstances an alert system can be built in notifying a user that a fraudulent attempt has been made which breaches their parameters, and can provide data on this in real time. This is the optimal method of security for credit cards, as it provides very high levels of security, control and awareness in the real and virtual world. Furthermore it requires no changes for merchants at all and is attractive to users, merchants and banks, as it not only detects fraud but prevents it.

Additionally, there are security features present on the physical card itself in order to prevent counterfeiting. For example, most modern credit cards have a watermark that will fluoresce under ultraviolet light.

A Visa card has a letter V superimposed over the regular Visa logo and a Mastercard has the letters MC across the front of the card. Older Visa cards have a bald eagle or dove across the front. In the aforementioned cases, the security features are only visible under ultraviolet light and are invisible in normal light. Similar security features are present in paper currency and certain ID cards in the United States, as well.

The Federal Bureau of Investigation and U.S. Postal Inspection Service are responsible for prosecuting criminals who engage in credit card fraud in the United States, but they do not have the resources to pursue all criminals. In general, federal officials only prosecute cases exceeding US$5,000.

Three improvements to card security have been introduced to the more common credit card networks but none has proven to help reduce credit card fraud so far. First, the on-line verification system used by merchants is being enhanced to require a 4 digit Personal Identification Number known only to the card holder.

Second, the cards themselves are being replaced with similar-looking tamper-resistant smart cards which are intended to make forgery more difficult. The majority of smart card based credit cards comply with the EMV standard. Third, an additional 3 or 4 digit Card Security Code is now present on the back of most cards, for use in "card not present" transactions.

Stakeholders at all levels in electronic payment have recognized the need to develop consistent global standards for security that account for and integrate both current and emerging security technologies. They have begun to address these needs through organizations such as PCI DSS and the Secure POS Vendor Alliance.

Code 10

Code 10 calls are made when merchants are suspicious about accepting a credit card. The phrase "Code 10 authorization" is used to avoid alerting the customer to the fact that the merchant is suspicious of their card.

The operator then asks the merchant a series of YES or NO questions to find out whether the merchant is suspicious of the card or the cardholder. The merchant may be asked to retain the card if it is safe to do so.

Credit History

The way credit card owners pay off their balances has a tremendous effect on their credit history. Two of the most important factors reported to a credit bureau are the timeliness of the debt payments and the amount of debt to credit limit.

Lenders want to see payments made as agreed, usually on a monthly basis, and a credit balance of around one-third the credit limit. The credit information stays on the credit report generally for 7 years. However, there are a few jurisdictions and situations where the timeframe might differ.

Profits and Losses

In recent times, credit card portfolios have been very profitable for banks, largely due to the booming economy of the late nineties.

However, in the case of credit cards, such high returns go hand in hand with risk, since the business is essentially one of making unsecured loans, and thus dependent on borrowers not to default in large numbers.

Costs

Interest Expenses

Banks generally borrow the money they then lend to their customers. As they receive very low-interest loans from other firms, they may borrow as much as their customers require, while lending their capital to other borrowers at higher rates. If the card issuer charges 15% on money lent to users, and it costs 5% to borrow the money to lend, and the balance sits with the cardholder for a year, the issuer earns 10% on the loan. This 10% difference is the "net interest spread" and the 5% is the "interest expense".

Operating Costs

This is the cost of running the credit card portfolio, including everything from paying the executives who run the company to printing the plastics, to mailing the statements, to running the computers that keep track of every cardholder's balance, to taking the many phone calls which cardholders place to their issuer, to protecting the customers from fraud rings. Depending on the issuer, marketing programmes are also a significant portion of expenses.

Charge Offs

When a consumer becomes severely delinquent on a debt, the creditor may declare the debt to be a charge-off. It will then be listed as such on the debtor's credit bureau reports. The item will include relevant dates, and the amount of the bad debt.

A charge-off is considered to be "written off as uncollectable." To banks, bad debts and even fraud are simply part of the cost of doing business. However, the debt is still legally valid, and the creditor can attempt to collect the full amount for the time periods permitted under state law, which is usually 3 to 7 years. This includes contacts from internal collections staff, or more likely, an outside collection agency. If the amount is large, there is the possibility of a lawsuit or arbitration.

In the United States, as the charge off number climbs or becomes erratic, officials from the Federal Reserve take a close look at the finances of the bank and may impose various operating strictures on the bank, and in the most extreme cases, may close the bank entirely.

Rewards

Many credit card customers receive rewards, such as frequent flyer points, gift certificates, or cash back as an incentive to use the card. Rewards are generally tied to purchasing an item or service on the card, which may or may not include balance transfers, cash advances, or other special uses.

Depending on the type of card, rewards will generally cost the issuer between 0.25% and 2.0% of the spread. Networks such as Visa or MasterCard have increased their fees to allow issuers to fund their rewards system. Some issuers discourage redemption by forcing the cardholder to call customer service for rewards.

On their servicing website, redeeming awards is usually a feature that is very well hidden by the issuers. Others encourage redemption for lower cost merchandise; instead of an airline ticket, which is very expensive to an issuer, the cardholder may be encouraged to redeem for a gift certificate instead.

With a fractured and competitive environment, rewards points cut dramatically into an issuer's bottom line, and rewards points and related incentives must be carefully managed to ensure a profitable portfolio. Unlike unused gift cards, in whose case the breakage in certain US states goes to the state's treasury, unredeemed credit card points are retained by the issuer.

Fraud

In relative numbers the values lost in bank card fraud are minor, calculated in 2006 at 7 cents per 100 dollars worth of transactions. In 2004, in the UK, the cost of fraud was over £500 million.

When a card is stolen, or an unauthorized duplicate made, most card issuers will refund some or all of the charges that the customer has received for things they did not buy. These refunds will, in some cases, be at the expense of the merchant, especially in mail order cases where the merchant cannot claim sight of the card. In several countries, merchants will lose the money if no ID card was asked for, therefore merchants usually require ID card in these countries. Credit card companies generally guarantee the merchant will be paid on legitimate transactions regardless of whether the consumer pays their credit card bill.

Most banking services have their own credit card services that handle fraud cases and monitor for any possible attempt at fraud. Employees that are specialized in doing fraud monitoring and investigation are often placed in Risk Management, Fraud and Authorization, or Cards and Unsecured Business.

Fraud monitoring emphasizes minimizing fraud losses while making an attempt to track down those responsible and contain the situation. Credit card fraud is a major white collar crime that has been around for many decades, even with the advent of the chip based card that was put into practice in some countries to prevent cases such as these. Even with the implementation of such measures, credit card fraud continues to be a problem.

Promotion

Promotional purchase is any purchase on which separate terms and conditions are set on each individual transaction unlike a standard purchase where the terms are set on the cardholder's account record and their pricing strategy.

All promotional purchases that post to a particular account will be carrying its own balance called as Promotional Balance.

Revenues

Interchange Fee

In addition to fees paid by the card holder, merchants must also pay interchange fees to the card-issuing bank and the card association. For a typical credit card issuer, interchange fee revenues may represent about a quarter of total revenues. These fees are typically from 1 to 6 per cent of each sale, but will vary not only from merchant to merchant, but also from card to card, with business cards and rewards cards generally costing the merchants more to process. The interchange fee that applies to a particular transaction is also affected by many other variables including: the type of merchant, the merchant's total card sales volume, the merchant's average transaction amount, whether the cards were physically present, how the information required for the transaction was received, the specific type of card, when the transaction was settled, and the authorized and settled transaction amounts.

In some cases, merchants add a surcharge to the credit cards to cover the interchange fee, encouraging their customers to instead use cash, debit cards, or even cheques.

Interest on Outstanding Balances

The major fees are for:

- Late payments or overdue payments
- Charges that result in exceeding the credit limit on the card, called overlimit fees
- Returned cheque fees or payment processing fees
- Cash advances and convenience cheques
- Transactions in a foreign currency. A few financial institutions do not charge a fee for this.
- Membership fees, sometimes a percentage of the credit limit.
- Exchange rate loading fees. The variation of exchange rates applied by different credit cards can be very substantial, as much as 10% according to a Lonely Planet report in 2009.

Controversy

Credit card debt has increased steadily. Since the late 1990s, lawmakers, consumer advocacy groups, college officials and other higher education affiliates have become increasingly concerned about the rising use of credit cards among college students.

The major credit card companies have been accused of targeting a younger audience, in particular college students, many of whom are already in debt with college tuition fees and college loans and who typically are less experienced at managing their own finances. Credit card debt may also negatively affect their grades as they are likely to work more both part and full time positions.

Another controversial area is the universal default feature of many North American credit card contracts. When a cardholder is late paying a particular credit card issuer, that card's interest rate can be raised, often considerably. With universal default, a customer's other credit cards, for which the customer may be current on payments, may also have their rates and/or credit limit changed.

The universal default feature allows creditors to periodically check cardholders' credit portfolios to view trade, allowing these other institutions to decrease the credit limit and/or increase rates on cardholders who may be late with another credit card issuer. Being late on one credit card will potentially affect all the cardholder's credit cards.

Citibank voluntarily stopped this practice in March 2007 and Chase stopped the practice in November 2007. The fact that credit card companies can change the interest rate on debts that were incurred when a different rate of interest was in place is similar to adjustable rate mortgages where interest rates on current debt may rise.

However, in both cases this is agreed to in advance, and is a trade off that allows a lower initial rate as well as the possibility of an even lower rate or perpetually keeping a below-market rate. It should be noted that the Universal Default practice was actually encouraged by Federal Regulators, particularly those at the Office of the Comptroller of the Currency as a means of managing the changing risk profiles of cardholders.

Another controversial area is the trailing interest issue. Trailing interest is the practice of charging interest on the entire bill no matter what percentage of it is paid. U.S Senator Carl Levin raised the issue of millions of Americans affected by hidden fees, compounding interest and cryptic terms. Their woes were heard in a Senate Permanent Subcommittee on

Investigations hearing which was chaired by Senator Levin, who said that he intends to keep the spotlight on credit card companies and that legislative action may be necessary to purge the industry. In 2009, the C.A.R.D. Act was signed into law, enacting protections for many of the issues Levin had raised.

In the United States, some have called for Congress to enact additional regulations on the industry; to expand the disclosure box clearly disclosing rate hikes, use plain language, incorporate balance payoff disclosures, and also to outlaw universal default. At a congress hearing around March 1, 2007, Citibank announced it would no longer practice this, effective immediately.

Opponents of such regulation argue that customers must become more proactive and self-responsible in evaluating and negotiating terms with credit providers. Some of the nation's influential top credit card issuers, who are among the top fifty corporate contributors to political campaigns, successfully opposed it.

Hidden Costs

In the United Kingdom, merchants won the right through The Credit Cards Order 1990 to charge customers different prices according to the payment method. As of 2007, the United Kingdom was one of the world's most credit-card-intensive countries, with 2.4 credit cards per consumer, according to the UK Payments Administration Ltd.

In the United States, until 1984 federal law prohibited surcharges on card transactions. Although the federal Truth in Lending Act provisions that prohibited surcharges expired that year, a number of states have since enacted laws that continue to outlaw the practice; California, Colorado, Connecticut, Florida, Kansas, Massachusetts, Maine, New York, Oklahoma, and Texas have laws against surcharges.

As of 2006, the United States probably had one of the world's if not the top ratio of credit cards per capita, with 984 million bank-issued Visa and MasterCard credit card and debit card accounts alone for an adult population of roughly 220 million people. The credit card per US capita ratio was nearly 4:1 as of 2003 and as high as 5:1 as of 2006.

Credit Card Numbering

The numbers found on credit cards have a certain amount of internal structure, and share a common numbering scheme.

The card number's prefix, called the Bank Identification Number, is the sequence of digits at the beginning of the number that determine the bank to which a credit card number belongs. This is the first six digits for MasterCard and Visa cards. The next nine digits are the individual account number, and the final digit is a validity check code.

In addition to the main credit card number, credit cards also carry issue and expiration dates, as well as extra codes such as issue numbers and security codes. Not all credit cards have the same sets of extra codes nor do they use the same number of digits.

Credit Cards in ATMs

Many credit cards can also be used in an ATM to withdraw money against the credit limit extended to the card, but many card issuers charge interest on cash advances before they do so on purchases. The interest on cash advances is commonly charged from the date the withdrawal is made, rather than the monthly billing date.

Many card issuers levy a commission for cash withdrawals, even if the ATM belongs to the same bank as the card issuer. Merchants do not offer cashback on credit card transactions because they would pay a percentage commission of the additional cash amount to their bank or merchant services provider, thereby making it uneconomical.

Many credit card companies will also, when applying payments to a card, do so at the end of a billing cycle, and apply those payments to everything before cash advances. For this reason, many consumers have large cash balances, which have no grace period and incur interest at a rate that is higher than the purchase rate, and will carry those balance for years, even if they pay off their statement balance each month.

Credit Cards as Funding for Entrepreneurs

Credit cards are a risky way for entrepreneurs to acquire capital for their start ups when more conventional financing is unavailable. It's widely reported that Len Bosack and Sandy Lerner used personal credit cards to start Cisco Systems. It is rumoured that Larry Page and Sergey Brin's start up of Google was financed by credit cards to buy the necessary computers and office equipment, more specifically "a terabyte of hard disks".

Similarly, filmmaker Robert Townsend financed part of Hollywood Shuffle using credit cards. Director Kevin Smith funded Clerks in part by maxing out several credit cards. Actor Richard Hatch also financed his production of Battlestar Galactica: The Second Coming partly through his credit cards. Famed hedge fund manager Bruce Kovner began his career in financial markets by borrowing from his credit card. UK entrepreneur James Caan financed his first business using several credit cards.

DEBIT CARD

A debit card is a plastic card that provides an alternative payment method to cash when making purchases. Functionally, it can be called an electronic cheque, as the funds are withdrawn directly from either the bank account, or from the remaining balance on the card. In some cases, the cards are designed exclusively for use on the Internet, and so there is no physical card.

In many countries the use of debit cards has become so widespread that their volume of use has overtaken the cheque and, in some instances, cash transactions. Like credit cards, debit cards are used widely for telephone and Internet purchases and, unlike credit cards, the funds are transferred immediately from the bearer's bank account instead of having the bearer pay back the money at a later date.

Debit cards may also allow for instant withdrawal of cash, acting as the ATM card for withdrawing cash and as a cheque guarantee card. Merchants may also offer cashback facilities to customers, where a customer can withdraw cash along with their purchase.

Types of Debit Card Systems

There are currently three ways that debit card transactions are processed: online debit, offline debit and the Electronic Purse Card System. It should be noted that one physical card can include the functions of an online debit card, an offline debit card and an electronic purse card.

Although many debit cards are of the Visa or MasterCard brand, there are many other types of debit card, each accepted only within a particular country or region, for example Switch and Solo in the United Kingdom, Interac in Canada, Carte Bleue in France, Laser in Ireland, "EC electronic cash" in Germany and EFTPOS cards in Australia and New Zealand.

The need for cross-border compatibility and the advent of the euro recently led to many of these card networks being re-branded with the internationally recognised Maestro logo, which is part of the MasterCard brand. Some debit cards are dual branded with the logo of the national card as well as Maestro.

The use of a debit card system allows operators to package their product more effectively while monitoring customer spending. An example of one of these systems is ECS by Embed International.

Online Debit System

Online debit cards require electronic authorization of every transaction and the debits are reflected in the user's account immediately. The transaction may be additionally secured with the personal identification number authentication system and some online cards require such authentication for every transaction, essentially becoming enhanced automatic teller machine cards.

One difficulty in using online debit cards is the necessity of an electronic authorization device at the point of sale and sometimes also a separate PINpad to enter the PIN, although this is becoming commonplace for all card transactions in many countries. Overall, the online debit card is generally viewed as superior to the offline debit card because of its more secure authentication system and live status, which alleviates problems with processing lag on transactions that may only issue online debit cards.

Offline Debit System

Offline debit cards have the logos of major credit cards or major debit cards and are used at the point of sale like a credit card. This type of debit card may be subject to a daily limit, and/or a maximum limit equal to the current/checking account balance from which it draws funds. Transactions conducted with offline debit cards require 2–3 days to be reflected on users' account balances.

In some countries and with some banks and merchant service organizations, a "credit" or offline debit transaction is without cost to the purchaser beyond the face value of the transaction, while a small fee may be charged for a "debit" or online debit transaction. Other differences are that online debit purchasers may opt to withdraw cash in addition to the amount of the debit purchase; also, from the merchant's standpoint, the merchant pays lower fees on online debit transaction as compared to "credit" debit transaction.

Electronic Purse Card System

Smart-card-based electronic purse systems are in use throughout Europe since the mid-1990s, most notably in Germany, Austria, the Netherlands, Belgium and Switzerland. In Austria and Germany, all current bank cards now include electronic purses.

Prepaid Debit Card

Prepaid debit cards, also called reloadable debit cards or reloadable prepaid cards, are often used for recurring payments. The payer loads funds to the cardholder's card account. Prepaid debit cards use either the offline debit system or the online debit system to access these funds. Particularly for companies with a large number of payment recipients abroad, prepaid debit cards allow the delivery of international payments without the delays and fees associated with international checks and bank transfers.

Providers include Caxton FX prepaid cards, Escape prepaid cards and Travelex prepaid cards. Whereas, web-based services such as stock photography websites, outsourced services, and affiliate networks have all started offering prepaid debit cards for their contributors/freelancers/vendors.

Advantages and Disadvantages

Debit and check cards, as they have become widespread, have revealed numerous advantages and disadvantages to the consumer and retailer alike.

The following allegations seem to be based only on the current situation within the U.S.A.

Advantages are as follows:

- A consumer who is not credit worthy and may find it difficult or impossible to obtain a credit card can more easily obtain a debit card, allowing him/her to make plastic transactions.
- For most transactions, a check card can be used to avoid check writing altogether. Check cards debit funds from the user's account on the spot, thereby finalizing the transaction at the time of purchase, and bypassing the requirement to pay a credit card bill at a later date, or to write an insecure check containing the account holder's personal information.
- Like credit cards, debit cards are accepted by merchants with less identification and scrutiny than personal checks, thereby making transactions quicker and less intrusive. Unlike personal checks, merchants generally do not believe that a payment via a debit card may be later dishonoured.
- Unlike a credit card, which charges higher fees and interest rates when a cash advance is obtained, a debit card may be used to obtain cash from an ATM or a PIN-based transaction at no extra charge, other than a foreign ATM fee.

The Debit card has many disadvantages as opposed to cash or credit:

- Use of a debit card is not usually limited to the existing funds in the account to which it is linked, most banks allow a certain threshold over the available bank balance which can cause overdraft fees if the customer does not depend on their own records of spending.
- Many banks are now charging over-limit fees or non-sufficient funds fees based upon pre-authorizations, and even attempted but refused transactions by the merchant.
- Many merchants mistakenly believe that amounts owed can be "taken" from a customer's account after a debit card has been presented, without agreement as to date, payee name, amount and currency, thus causing penalty fees for overdrafts, over-the-limit, amounts not available causing further rejections or overdrafts, and rejected transactions by some banks.
- In some countries debit cards offer lower levels of security protection than credit cards. Theft of the users PIN using skimming devices can be accomplished much easier with a PIN input than with a signature-based credit transaction. However, theft of users' PIN codes using skimming devices can be equally easily accomplished with a debit transaction PIN input, as with a credit transaction PIN input, and theft using a signature-based credit transaction is equally easy as theft using a signature-based debit transaction.
- In many places, laws protect the consumer from fraud much less than with a credit card. While the holder of a credit card is legally responsible for only a minimal amount of a fraudulent transaction made with a credit card, which is often waived by the bank, the consumer may be held liable for hundreds of dollars, or even the entire value of fraudulent debit transactions. The consumer also has a shorter time

to report such fraud to the bank in order to be eligible for such a waiver with a debit card, whereas with a credit card, this time may be up to 60 days. A thief who obtains or clones a debit card along with its PIN may be able to clean out the consumer's bank account, and the consumer will have no recourse.

Table. Federally Imposed Maximum Liability for Unauthorized Card Use (United States)

Reported	Maximum Card Holder Liability	
	Credit Card	Debit Card
Before Use	$0	$0
Within 2 business days	$50	$50
After 2 but before 60 business days	$50	$500
After 60 business days	Unlimited	Unlimited

- In the UK and Ireland, among other countries, a consumer who purchases goods or services with a credit card can pursue the credit card issuer if the goods or services are not delivered or are unmerchantable. While they must generally exhaust the process provided by the retailer first, this is not necessary if the retailer has gone out of business. This protection is not provided by legislation when using a debit card but may be offered to a limited extent as a benefit provided by the card network, e.g. Visa debit cards.
- When a transaction is made using a credit card, the bank's money is being spent, and therefore, the bank has a vested interest in claiming its money where there is fraud or a dispute. The bank may fight to void the charges of a consumer who is dissatisfied with a purchase, or who has otherwise been treated unfairly by the merchant. But when a debit purchase is made, the consumer has spent his/her own money, and the bank has little if any motivation to collect the funds.
- In some countries, and for certain types of purchases, such as gasoline, lodging, or car rental, the bank may

place a hold on funds much greater than the actual purchase for a fixed period of time. However, this isn't the case in other countries, such as Sweden. Until the hold is released, any other transactions presented to the account, including checks, may be dishonoured, or may be paid at the expense of an overdraft fee if the account lacks any additional funds to pay those items.

- While debit cards bearing the logo of a major credit card are accepted for virtually all transactions where an equivalent credit card is taken, a major exception in some countries is at car rental facilities. In some countries car rental agencies require an actual credit card to be used, or at the very least, will verify the creditworthiness of the renter using a debit card. In these unspecified countries, these companies will deny a rental to anyone who does not fit the requirements, and such a credit check may actually hurt one's credit score, as long as there is such a thing as a credit score in the country of purchase and/or the country of residence of the customer.

Consumer Protection

Consumer protections vary, depending on the network used. Visa and MasterCard, for instance, prohibit minimum and maximum purchase sizes, surcharges, and arbitrary security procedures on the part of merchants. Merchants are usually charged higher transaction fees for credit transactions, since debit network transactions are less likely to be fraudulent.

This may lead them to "steer" customers to debit transactions. Consumers disputing charges may find it easier to do so with a credit card, since the money will not immediately leave their control.

Fraudulent charges on a debit card can also cause problems with a checking account because the money is withdrawn immediately and may thus result in an overdraft or bounced checks. In some cases debit card-issuing banks will promptly refund any disputed charges until the matter can be settled, and in some jurisdictions the consumer liability for unauthorized charges is the same for both debit and credit cards.

In some countries, like India and Sweden, the consumer protection is the same regardless of the network used. Some banks set minimum and maximum purchase sizes, mostly for online-only cards.

However, this has nothing to do with the card networks, but rather with the bank's judgement of the person's age and credit records. Any fees that the customers have to pay to the bank are the same regardless of whether the transaction is conducted as a credit or as a debit transaction, so there is no advantage for the customers to choose one transaction mode over another.

Shops may add surcharges to the price of the goods or services in accordance with laws allowing them to do so. Banks consider the purchases as having been made at the moment when the card was swiped, regardless of when the purchase settlement was made.

Regardless of which transaction type was used, the purchase may result in an overdraft because the money is considered to have left the account at the moment of the card swiping.

Financial Access

Debit cards and secured credit cards are popular among college students who have not yet established a credit history. Debit cards may also be used by expatriated workers to send money home to their families holding an affiliated debit card.

Issues With Deferred Posting of Offline Debit

To the consumer, a debit transaction is perceived as occurring in real-time; *i.e.* the money is withdrawn from their account immediately following the authorization request from the merchant, which in many countries, is the case when making an online debit purchase. However, when a purchase is made using the "credit" option, the transaction merely places an authorization hold on the customer's account; funds are not actually withdrawn until the transaction is reconciled and hard-posted to the customer's account, usually a few days later. However, the previous sentence applies to all kinds of transaction types, at least when using a card issued by a European bank.

This is in contrast to a typical credit card transaction; though it can also have a lag time of a few days before the transaction is posted to the account, it can be many days to a month or more before the consumer makes repayment with actual money.

Because of this, in the case of a benign or malicious error by the merchant or bank, a debit transaction may cause more serious problems than in the case of a credit card transaction. This is especially true in the United States, where cheque fraud is a crime in every state, but exceeding your credit limit is not.

Internet Purchases

Debit cards may also be used on the Internet. Internet transactions may be conducted in either online or offline mode, although shops accepting online-only cards are rare in some countries, while they are common in other countries. For a comparison, PayPal offers the customer to use an online-only Maestro card if the customer enters a Dutch address of residence, but not if the same customer enters a Swedish address of residence.

Internet purchases may be conducted in either online or offline mode, and just as in the case where you use your card in a shop, it is impossible to tell whether the transaction was conducted in online or offline mode, since the mode isn't mentioned on any receipt or similar.

Internet purchases use neither a PIN code nor a signature for identification. Transactions may be conducted in either credit or debit mode, and this has nothing to do with whether the transaction was conducted on online or offline mode, since both credit and debit transactions may be conducted in both modes.

Overdraft Fees

On banks' lucrative debit card overdraft fees - pointed out that debit card issuers could notify customers electronically, allowing them to avoid overdraft fees. Nessa Feddis, banking industry spokesperson and lobbyist, contended that "current technology makes real-time notification of overdrafts cost-prohibitive."

The contended that "financial institutions don't want to change the status quo because they make good and easy money off their own customers' mistakes and irresponsibility."

Debit Cards Around the World

In some countries, banks tend to levy a small fee for each debit card transaction. In some countries the merchants bear all the costs and customers are not charged. There are many people who routinely use debit cards for all transactions, no matter how small.

Some retailers refuse to accept debit cards for small transactions, where paying the transaction fee would absorb the profit margin on the sale, making the transaction uneconomic for the retailer.

Australia

Debit cards in Australia are called different names depending on the issuing bank: Commonwealth Bank of Australia: Keycard; Westpac Banking Corporation: Handycard; National Australia Bank: FlexiCard; ANZ Bank: Access card; Bendigo Bank: Cashcard.

EFTPOS is very popular in Australia and has been operating there since the 1980s. EFTPOS-enabled cards are accepted at almost all swipe terminals able to accept credit cards, regardless of the bank that issued the card, including Maestro cards issued by foreign banks, with most businesses accepting them, with 450,000 Point Of Sale terminals.

EFTPOS cards can also be used to deposit and withdraw cash over the counter at Australia Post outlets participating in giroPost, just as if the transaction was conducted at a bank branch, even if the bank branch is closed. Electronic transactions in Australia are generally processed via the Telstra Argent and Optus Transact Plus network - which has recently superseded the old Transcend network in the last few years. Most early keycards were only usable for EFTPOS and at ATM or bank branches, whilst the new debit card system works in the same ways a credit card, except it will only use funds in the specified bank account. This means that, among other advantages, the new system is suitable for electronic purchases without a delay of 2 to 4 days for bank-to-bank money transfers.

Australia operates both electronic credit card transaction authorization and traditional EFTPOS debit card authorization systems, the difference between the two being that EFTPOS transactions are authorized by a personal identification number while credit card transactions are usually authorized by the printing and signing of a receipt. If the user fails to enter the correct pin 3 times, the consequences range from the card being locked out and requiring a phone call or trip to the branch to reactivate with a new PIN, the card being cut up by the merchant, or in the case of an ATM, being kept inside the machine, both of which require a new card to be ordered.

Generally credit card transaction costs are borne by the merchant with no fee applied to the end user while EFTPOS transactions cost the consumer an applicable withdrawal fee charged by their bank. The introduction of Visa and MasterCard debit cards along with regulation in the settlement fees charged by the operators of both EFTPOS and credit cards by the Reserve Bank has seen a continuation in the increasing ubiquity of credit card use among Australians and a general decline in the profile of EFTPOS. However, the regulation of settlement fees also removed the ability of banks, who typically provide merchant services to retailers on behalf of Visa, MasterCard or Bankcard, from stopping those retailers charging extra fees to take payment by credit card instead of cash or EFTPOS.

Though only a few operators with strong market power have done so, the passing on of fees charged for credit card transactions may result in an increased use of EFTPOS.

Brazil

In Brazil debit cards are called cartão de débito and are getting increasingly popular as a replacement of cheques, that are still uncommonly popular in the country.

Canada

Canada has a nation-wide EFTPOS system, called Interac Direct Payment. Since being introduced in 1994, IDP has become the most popular payment method in the country. Previously, debit cards have been in use for ABM usage since the early 1980s.

In the early 1990s, pilot projects were conducted among Canada's six largest banks to gauge security, accuracy and feasibility of the Interac system. Slowly in the later half of the 1990s, it was estimated that approximately 50% of retailers offered Interac as a source of payment. Retailers, many small transaction retailers like coffee shops, resisted offering IDP to promote faster service. In 2009, 99% of retailers offer IDP as an alternative payment form.

In Canada, the debit card is sometimes referred to as a "bank card". It is a client card issued by a bank that provides access to funds and other bank account transactions, such as transferring funds, checking balances, paying bills, etc., as well as point of purchase transactions connected on the Interac network.

Since its national launch in 1994, Interac Direct Payment has become so widespread that, as of 2001, more transactions in Canada were completed using debit cards than cash. This popularity may be partially attributable to two main factors: the convenience of not having to carry cash, and the availability of automated bank machines and Direct Payment merchants on the network.

Canadians, in fact, rank as the undisputed world leaders in debit card use, making 71.7 debit transactions per person in 2001, which is significantly more than consumers in the next closest country. The average value of a debit transaction in Canada was the lowest in an 11-country comparison, with Japan and Switzerland markedly standing out.93 Thus, compared to consumers in other countries, Canadians appear to be using their debit cards more often, even for frequent low-cost transactions. Debit cards may be considered similar to stored-value cards in that they represent a finite amount of money owed by the card issuer to the holder. They are different in that stored-value cards are generally anonymous and are only usable at the issuer, while debit cards are generally associated with an individual's bank account and can be used anywhere on the Interac network.

In Canada, the bank cards can be used at POS and ABMs. Interac Online has also been introduced in recent years allowing clients of most major Canadian banks to use their debit cards for online payment with certain merchants as well. Certain financial institutions also allow their clients to use their debit cards in the United States on the NYCE network.

Consumer Protection in Canada

Consumers in Canada are protected under a voluntary code* entered into by all providers of debit card services, The Canadian Code of Practice for Consumer Debit Card Services. Adherence to the Code is overseen by the Financial Consumer Agency of Canada, which investigates consumer complaints.

The FCAC website, revisions to the Code that came into effect in 2005 put the onus on the financial institution to prove that a consumer was responsible for a disputed transaction, and also place a limit on the number of days that an account can be frozen during the financial institution's investigation of a transaction.

Chile

Chile has an EFTPOS system called Redcompra which is currently used in at least 23,000 establishments throughout the country. Goods may be purchased using this system at most supermarkets, retail stores, pubs and restaurants in major urban centres.

Colombia

Colombia has a system called Redeban-Multicolour and

Credibanco Visa which are currently used in at least 23,000 establishments throughout the country. Goods may be purchased using this system at most supermarkets, retail stores, pubs and restaurants in major urban centres. Colombian debit cards are Maestro, Visa Electron, Visa Debit and MasterCard-Debit.

Denmark

The Danish debit card Dankort was introduced on 1 September 1983, and despite the initial transactions being paper-based, the Dankort quickly won widespread acceptance in Denmark. By 1985 the first EFTPOS terminals were introduced, and 1985 was also the year when the number of Dankort transactions first exceeded 1 million. It is not uncommon that Dankort is the only card accepted at smaller stores, thus making it harder for tourists to travel without cash.

Miscellaneous Facts and Numbers

- In 2007 PBS, the Danish operator of the Dankort system, processed a total of 737 million Dankort transactions. Of these, 4.5 million just on a single day, 21 December. This remains the current record.
- At the end of 2007, there were 3.9 million Dankort in existence.
- More than 80,000 Danish shops have a Dankort terminal. Another 11,000 internet shops also accept the Dankort.

France

Carte Bancaire, the national payment scheme, in 2008, had 57,5 milion carts carrying its logo and 7,76 billion transactions were processed through the e-rsb network. Most CB cards are debit cards, either debit or deferred debit. Less than 10% of CB cards were credit cards. Banks in France charge annual fees for debit cards, yet they do not charge personal customers for checkbooks or processing checks.

This imbalance most probably dates from the unilateral introduction in France of Chip and PIN debit cards in the early

1990s, when the cost of this technology was much higher than it is now. Credit cards of the type found in the United Kingdom and United States are unusual in France and the closest equivalent is the deferred debit card, which operates like a normal debit card, except that all purchase transactions are postponed until the end of the month, thereby giving the customer between 1 and 31 days of interest-free credit.

The annual fee for a deferred debit card is around €10 more than for one with immediate debit. Most France debit cards are branded with the Carte Bleue logo, which assures acceptance throughout France. Most card holders choose to pay around €5 more in their annual fee to additionally have a Visa or a MasterCard logo on their Carte Bleue, so that the card is accepted internationally.

A Carte Bleue without a Visa or a MasterCard logo is often known as a "Carte Bleue Nationale" and a Carte Bleue with a Visa or a MasterCard logo is known as a "Carte Bleue Internationale", or more frequently, simply called a "Visa" or "MasterCard". Many smaller merchants in France refuse to accept debit cards for transactions under a certain amount because of the minimum fee charged by merchants' banks per transaction. But more and more merchants accept debit cards for small amounts, due to the massive daily use of debit card nowadays. Merchants in France do not differentiate between debit and credit cards, and so both have equal acceptance. This is legal in France to set a minimum amount to transactions but the merchants must display it clearly.

Germany

Debit cards have enjoyed wide acceptance in Germany for years. Facilities already existed before EFTPOS became popular with the Eurocheque card, an authorization system initially developed for paper checks where, in addition to signing the actual check, customers also needed to show the card alongside the check as a security measure. Those cards could also be used at ATM Terminals and for card-based electronic funds transfer. These are now the only functions of such cards: the Eurocheque system was abandoned in 2002 during the transition from the Deutsche Mark to the euro. As of 2005, most stores and petrol outlets have EFTPOS facilities. Processing fees are paid by the businesses, which leads to some business owners refusing debit card payments for sales totalling less than a certain amount, usually 5 or 10 euro.

To avoid the processing fees, many businesses resorted to using direct debit, which is then called electronic direct debit. The point-of-sale terminal reads the name and account number from the card but instead of handling the transaction through the ec network it simply prints a form, which the customer signs to authorise the debit note.

However, this method also avoids any verification or payment guarantee provided by the network. Further, customers can return debit notes by notifying their bank without giving a reason. This means that the beneficiary bears the risk of fraud and illiquidity. Some business mitigate the risk by consulting a proprietary blacklist or by switching to electronic cash for higher transaction amounts.

Around 2000, an Electronic Purse Card was introduced, dubbed Geldkarte. It makes use of the smart card chip on the front of the standard issue debit card. This chip can be charged with up to 200 euro, and is advertised as a means of making medium to very small payments, even down to several euros or cent payments. The key factor here is that no processing fees are deducted by banks. It did not gain the popularity its inventors had hoped for. However, this could change as this chip is now used as means of age verification at cigarette vending machines, which has been mandatory since January 2007. Furthermore, some payment discounts are being offered when paying with "Geldkarte". The "Geldkarte" payment lacks all security measures, since it does not require the user to enter a PIN or sign a sales slip: the loss of a "Geldkarte" is similar to the loss of a wallet or purse - anyone who finds it can then use their find to pay for their own purchases.

Hong Kong

One popular payment method that is widely used in Hong Kong which is similar to the debit card is called EPS. EPS is a payment method that lets customers use their ATM Card like a debit card. Most of the big banks in Hong Kong provide the customer with an ATM card with EPS.

Hungary

In Hungary debit cards are far more common and popular than credit cards. Many Hungarians even refer to their debit card mistakenly using the word for credit card.

India

The debit card has limited popularity in India as the merchant is charged for each transaction. The debit card therefore is mostly used for ATM transactions. Most of the banks issue VISA debit cards, while some banks issue Maestro cards.

The debit card transactions are routed through the VISA or MasterCard networks rather than directly via the issuing bank The National Payments Corporation of India is introducing a payment network and debit card dubbed 'india card'.

The Reserve Bank of India is expecting this system will gradualy replace the overseas run networks from Visa and MaterCard for Indian ATM, debit and credit card services.

Italy

Debit cards are quite popular in Italy. There are both classic and prepaid cards. The main classic debit card in Italy is PagoBancomat: this kind of card is issued by Italian banks, often with a credit card. It allows access to the owner's bank account funds and it is widely accepted in most shops, although on the Internet it is allowed only the credit card mode.

The major debit prepaid card is issued by Poste Italiane S.p.A., is called Postepay and runs on the Visa Electron circuit. It can be used on Poste Italiane's ATMs and on Visa Electron-compatible bank ATMs all over the world. It has no fees when used on the Internet and in POS-based transactions. Other cards are issued by other companies, such as Vodafone

CashCard, Banca di Milano's Carta Jeans and Carta Moneta Online.

Japan

In Japan people usually use their cash cards, originally intended only for use with cash machines, as debit cards. The debit functionality of these cards is usually referred to as J-Debitand only cash cards from certain banks can be used. A cash card has the same size as a VISA/MasterCard. As identification, the user will have to enter his or her four-digit PIN when paying. J-Debit was started in Japan on March 6, 2000.

Kuwait

In Kuwait, all banks provide a debit card to their account holders. This card is branded as KNET, which is the central switch in Kuwait. KNET card transactions are free for both customer and the merchant and therefore KNET debit cards are used for low valued transactions as well.

KNET cards are mostly co-branded as Maestro or Visa Electron which makes it possible to use the same card outside Kuwait on any terminal supporting these payment schemes.

The Netherlands

In the Netherlands using EFTPOS is known as pinnen, a term derived from the use of a Personal Identification Number. PINs are also used for ATM transactions, and the term is used interchangeably by many people, although it was introduced as a marketing brand for EFTPOS. The system was launched in 1987, and in 2006 there were 166,375 terminals throughout the country, including mobile terminals used by delivery services and on markets. All banks offer a debit card suitable for EFTPOS with current accounts.

PIN transactions are usually free to the customer, but the retailer is charged per-transaction and monthly fees. Equens, an association with all major banks as its members, runs the system, and until August 2005 also charged for it. Responding to allegations of monopoly abuse, it has handed over contractual responsibilities to its member banks, who now offer competing contracts. Interpay, a legal predecessor of Equens, was fined EUR 47 million in 2004, but the fine was later dropped, and a related fine for banks was lowered from EUR 17 to €14 million. Per-transaction fees are between 5-10 eurocents, depending on volume.

Credit cards use in the Netherlands is very low, and most credit cards cannot be used with EFTPOS, or charge very high fees to the customer. Debit cards can often, though not always, be used in the entire EU for EFTPOS. Most debit cards are Maestro cards. Electronic Purse Cards were introduced in 1996, but have never become very popular.

New Zealand

The EFTPOS system is highly popular in New Zealand, with more debit card terminals per head of population than any other country, and being used for about 60% of all retail transactions.

The largest EFTPOS network provider, "New Zealanders use EFTPOS twice as much as any other country." It is not unusual for a New Zealander to have more than one EFTPOS card and for banks to offer fixed monthly fees for unlimited EFTPOS transactions during that month. EFTPOS systems are capable of handling huge volumes of transactions during busy periods such as Christmas. The networks are highly sophisticated and have a number of safeguards in place to ensure security and to minimise the risk of disruption even during peak transaction periods.

Virtually all retail outlets have EFTPOS terminals, particularly supermarkets, "dairies", service stations, and bars. Increasingly Taxi operators, businesses operating from stands at events and even pizza delivery people have mobile EFTPOS terminals.

New Zealanders use EFTPOS for both small and large transactions. It would not be unusual for a New Zealander to use an EFTPOS card to pay for an amount as small as 50 cents NZD. Because EFTPOS is such an integral part of spending in New Zealand, rare network failures cause tremendous delays, inconvenience and lost income to businesses who must resort to manual "zip-zap" swipe machines to process EFTPOS transactions until the network returns to service. Typically New Zealand merchants do not pay a fee per transaction as is the case in Australia and other countries.

Transaction fees are typically borne by the customer, and retailers pay a fixed monthly equipment rental fee. As bank accounts for students and children under 18 years old typically attract low or no electronic transaction fees, the use of EFTPOS by the younger generations has become virtually ubiquitous. In recent times, major banks have started to offer accounts with no EFTPOS transaction fees.

The Bank of New Zealand introduced EFTPOS to New Zealand in 1985 through a pilot scheme with petrol stations. EFTPOS is operated through two primary networks. One, EFTPOS NZ, owned by ANZ, and a second operated by Paymark Limited which is owned by ASB Bank, Westpac, and the Bank of New Zealand.

The Paymark network processes approximately 75% of all EFTPOS transactions in New Zealand on their Paymark EFTPOS network and has over 73,000 points of sale. During July 2006 the five billionth EFTPOS payment flowed across the ETSL/Paymark EFTPOS network since the electronic form of payment was introduced in New Zealand in 1989. On 9 May 2007, Payment Express was certified as the first IP/broadband certified terminal allowing EFTPOS transactions to be transmitted securely over the Internet.

However security issues regarding EFTPOS payments over the public Internet and the costs associated with legacy terminal replacement has hampered the growth of the IP medium in New Zealand. One company, Merchant IP Services offers an alternative IP-POS solution allowing for the secure IP connection of most legacy terminals without the need for terminal replacement.

The PCI compliant and Paymark certified MIPS IP-POS system consists of a MIPS WebNAC connected to the legacy EFTPOS terminal converting dial up transaction data to IP before transporting the payment securely to the bank switch.

In March 2008 Paymark partnered with virtual wallet payment system pago to create New Zealands first debit or "stored value" system for online shopping. The New Zealand eftpos system was one of the first in the world to be designed and its success and popularity have ironically meant that little has been done to incorporate it with systems from other countries as they were developed.

Cards can only be used within New Zealand and only when physically at a merchant terminal. In response most banks started issuing eftpos cards co-branded as maestro so they could be used overseas. In 2009 a number of banks started introducing eftpos cards that, as well as having New Zealand eftpos facility also incorporated the Visa Debit system so that clients could use them on-line as well as overseas.

Philippines

In the Philippines, all three national ATM network consortia offer proprietary PIN debit. This was first offered by Express Payment System in 1987, followed by Megalink with Paylink in 1993 then BancNet with the Point-of-Sale in 1994. Express Payment System or EPS was the pioneer provider, having launched the service in 1987 on behalf of the Bank of the Philippine Islands.

The EPS service has subsequently been extended in late 2005 to include the other Expressnet members: Banco de Oro and Land Bank of the Philippines. They currently operate 10,000 terminals for their cardholders. Megalink launched Paylink EFTPOS system in 1993. Terminal services are provided by Equitable Card Network on behalf of the consortium. Service is available in 2,000 terminals, mostly in Metro Manila.

BancNet introduced their Point of sale System in 1994 as the first consortium-operated EFTPOS service in the country. The service is available in over 1,400 locations throughout the Philippines, including second and third-class municipalities. In 2005, BancNet signed a Memorandum of Agreement to serve as the local gateway for China UnionPay, the sole ATM switch in the People's Republic of China. This will allow the estimated 1.0 billion Chinese ATM cardholders to use the BancNet ATMs and the EFTPOS in all SM Supermalls. Visa debit cards are issued by Union Bank of the Philippines, Chinatrust, Equicom Savings Bank, Banco De Oro, HSBC, HSBC Savings Bank and Sterling Bank of Asia. Union Bank of the Philippines cards, Equicom Savings Bank and Sterling Bank of Asia EMV cards which can also be used for internet purchases.

Sterling Bank of Asia has released its first line of prepaid and debit Visa cards with EMV chip. MasterCard debit cards are issued by Banco de Oro, Security Bank and Smart Communications tied up with Banco De Oro. MasterCard Electronic cards are issued by BPI and Security Bank. All VISA and MasterCard based debit cards in the Philippines are non-embossed and are marked either for "Electronic Use Only" or "Valid only where MasterCard Electronic is Accepted"

Poland

In Poland, local debit cards, such as PolCard, have become largely substituted with international ones, such as Visa, MasterCard, or the unembossed Visa Electron or Maestro. Most banks in Poland block Internet and MOTO transactions with unembossed cards, requiring the customer to buy an embossed card or a card for Internet/MOTO transactions only. The number of banks which do not block MOTO transactions on unembossed cards has recently started to increase.

Russia

In addition to VISA and Master Card, there are some local payment system based in general on Smart Card technology:

- *Sbercard*: This payment system was created by Sberbank around 1995–1996. It uses BGS Smartcard Systems AG smart card technology *i.e.* DUET. Sberbank was a single retail bank in USSR before 1990. De facto this is a payment system of the SberBank.
- *Zolotaya Korona*: This card brand was created in 1994. Zolotaya Korona is based on CFT technology.
- *STB Card*: This card uses the classic magnetic stripe

technology. It almost fully collapsed after 1998 with STB bank failure.

- *Union Card*: The card also uses the classic magnetic stripe technology. This card brand is on the decline. These accounts are being reissued as Visa or MasterCard accounts.

Nearly every transaction, regardless of brand or system, is processed as an immediate debit transaction. Non-debit transactions within these systems have spending limits that are strictly limited when compared with typical Visa or MasterCard accounts.

Saudi Arabia

In Saudi Arabia, all debit card transactions are routed trough Saudi Payments Network, the only electronic payment system in the Kingdom and all banks are required by the Saudi Arabian Monetary Agency to issue cards fully compatible with the network.

It connects all point of sale terminals throughout the country to a central payment switch which in turn re-routes the financial transactions to the card issuer, local bank, VISA, AMEX or MasterCard. As well as its use for debit cards, the network is also used for ATM and credit card transactions.

Singapore

Singapore's debit service is managed by Network for Electronic Transfers, founded by Singapore's leading banks, DBS, Keppel Bank, OCBC, OUB, POSB, Tat Lee Bank and UOB in 1985 as a result of a need for a centralised e-Payment operator.It will deduct money from your bank directly when you buy things using debit cards.

United Kingdom

In the UK debit cards are an established part of the retail market and are widely accepted both by bricks and mortar stores and by internet stores. The term EFTPOS is not widely used by the public, debit card is the generic term used. Cards commonly in circulation include Maestro, Solo, Visa Debit and

Visa Electron. Banks do not charge customers for EFTPOS transactions in the UK, but some retailers make small charges, particularly where the transaction amount in question is small. The UK has converted all debit cards in circulation to Chip and PIN, based on the EMV standard, to increase transaction security; however, PINs are not required for internet transactions.

In the United Kingdom, banks started to issue debit cards in the mid 1980s in a bid to reduce the number of cheques being used at the point of sale, which are costly for the banks to process; the first bank to do so was Barclays with the Barclays Connect card. As in most countries, fees paid by merchants in the United Kingdom to accept credit cards are a percentage of the transaction amount, which funds card holders' interest-free credit periods as well as incentive schemes such as points, airmiles or cashback.

Debit cards do not usually have these characteristics, and so the fee for merchants to accept debit cards is a low fixed amount, regardless of transaction amount. For very small amounts, this means it is cheaper for a merchant to accept a credit card than a debit card. Although merchants won the right through The Credit Cards Order 1990 to charge customers different prices according to the payment method, few merchants in the UK charge less for payment by debit card than by credit card, the most notable exceptions being budget airlines, travel agents and IKEA.

Debit cards in the UK lack the advantages offered to holders of UK-issued credit cards, such as free incentives, interest-free credit and protection against defaulting merchants under Section 75 of the Consumer Credit Act 1974. Almost all establishments in the United Kingdom that accept credit cards also accept debit cards but a minority of merchants, for cost reasons, accept debit cards and not credit cards.

United States

In the U.S., EFTPOS is universally referred to simply as debit. The same interbank networks that operate the ATM network also operate the POS network. Most interbank networks, such as Pulse, NYCE, MAC, Tyme, SHAZAM, STAR, etc. are regional and do not overlap, however, most ATM/POS networks have agreements to accept each other's cards. This means that cards issued by one network will typically work anywhere they accept ATM/POS cards for payment.

For example, a NYCE card will work at a Pulse POS terminal or ATM, and vice versa. Many debit cards in the United States are issued with a Visa or MasterCard logo allowing use of their signature-based networks.

The liability of a U.S. debit card user in case of loss or theft is up to 50 USD if the loss or theft is reported to the issuing bank in two business days after the customer notices the loss. The fees charged to merchants on offline debit purchases—and the lack of fees charged merchants for processing online debit purchases and paper checks—have prompted some major merchants in the U.S. to file lawsuits against debit-card transaction processors such as Visa and MasterCard. In 2003, Visa and MasterCard agreed to settle the largest of these lawsuits and agreed to settlements of billions of dollars.

Some consumers prefer "credit" transactions because of the lack of a fee charged to the consumer/purchaser; also, a few debit cards in the U.S. offer rewards for using "credit". However, since "credit" costs more for merchants, many terminals at PIN-accepting merchant locations now make the "credit" function more difficult to access.

For example, if you swipe a debit card at Wal-Mart in the U.S., you are immediately presented with the PIN screen for online debit; to use offline debit you must press "cancel" to exit the PIN screen, then press "credit" on the next screen.

One additional problem surrounding the use of debit cards is their use at a self-service gas pump like those common in the U.S. The customer might want to purchase fuel on their debit card, but the pump's computer does not know how much fuel the customer wants. The pump is activated by the customer presenting their card to a card reader and possibly entering a PIN. At this point the pump will dispense fuel, though no sales transaction has completed. The pump has no way of knowing how much fuel will be sold, nor how much money is available in the customer's debit account. In a typical sale transaction, trying to spend more money than is available in your account will result in a "no-sale" alert to the merchant, and the sale does not occur. At a self-serve fuel pump, the fuel is already in the customer's tank by the time the bank knows the final sale price.

Several solutions to this problem are in place, such as denying $1 pre-authorizations when an account holds less than $10 while still allowing transactions for specific amounts, but the concept of delivering the merchandise before the sales transaction plagues the debit card system.

The commission is sometimes so high that the gas station sometimes actually loses money when someone pays for gas with credit. When pay at the pump started in the 1980s, many gas stations offered a discount for paying with cash. Most of them stopped doing that because the discount did not significantly increase their cash sales.

2009-07-08: Minimum and Maximum Charges for Visa in USA The Merchants Agreement for Visa states:

Always honour valid Visa cards in your acceptance category, regardless of the dollar amount of the purchase. Imposing minimum or maximum purchase amounts in order to accept a Visa card transaction is a violation of the Visa rules.

FSA, HRA, and HSA Debit Cards

In the U.S.A, a FSA debit card only allows medical expenses. It is used by some banks for withdrawals from their FSAs, MSAs, and HSAs as well. They have Visa or MasterCard logos, but cannot be used as "debit cards", only as "credit cards"", and they are not accepted by all merchants that accept debit and credit cards, but only by those that accept FSA debit cards.

Merchant codes and product codes are used at the point of sale to restrict sales if they do not qualify. Because of the extra checking and documenting that goes on, later, the statement can be used to substantiate these purchases for tax deductions. In the occasional instance that a qualifying purchase is rejected, another form of payment must be used. In the more likely case that non-qualifying items are accepted, the consumer is technically still responsible, and the discrepancy could be revealed during an audit.

A small but growing segment of the debit card business in the U.S. involves access to tax-favoured spending accounts such as flexible spending accounts, health reimbursement accounts, and health savings accounts. Most of these debit cards are for medical expenses, though a few are also issued for dependent care and transportation expenses.

Traditionally, FSAs were accessed only through claims for reimbursement after incurring, and often paying, an out-of-pocket expense; this often happens after the funds have already been deducted from the employee's paycheck. The only method permitted by the Internal Revenue Service to avoid this "double-dipping" for medical FSAs and HRAs is through accurate and auditable reporting on the tax return.

Statements on the debit card that say "for medical uses only" are invalid for several reasons:

- The merchant and issuing banks have no way of quickly determining whether the entire purchase qualifies for the customer's type of tax benefit;
- The customer also has no quick way of knowing; often has mixed purchases by necessity or convenience; and can easily make mistakes;
- Extra contractual clauses between the customer and issuing bank would cross-over into the payment processing standards, creating additional confusion.

Therefore, using the card exclusively for qualifying purchases may be convenient for the customer, but it has nothing to do with how the card can actually be used. If the bank rejects a transaction, for instance, because it is not at a recognized drug store, then it would be causing harm and confusion to the cardholder.

In the United States, not all medical service or supply stores are capable of providing the correct information so an FSA debit card issuer can honour every transaction-if rejected or documentation is not deemed enough to satisfy regulations, cardholders may have to send in forms manually.

PROS AND CONS

Pros and cons are arguments for or against a particular issue. Pros are arguments which aim to promote the issue, while cons suggest points against it. The term has been in use since the 16th century and is a shortening of a Latin phrase, *pro et contra,* which means "for and against." Considering the pros and cons of an issue is a very useful way to weigh the issue thoughtfully and reach an informed decision.

Many people find themselves considering pros and cons in daily life, although they may not be aware of it. For example, someone shopping at a supermarket might weigh the cost of an item and the quality to decide whether or not to purchase it. People making larger decisions, like purchasing a new car or home, often spend a great deal of time thinking about the pros and cons of the purchase so that they can be sure that the right choice will be made.

In addition to being useful in daily life, pros and cons can also strengthen academic papers and debates. By weighing the pros and cons beforehand, someone can consider potential objections to a point, as well as ways to dismiss a counter-argument.

Skilled authors will often include pros and cons in a paper to indicate that they have considered all sides of an issue and are confident that their feelings are correct. They can also be used to identify weaknesses in an argument: if you notice a lack of discussion of the cons of an issue, for example, it is probably too good to be true.

Many politicians have highly refined the art of examining pros and cons, especially when it comes to major issues. Campaign and staff advisers are kept on staff to thoroughly and carefully research issues and ultimately provide a list of pros and cons.

This list can be used to build solid, well thought out persuasive arguments that can be used on the campaign trail, in political debates, on the floor of a legislative body, or to counter statements made by opponents. When using pros and cons to reach a difficult decision, many people find it helpful to divide a piece of paper into two columns, writing the pros in one column and the cons in another.

Sometimes providing a clear visual guide allows the decision to become obvious, as one side may overwhelmingly outweigh the other. If nothing else, weighing the pros and cons will allow someone to consider every aspect of a situation.

8

Role of Commercial Banking Industry

STRATEGIC IMPLICATIONS FROM A US PERSPECTIVE

The banking industry provides an interesting and important case study of how changes in technology and regulation influence competitive structure, business strategy and industrial evolution. Indeed a narrow focus on traditional bank products and performance measures conditioned on the rapid pace of technological change confronting the industry would lead one to conclude that banking is essentially a declining industry.

In fact, according to some observers the commercial bank-an institution that conducts the twin activities of accepting deposits payable on demand and originating loans-has outlived its usefulness. Such a focus, however, misses most of the true innovations that have taken place in the industry in recent years-most notably the move towards off-balance-sheet and information-based activities.

A broader perspective shows banks evolving in ways that are enabling them to provide the same basic functions as before, but in new, more efficient ways. In the past most banks thought of themselves as delivering a set of specific, largely unrelated products to different sets of customers. Today, as a result of technological change and competitive pressures, many banks are pursuing strategies that aim to strengthen their ability to perform various functions, including, for example, financial planning for retail clients and raising capital for middle-market companies, which tend to cut across old product lines.

As a result, and in contrast to most industrial firms, many banks are offering a more diversified range of products and services than ever before with the aim of exploiting potential synergies among those products. Much of this has been made possible by the recent advances in technology, typically associated with the so-called electronic banking revolution and spurred on by the rapid development and application of the Internet.

The economic rationale for banks' past existence relates directly to their two core activities-taking in deposits payable on demand and providing non-marketable loans. It seems clear that both activities essentially require the institution to come up with cash at short notice-that is, to provide liquidity. Economy of scale in the provision of liquidity thus explains why both activities are provided by the same entity.

Deregulation and technological innovations have served to increase competition in the financial services industry, which has forced commerical banks to concentrate on the essentials of liquidity provision. This is why the outward nature of bank activities has changed significantly for both retail and wholesale customers. For example banks around the globe often sell their loans instead of holding them on their balance sheets, offer consumers unsecured personal credit lines through credit cards and provide back-up lines for commercial paper instead of extending loans. Despite these different types of activity, it should be obvious to the astute observer that the underlying economic rationale for these activities-the provision of liquidity-has not changed.

Beneath the surface of the dramatic changes in financial products and services, the fundamental banking business of liquidity provision seems alive and well. Moreover, in the course of performing their traditional activities banks have acquired competencies that enable them to perform a variety of other financial and non-financial activities that deregulation and innovation have opened up to them.

RECENT TRENDS IN THE US BANKING INDUSTRY

Since the 1970s, what is commonly called the commercial banking industry in the US has evolved into two distinct and, for the most part, differently focused industries: the 'global banking industry' and the 'community', 'local' or regional banking industry.

As might be expected, banks operating in the global banking industry or market compete in national and international markets while community banks compete largely in local markets. This is at least partly because global banks have large corporate customers with special financing and information requirements compared with consumers and small businesses.

Thus US global banks face competition from different sources than those faced by community banks. For example global banks face competition from the commercial paper market, investment and merchant banks and major foreign banks, all of which compete in national or international markets.

Consequently the geographical market for many of these global bank customers and services is at least national in scope but is more often global. In contrast, the geographical market of the community banking industry is still largely local, approximated by metropolitan statistical areas (MSAs) or non-MSA counties. The preference of consumers and small businesses for local banks is presumably due to the lower information and transaction costs relative to their funds and may also reflect the information costs facing non-local financial firms.

Whatever the reason, it is apparent that US bankers are keenly aware of this preference and treat community or regional banking as a very localised activity that often requires a local presence. For example the number of bank branches in the US increased by about 74 per cent between 1970 and 1990, even as the number of banks and banking organisations declined. For many years it has been apparent that community banks are significantly influenced by local market conditions that may influence only some, if any, of the activities of global banks. This has provided support for the view that local banking is a separate industry from the global banking industry. This view is also supported by studies of the cost structure of the US banking industry.

Many of these studies have found that global and community banks do indeed operate on different long-term average cost curves, that is, these banks operate in different industries. While firms in both of these industries operate as financial intermediaries, offer insured deposits and the other standard packages of services, local banks have traditionally served a distinctly separate class of customer and competed in fairly protected local markets. As a result it has been generally assumed that developments in the global banking industry will only marginally affect community or regional banks.

However, with the advent of dramatic technological change in the form of various electronic or Internet banking developments and the increase in the minimum efficient size of banks as a result of technological developments, local banks can no longer assume that their local markets will remain unattractive or inaccessible to global banks and their global networks.

Thus local and regional banks should be aware that their market share is at risk. This is easy to see given that the overlap between these two industries is limited in an important way that is indicative of the basic difference between the two industries. Specifically, while banking organis-ations that operate in the global banking industry can and do operate in the community or local banking industry, the reverse does not hold.

That is, community and local banks tend not to operate in the global banking industry. However, just as technological developments represent a threat to the long-term viability of community banks, when used appropriately they also present an opportunity for these banks to access the global banking market through the electronic networks offered by members of the global banking industry. Two interesting avenues for examining technological change and its influence on the banking industry are

- Regulation and the legal environment resulting from changes in banking technology, and
- Changes in the competitive environment facing financial institutions.

Regarding the regulation of Internet banking and related changes induced by technology, the current consensus among US banking scholars seems to be that market arrangements for electronic money and Internet banking should be allowed to evolve unencumbered by regulation and government intervention. This should remain the case as long as the safety, soundness and stability of the payments and financial system are not impaired by these developments.

This essentially means that regulatory intervention in electronic money and internet banking will take place in a parallel fashion to the regulation that already exists for non-electronic non-Internet banking. That is, if the paper equivalent of an electronic transaction is regulated, then so should the electronic transaction. In this environment, regulatory attention is focused on evaluating the threat of those electronic transactions which have no paper equivalent to the safety and soundness of the payments and financial system.

Many concerns have also been expressed about the nature and structure of the US banking industry in the next 20 to 30 years; in particular, whether local and regional banks will be able to compete with the larger global banks and whether banking services will continue to be owned by traditional bankers or by software developers or telecommunications firms. As should be clear from this introduction, there is reason to believe that banking services will continue to be provided by banks (both global and regional), albeit in a much more competitive environment.

TECHNOLOGICAL CHANGE AND THE INDUSTRIAL ORGANISATION OF US BANKING MARKETS

The impact of technological change on the banking industry (both globally and locally), particularly the development of

Internet banking, is best examined using the tools of modern industrial organisation theory. Though many banks might eventually offer combinations of electronic cash and electronic money, the decision to become a fully fledged provider of electronic or Internet banking services involves irreversible investment and output decisions.

This irreversibility, combined with uncertainty about customer demand for electronic banking services, implies that banks (and other firms for that matter) will typically face a precommitment decision when deciding whether to enter the Internet banking business and the scope of such involvement. This decision will uniquely influence the environment surrounding the emergence of an electronic or Internet banking technology.

Given these elements of irreversibility and demand uncertainty, if banks are profit-maximising firms we can expect incumbent or dominant banks (typically the large global banks in the US) to act strategically when deciding the scope of their involvement in Internet banking. Hence they can be expected to undertake entry-deterring investments to the extent that the marginal benefit of such investments (the profit that flows from reduced future competition) exceeds their current cost.

Investment in excess capacity is one such strategy. Whether or not investment in excess capacity constitutes a credible threat by dominant firms depends on what potential entrants think the post-entry regime will be, on whether or not there are economies of scale and scope in the provision of electronic and Internet banking services, and on the size of minimum output relative to the market.

Whether incumbents find investment in excess capacity profitable depends on their certainty that such investment will deter entry, and perhaps on the possibility of free-riding by other incumbent firms. Investment could also be used as a way of responding to entry rather than as a device for precluding entry.

If customers incur costs by switching from their current bank to a new provider of financial services, then incumbents or dominant firms may strategically expand output to attract customers and make entry more difficult. This involves some sacrifice of short-term profits and should be considered as a strategic investment in the customer base.

It is clearly costly for incumbent or dominant firms to carry excess capacity or to make other strategic investments to deter entry. If incumbents can raise the costs incurred by actual or potential rivals while suffering smaller cost increases themselves, they will generally find it profitable to do so.

The existence of significant demand uncertainty also implies that dominant firms find it worthwhile to engage in predatory or entry-limiting behaviour in order to create and maintain a reputation as a firm that will fight entry, or as a low-cost firm.

Although such a strategy may be unprofitable in the particular market in which it is carried out, it does discourage entry into other markets and thus may be optimal for dominant firms from an overall point of view.

Barring the success of the above strategies, cooperation may emerge as a key force behind the evolution of electronic and Internet banking. Such cooperative arrangement are commonly referred to as strategic alliances or joint ventures.

RECENT CHANGES CONSISTENT WITH THE PREDICTIONS OF MODERN INDUSTRIAL ORGANISATION THEORY

Two developments are responsible for the interest and growth in electronic and Internet banking around the globe. These developments are significant for both global banks and community and local banks in the US and elsewhere. First, computing costs have dropped steeply in recent years; second, electronic telecommunications innovations have simultaneously increased the capacity for communication usage in financial services and reduced the importance of geographically based financial services.

Historically, both global and local bankers viewed themselves as owning customers. They provided a range of services to customers, including current and savings accounts, credit cards and settlement and clearing procedures.

Customers only had to choose a bank, deposit their money and withdraw it in whatever form they chose at some future date. In many countries, and especially the US, the types of service that banks and other financial firms could offer customers were restricted by law-for example, until recently US firms that issued securities were not allowed to accept deposits.

In addition there were statutory restrictions on the types of entity that could accept customer deposits. A prime example of this was the US Bank Holding Company Act, which prohibited companies from owning banks if the parent company was engaged in activities that were not closely related to banking.

The deregulation of banking and bank deposit activities has brought deposit rates to competitive levels in most banking markets. Indeed, with the depositor's cost of telephoning or e-mailing competitors falling to zero, banks have had to rethink their deposit and retail business. While synergies remain in liquidity provision, all banks enjoy this synergy, so the challenge is to build a competitive deposit business in ways that create rents for the bank.

In fact there are only a limited number of ways in which long-term profits can be made. The holy grail for all banks (both global and local) continues to be captive customers who are price-insensitive, that is, have inelastic demand curves. In the absence of this, banks must innovate continuously or find scale economies that enable them to become low-cost producers.

It helps, of course, if there is substantial first-mover advantage in a product so that the profits from innovation or scale can be reaped over a longer period. In the days when a customer had to be physically present to undertake most banking activities, proximity to a bank branch was important. A bank's customers were those who lived closest to the branch. Higher prices could be charged or lower interest rates paid to their customers because the customer's costs of switching to another bank were high. But today it is no longer clear which customers a bank should target. The geographical reach of any given bank has increased as a result of lower communication costs. At the same time the cost to the customer of switching banks has fallen.

Banks, both global and regional, have one big advantage when deciding who to target, how to bring them in and how to increase their switching costs: so-called customer inertia. Many customers have been slow to use the phone or other telecommunications media to reach other financial service providers-there seems to be considerable inertia and the learning curve is apparently steep.

For example, while the number of ATMs in the US went up from 13 800 in 1979 to about 187 000 in 1998, the number of bank branches also went up over the same period. Many customers in the US still prefer to use bank branches for such activities as depositing cheques despite the fact that ATMs can do the job just as well as tellers in manned branches.

Local branches provide some human interaction, and hence are less technologically intimidating. Moreover bankers (at least in the US) have been seen as more trustworthy than other financial service providers, such as stockbrokers and insurance agents.

Some bankers correctly view their branch network and current depositor base as an opportunity. Their idea is to use the branch as the gateway through which the depositor can access the entire financial system. They would like to convert the physical contact and trust they currently enjoy with depositors into high switching costs so that when depositors become more technically sophisticated, or when access costs diminish further, they are not tempted to switch banks.

There are a number of ways in which financial service companies can increase switching costs. Providing personal advisory services may be the costliest approach, but it also has the most potential to build personal bonds that are hard to break. Another approach is to offer a variety of services and to integrate them so that they appear seamless to the customer. For instance a bank that can offer to the customer mortgage, credit card and insurance services can link all these accounts to the deposit account, as well as to overdraft facilities and home equity loans. Within limits, authorised payments can be made automatically, if necessary by borrowing on behalf of the customer at the least-cost rate. The bank can also provide a consolidated statement to the customer at the end of every month. The advantage of being the sole access point is that the cost of switching to a different access point increases with the number of services provided (and if the customer uses software, with the degree of specialisation of the software needed to gain access).

Clearly this strategy is so designed that convenience is the most important feature, but this raises an interesting question: should the bank offer access to more than its own products and services? It should, and not simply because it will become more attractive as an access point if it is able to offer the best services.

By offering other firms' services, it can also promise its customers that they will not be overcharged, ripped-off or gouged later if they lock themselves into the bank (economists call this technique a second sourcing). Moreover the bank that controls access is in a position to extract rents from the other service providers because it controls the prime asset: captive customers.

This approach has been successfully followed by the discount broker Charles Schwab, and by Intuit Home Banking. For example Schwab's mutual fund provides its customers with access to over 1100 mutual funds from over 100 fund families, consolidating all fund statements into one statement for the customer.

The market power gained by Schwab through its customer control access is evident in Fidelity's decision to withdraw most of its popular funds from this scheme.

INNOVATION

Innovation is clearly one way in which a financial institution can differentiate itself from the pack. But most successful product innovations on the retail side are easily imitated (except those based on proprietary technology). One way to build sustained advantage is to use innovation to build a captive customer base. In a sense this is what Charles Schwab has done. It was one of the first brokers to allow customers to trade electronically. In the process it cross-sold a variety of products, including information services and mutual fund services that locked the electronic customer into a relationship with Schwab. At the same time these customers give Schwab the necessary scope to pursue further innovation.

Another kind of innovation is to identify activities with high transaction costs and to reduce those costs by internalising the transactions. To the extent that there are first-mover advantages to this approach, a bank can build a long-term franchise. For example Citibank recognised that there were still very high costs involved in making cross-border payments.

By setting up a global network of branches and developing tremendous expertise in foreign exchange transactions it succeeded in internalising cross-border payments. The savings in transactions costs coupled with the very high volume of transactions have made this a very profitable franchise. Moreover other banks are unlikely to challenge this franchise because of the high cost of setting up a competing network and the formidable position now occupied by Citibank.

TECHNOLOGY

It is clear that nothing beats being a low-cost financial services provider and that automation is a proven way to reduce costs. For example the real cost of an electronic deposit in the US fell from four times the cost of processing a cheque in 1979 to less than half the cost in 1998.

Since automation requires a substantial investment, large global banks have a competitive advantage. Indeed this may also explain the large-scale consolidation taking place in the US banking industry.

In recent years the percentage of assets in banks with over $100 billion more than doubled between 1979 and 1998 while the percentage of assets in small banks dropped by more than 50 per cent. Most economic analysts of the payments business suggest that it is a large-fixed-cost business. Thus the economics of the situation require the service provider to maximise its customer contacts in order to spread these fixed costs over a larger base.

Since variable costs are low, maximising the customer base maximises profits. Hence the private provider will be motivated to control a larger and larger share of the market. This could lead to increased market concentration and market (monopoly) power, with adverse consequences for small community and regional banks.

Given that there are large sunken costs in the business, standard economic theory implies that the incumbent provider will be able to sustain its monopoly position, that is, market forces will not keep the firm from exploiting its monopoly position. Being in a business that is subject to mild increasing returns to scale-that is, the larger the firm the cheaper its average cost of producing electronic financial services-dominant firms will naturally seek to become larger and will engage in entry-limiting and/or pricing behaviour to limit competition.

Again, this implies that small regional banks will find it difficult to compete. Finally, electronic payments systems are subject to significant network externalities, scope economies and economies of sequencing. A dominant firm with the industry standard software or hardware will have a definite competitive advantage over all new entrants, which must adopt this software or hardware in order to offer complete access.

The dominant firm is thus able to exploit scope economies and gain access to additional customers, again leading to increased market share and power. The business also has elements of economies of sequencing, which are present if an integrated technology is more productive than separate technologies.

ECONOMIES OF SCALE AND SCOPE

Scale and scope economies typically have important implications for the structure of an industry. If such economies are substantial, ceteris paribus an industry will tend to be relatively concentrated and entry will be difficult. There is a large body of literature on scale and scope economies in the commercial banking industry in most developed countries. Most of this literature focuses on data for banks with under $1 billion in total assets, which in essence are part of the community or regional banking industry.

The evidence suggests that scale economies (especially in US banking) are quite modest and are exhausted at low levels of output. This bodes well for the competitive viability of smaller regional and community banks. On the other hand, more recent studies of larger global-type banks show that significant scale economies are possible for these banks. This raises questions about the viability of local and regional banks throughout the developed world. What is one to make of these mixed findings?

Since the 1970s, with the onset of deregulation, increased expansion and new electronic technologies, questions have been raised about the competitive viability of small and regional banks. A fairly wide range of empirical evidence suggests that small banks are both viable and profitable. For example it has been argued that the scale economy research findings imply that smaller banks are able to compete on an equal footing with large global banks, or at least with respect to basic banking services.

Moreover, recent research on managerial inefficiency in US banking suggests that these types of inefficiencies dominate those identified with inefficient scale. If one believes these findings, small community and regional banks do indeed have a continuing role to play in the industry. Nonetheless there is reason to believe that small and regional banks will continue to be threatened by developments arising from technological change.

Studies of the impact of technological change in the US banking industry suggest that the minimum efficient size of banks (especially in the US) has increased as a result of technological change. This combined with the probable impact of electronic or Internet banking on the structure of the industry, strongly suggests that regional and small local banks will have a tougher time competing in the future.

STRATEGIES FOR SURVIVAL IN AN INTERNET BANKING WORLD AND THE ROLE OF LOCAL BANKS

Even though fundamental competencies have not changed, in order to compete, global banks and community and regional banks can pursue different strategies in the world of Internet banking. Banking scholars have identified several strategies to deal with the technological revolution in the financial services industry. These strategies involve serving different customer segments in a variety of ways. Strategic decisions involve both operating decisions and product decisions and can be made locally on a decentralised basis or on a centralised basis.

Decentralised operating and product or service decision making has the advantage of keeping local bank decision makers in close proximity with the customer and local information. The disadvantage of this approach is that senior management may not have complete control over the operations side, while on the product or service side the bank may miss opportunities to exploit economies of scope and scale.

By default, this strategy is a natural one for small community and regional banks, given their size and/or lack of extensive branch networks. However some small banks have attempted to mitigate the disadvantages of the strategy by outsourcing back office operations and joining large electronic networks to enhance their customers' access. However, in attempting to circumvent the weaknesses of the decentralised strategy these banks may have to share a substantial proportion of the profits from their customer base with the access providers, and they also risk their customers being captured or stolen by the access providers.

Clearly the decentralisation strategy will pose significant risks and problems for small banks in the future as geographical location becomes less important in defining a bank's customer base. A strategy of decentralised operational decision making and centralised product and service decision making makes sense for banks that possess special localised knowledge about their markets, but recognise that retail customers (in all but the most remote and isolated markets) in an Internet banking world will have fairly low switching costs.

It will also be difficult for banks to make significant profits from traditional products that come to be offered on a commodity basis. Thus, it will become important for banks to offer customers a wide choice of a products and services (which emerge from a centralised product and services strategy) and to offer local or decentralised pricing differences and advice only for those products that are deemed to be of high value-added.

A strategy of centralised operational and product and service decision making recognises the growing standardisation of banking products generally, though not exclusively. Such a strategy also implies more uniformity in operations and products regardless of location, since location is less relevant in an increasingly electronic world.

Like the findings of studies on the cost effectiveness of banks using decentralised and centralised decision making more generally, it is likely that a totally centralised strategy will not be optimal for most banks. Such a strategy seems to work for the McDonald restaurant chain but it probably will not for most banks, given their special competency in local information gathering and processing.

Based on this discussion, it seems fairly obvious that a totally decentralised strategy, especially on the retail side, will become less and less profitable as we move into a more integrated electronic and Internet banking world. Customers will become more sophisticated, they will move up the learning curve, and the cost of electronic hardware and software will continue to decline, making this mode of transacting even more cost effective relative to paper and face-to-face contact. To be sure, no one knows exactly how long this will take, so the strategy may be profitable in the short run. A global strategy, on the other hand, is likely to be beyond the means of most small and medium-sized banks. For most banks, then, a strategy that exploits local market-information advantages and product synergies, scale economies and innovation seems most appropriate.

FINANCIAL INSTITUTION IN THE EURO ERA

The euro has been transforming and will continue to transform the financial industry in Europe. It has had the impact of a tidal wave hitting the shore: forex margins in the euro-zone are gone, lending margins are under pressure and so on.

FIRST IMPERATIVE: MANAGE YOUR COSTS

The challenges and opportunities brought by the euro are in general the same as those brought by any market-broadening event. To some degree, the gradual removal of the Glass-Steagall Act will have similar effects in the US. Consolidation will accelerate, customers will become more demanding, distribution channels will proliferate.

All these effects will increase the pressure significantly to lower costs. The need to manage costs in general and the cost income ratio in particular is the first imperative observed here: the need for cost reduction in order to keep pace as an incumbent financial institution. New attackers from within the industry, Internet-related such as ConSors and DAB or not, or from outside the industry, such as retailers and telecom operators, often enter the industry with tailored propositions at very low cost.

The existing financial institutions are faced with matching the new offering while maintaining the existing offering. This matching does not imply the same value at the same price, but the essence of a competitive offering should be present in terms of cost/benefit. This is the core of the multichannel strategy, and the resulting complexity makes a low-cost position very difficult to achieve.

It represents a new development compared with previous years' when there was a trend to make better use of IT and to move to bigger branches to deliver a full service at acceptable costs. Besides the tidal wave of the euro there are less visible but more powerful forces at work in the financial industry: technological change, regulatory issues, globalisation and demographics.

SECOND IMPERATIVE: OFFER YOUR CUSTOMERS A GLOBAL WINDOW

One particular implication of globalisation is that financial institutions will increasingly concentrate certain activities in 'hot spot' financial centres such as London or New York because they offer access to a larger pool of talent, and there are no hurdles in the Internet age against serving customers from these centres.

This is what happens in advisory investment banking, in custody and increasingly in brokerage. This implies that all financial institutions will be forced to rely upon the talent pool of those centres and to open shop there. These centres are very competitive markets, and it may take years to establish a good position for newcomers, given the risks of trying to move forward.

On a more general note, globalisation will increasingly change the financial industry because technology and deregulation facilitate trade. For years the total value of international trade has been growing at a multiple of the growth rate of world GDP, and the advent of e-commerce will only accelerate this trend.

Increased global trade, the growth of business and personal travel, and the seamless information flow through classical and new media such as the Internet are causing a paradigm shift. The typical local banking customer-even a small business or a well-experienced individual-will increasingly demand a window on the world within the local banking relationship. Financial institutions therefore need to offer this to virtually all customers.

Offering a global service with a local rooting is a new paradigm for the industry and those who can deliver this have the best chance of retaining their customers. At this point disintermediation can stop: if customers receive cost-effective, quality advice the financial institution can claim the relationship. The question facing all financial institutions is how to implement this global/local strategy.

THIRD IMPERATIVE: DEVELOP THE SKILLS OF YOUR PEOPLE

Demographics are a second powerful current of change. There will not only be a much older population, which traditionally owns the majority of all savings, but lower birth rates will concentrate wealth over generations through the mechanism of inheritance.

So customers will be fewer, more affluent and in need of advice. Retaining customers, who will be faced with a seamingly endless choice of financial institutions, will be the key for growth. Hence the increasing power of brand as a vehicle to inspire and maintain customer attention and loyalty. Secondly, these customers will be very sensitive to the quality of service and advice, including a clear appreciation of the risks they are facing.

But qualified advisors will be scarcer: not only will the proportion of the working population shrink, but all industries will compete with the financial industries for the talent available. The pressure on financial institutions to engage in productivity improvement and skill development will be tremendous.

Financial institutions will be forced to invest even more in the quality of their people, because these people will be the key advisors to customers, and therefore their quality will be the institution's quality.

The case of Almanij: In Belgium, Almanij and its group companies have been relentlessly striving to meet these imperatives. The creation of KBC is a good example of this.

- The creation of KBC has met the first imperative of cost reduction, because the merger of the former Kredietbank with CERA Bank allows it to rationalise its distribution network in Belgium without losing coverage. This is a tedious process, since the net present value of merger benefits can only be captured after meeting the costs of integration. Secondly, such a merger needs to be well prepared, manage the organisational culture and maintain the growth momentum of the initial positive goodwill from the public's reaction. Fifty per cent of all mergers fail on one or more of these criteria. However Almanij is confident that it can successfully conclude this integration, given the track record of the former Kredietbank.

- The creation of KBC has also significantly strengthened Almanij's capital base, creating options for international expansion. This is helping the Almanij Group to meet the second imperative: to create a window on the world in a local relationship. Needless to say, many things still need to be done. The merger enabled the Almanij Group to strengthen its position in Belgium (its home market), to finance its expansion into Central Europe, and to maintain or improve its position in certain niche markets, such as trade finance. The concept of a second home market is still under investigation. The key challenge is to preserve its focus in its growth process.
- Finally: embracing the bancinsurance concept is helping the Almanij Group to develop new skills in product development and marketing.

INNOVATION AND GROWTH

There is a common theme at the core of meeting these three imperatives. It has to do with growth and innovation. The importance of innovation is well known, and meeting the three imperatives only stresses its importance:

- Reducing costs while expanding the availability and quality of customer service requires innovation.
- Opening a window on the world and making it available to all local customers requires new ways of leveraging technology and alliances.
- Achieving new standards of productivity and skills for bank personnel requires innovations in working

methods, the use of computers and the training of employees. Growth is essential to offer these people a career, to retain them and to preserve the investment made in them.

The importance of growth is equally clear. Growth is necessary to broaden the earnings base and to motivate good people. However, organic growth opportunities in traditional markets are limited.

Capital markets' expectations for earnings growth are exceeding the business growth rate. Consequently growth raises the issue of size in the financial industry. Almanij's decision to create KBC is a good illustration of how it thinks about this issue.Almanij believes that shareholder value is the result of many factors, of which scale is only one.

But it recognises that scale and size make a huge difference in certain lines of business, for example in most activities in investment banking and custody. In other lines of business, the jury is still out. An example here is asset management, where some players prosper by going after scale, while others specialise and equally prosper.

Other businesses are much more skill- and reputation-driven. Private banking is an example.Almanij believes in the importance of scale in any line of business, influenced by factors such as regulation and technology.

Constant evaluation of position in terms of size is necessary in any line of business, as is assessment of the potential of business unit leaders and the quality of customer service.

Almanij and its group companies realise that growth and innovation lie at the core of competition. Not all innovations, though, have the nature of a breakthrough: some are small and even barely visible, but can help to meet the imperatives described above.

The following are a few examples:

- Almanij developed a strong position in the ECU trading market, a market that has now gone but gave Almanij some quality business over a number of years.

- Almanij pioneered new mutual funds with embedded options for its affluent customers and gained a significant market share.
- It expanded into new markets, including Eastern Europe, for their growth potential. Such expansion takes time, although there is a limited opportunity to enter such markets and it can soon be too late, as in China. Almanij's initial hesitation to enter unknown territory has been compensated by a pace of development that time exceeded expectations.
- It developed new types of collaboration between employees in bank branches and independent specialist exclusive agents in insurance in order to increase service quality.
- It was the ambition of one of the founders of IBOS, an international network for cash management and payment services, to start building more international service line.

Of course growth and innovation have no limits. Therefore Almanij must aggressively seek all growth opportunities and explore all ways to innovate. However the reality is that any advantage will be short-lived, and that there is a price to pay for innovation, which occasionally makes coming in second just fine.

PERVASIVE COMPUTING

REALLY GETTING TO KNOW YOUR TOASTER

The avalanche of technologies developed in the last twenty years has conditioned consumers to expect a new wave of devices in ever-shortening cycles, yet the pervasiveness of technology is the least understood aspect, and its implications for a global society are only just beginning to come to light. Studying the application of bio-integration to the socio-economic fabric of human relationships and the interface to contemporary business has barely begun.

It is apparent that the consumer's love affair with electronic gadgetry is far from over; in fact, it could be argued that it is only just starting. The rate of technology adoption is increasing with each new generation of potential users. Although all members of society do not share this affection for technology, the pervasiveness of technology continues to impact each individual either by direct participation or as an indirect consequence. The pervasiveness of computing has many implications for financial services companies, and in some cases distracts from a clear value proposition.

Is new technology spawning a revolution in how we work and live or is our lifestyle driving the need for new technology? The architect/philosopher Richard Buckminster Fuller noted in 1980 that the time between the creation of a technology and its practical adoption by society varied by technical category and application. In his words:

My half-century experience also discovered the natural, unacceleratable lags existing between inventions and industrial uses in various technical categories, which occur as follows: in electronics – two years; aerodynamics – five years; automobiles – ten years; railroading – fifteen years; big-city buildings twenty-five years; single family dwellings – fifty years.

This commercialization time lag in technology represents the time span necessary to educate the population about the benefits of new technologies, convince society of the improvements that such new technologies bring and allow the business infrastructure to reach a point of production that will make it economically viable. Architects incorporate the practical advantages of new technology into structures that shape our behaviour, while architecture involves employing a more complex process of changing social taste. The matter of adoption of any sort of technology by individuals is an exercise in shaping the behaviour of consumers as new technological marvels emerge.

The same technological time lag can be equated to financial services products and the technologies found in the four bands in the technology spectrum (for example ATMs, credit cards, retina scanners, and the Internet) and should be a critical part of strategic technology planning. Individual technologies can be plotted along a maturity curve and compared to a similar curve indicating the level of social acceptance. The delta between the curves represents the opportunity to experiment and refine the application of the technology as well as a barometer to set the expectations of the firm on the return on investment.

Technologies mature at a predictable rate determined by the innovation of their components. However, social acceptance of technology occurs at a rate that varies from culture to culture or even within the socio-economic classes in one given culture.

For example, the use of mobile phones for banking is more popular in Scandinavia than high-tech Boston, Massachusetts. Furthermore, there is a synergistic relationship between technology, people, and how people work in the lifecycle of technology creation, adoption, impact and design. Fuller's observation on technological latency brings into question the accelerating rate at which society is adopting technology. Technological visions such as Microsoft's Home of the Future and the Halifax's Future Retail Bank are early indications that the nature of work will radically change during the next twenty years.

It can be argued that not only will the nature of work change, but where one works will undergo a transformation. For example, retail banking will need to rethink how branches are designed in order to accommodate the shift from a transaction to an advisory business, which will indeed be different in each culture serviced. Organizations such as BWA\Chiat\Day, which have radically altered the way in which people think and work by inventing work spaces that stretch beyond the conventional designs of today's business, inadvertently provided financial services firms with a glimpse into the future of financial services.

Technological gadgetry – and the pervasiveness of computing – carries with it a familiar technology banner, resembling the messages from the early twentieth-century electric companies about removing the complexity of life and enabling users greater work efficiencies, that it will provide members of our modern society with additional leisure time. Alluring words, which should be remembered as you carry your laptop, mobile phone and personal digital assistant (PDA) on your next family vacation.

Stripping away the marketing hype, pervasive computing is capable of placing the user in the centre of the technological universe, allowing the individual to control the amount of intrusion permissible by other members in the connected society.

Technology is as pervasive as you will allow it to become. Business looks at pervasive computing as a new method of interacting with consumers, whereas consumers should view it as a way of employing technology to perform tasks on their behalf. The underlying dilemma that pervasive computing brings to the surface is the new balance that individuals must strike between work, leisure and social interactions. The product of this balance is a redefinition of when, where and how people work.

A strong argument can be made that the impact of technology will be the redefinition of the socio-economic contract with business and a reexamination of the nature of work. It is not incomprehensible that the result of society embracing pervasive computing is anytime, anywhere work. Technology is redefining where and how organizations work by removing the need to be in a specific geography, at a specific time. Many financial services firms, organized under traditional hierarchical command and control structures that were established because of the need to regulate the activities of subordinates, will find moving into a matrix structure difficult unless ample investment is made in training and education.

In today's world, manufacturing, consulting and research organizations are realizing that the ability to act unfettered by work hours, geography or corporate bureaucratic structure is not creating more leisure time for employees; in practice it is enabling a freeing up of work time, resulting in additional capacity. The proliferation of technology also creates opportunities to redefine the structure of organizations and establish new functional disciplines. A new skill that individuals will need to develop is striking a balance between these two diametrically opposed forces of work and leisure. As the lines between work and play become blurred, there may be opportunities for comingled activities to occur.

For example, an employee working at home for some portion of the week can order supplies for the office and home at the same time on the same Internet site using two different payment technologies, as well as communicating with colleagues and customers on the telephone and Internet while performing many other traditional in-house tasks without commuting.

Described in a business context, pervasive technology operates within a framework which can be represented by a diagram comprising four levels of conductivity similar to concentric circles in which you are at the epicentre. Individuals can add 'layers' to their epicentre as they grow more accepting of technology and more adept at using its capabilities.

LEVEL ONE TECHNOLOGIES

The first level is composed of smart devices equipped with microprocessors, called appliances, which are attached to you and facilitate your lifestyle, including home devices, wearable computing and biometric feedback mechanisms. These devices are basically automated methods of recognizing a person based on a physiological or behavioural characteristic.

For financial services companies, these devices provide new avenues for secure transactions because of their ability to identify a single individual or entity. Level one technologies centre on the point of interaction or an interchange of value, either monetary, informational or data. Micropayments, billing data, usage information and other transactions can be used to develop a profile of customer behaviour in retail banking applications.

The same model can be applied to small businesses and other entities such as government departments, not to act as Big Brother, but to optimize operating expenses and plan future budgetary requirements.

LEVEL TWO TECHNOLOGIES

Level two technologies that represent you and perform duties on your behalf are commonly referred to as agents, including bio-enhancement, intelligent agents, robots and avatars. Intelligent agents are autonomous, adaptive computer programmes that operate within software environments such as operating systems and database networks. They assist users with routine computer tasks being tailored to accommodate individual user habits.

Avatars are three-dimensional representations of individuals in cyberspace that users may utilize to represent themselves in both form and task. At the moment, avatars are inanimate objects. However, in the near future they may be animated to further express the personality that end users wish to portray. These technologies give you the ability to represent yourseif in the eEconomy, proposing the following question: When you select the physical appearance and personality of your avatar, will it reflect you or someone you would like to be?

Concerning the financial services community, level two technologies are a treasure-trove of opportunities in the development of intelligent agents that can seek out the highest yielding savings rate or the best mortgage terms to fit individual circumstances.

These agents could be employed to assess conditions on the stock market, interrogate individual securities, analyse currency rates and evaluate foreign market fluctuations. Intelligent agents will be crafted into a host of highly specialized functions that have yet to be imagined.

LEVEL THREE TECHNOLOGIES

Mechanisms on the third level are designed to keep you interfaced to the relentless stream of data generated by society by linking you to the information that is relevant to you. Technologies such as global positioning satellites (GPSs), bluetooth, wireless application protocol (WAP) and a host of new devices will act as data interchange brokers. Interface technologies are an integral part of the following example.

With your smart card's stored value-chip in your mobile phone, you approach a cold beverage machine, make a selection and then transmit digital currency to it by pressing a key on the phone.

The machine accepts your token and dispenses the beverage, sends the token to the bank via its cellular modem and transmits the reduction in inventory to the beverage distributor.

In this scenario, cash has moved from your account to your card, from your card to the dispenser, and finally to the accounts receivable of the beverage company, eliminating the need for physical cash pick-up, armoured car services, lock box operations and a suite of support services.

Level three technologies present financial services firms with an opportunity to facilitate transactions across markets, suppliers, consumers, nations and all parts of the Internet. Put simply, these technologies are the tools of the twenty-first-century intermediary. The fees associated with these types of transaction will obviously be commoditized over time and command very thin margins, indicating that operational efficiency will be the key factor in sustaining long-term viability.

LEVEL FOUR TECHNOLOGIES

Finally, fourth level prescriptive technologies, called regulators, are designed to keep you within the designated limits of a process or a set of rules in society. They include radio-controlled ankle restraints, anti-theft devices for automobiles and the pet chip, an electronic dog tag that is inserted under the skin of your pet. These technologies can act both passively and actively.

The application of these technologies to financial services is in its infancy. One can imagine microsensors embedded throughout an automobile providing an insurance adjuster with the data to assess damage incurred during an accident.

DATA, INFORMATION AND EVERYDAY LIFE

Another aspect of pervasive computing is the challenge

that it creates for data replication and information usability, including establishing corporate data-sharing policies to regulate the level and detail of information being passed to value chain partners.

One can speculate that if there is a direct relationship between data and value, the underlying value of information will be commoditized or worth less over time. Every piece of information has a half-life of usefulness to the individual or organization that assigns.

its original value. For example: for a stock trader, the value of up to the minute stock price information is extremely high; that same data on the following day is less valuable as a single piece of data, although it may still be valuable when plotted with similar pieces of data to form a chart or graph. Ultimately, to the stock trader, the individual stock quotation is almost valueless at some point in the future.

However, as that same element of data becomes less valuable to the trader, it increases in value to a stock analyst or fund manager. One can conclude that there is a direct relationship between information and its perceived value which is relative to who set the value on the information. This relationship between information and value is critically important to financial services organizations because of the nature of the data, received from third-party sources, passing through the business process within the firm to value chain partners.

Surprisingly, organizations are continually disappointed when they discover the often dysfunctional state of customer data that was in many cases a critical element in merger or acquisition negotiations. Often the value of the customer data is drastically reduced when the labour cost associated with bringing it up to date is applied.

Regardless of the data produced by these new technologies, it is difficult to predict how people during the next five years will use these technologies in everyday life. The more information that is collected about an individual, the greater the possibility that it can be mishandled and simply increase the cost of operations.

THE INTENT OF TECHNOLOGY

Often the purpose of a technology's initial design is derailed by the necessities of business or the way it is embraced by society. For example, the developers of television thought that its primary application was to give everyone the opportunity to receive a college education at home; however, today's television programming schedules are a long way from that ideal.

From the noble ideal of television's forefathers, its use was quickly transformed into an entertainment delivery device supported by product advertising, moving to its present state as a mechanism for selling products interrupted by entertainment programming. In order to draw a parallel between the pervasiveness of technology in everyday life, one can examine the pervasiveness of product advertising on television.

Television programming was merely supported by product commercials that provided the viewer with a view of life with the product in 10–30 seconds. Now, the products are simply integrated into the programming, noticeable as the actors or actresses in the programme strategically hold a beverage can so that the audience is able to read the label. Financial services organizations are presented with a wide range of opportunities to leverage these technologies into product offerings that supplement our everyday lives and streamline core banking services.

Pervasive technologies provide a financial services firm with the opportunity to rethink what they offer, how it is delivered and, more importantly, why a product or service offering is valuable to a customer. The long-term implications of these technologies are to change our view of technology as an asset and begin to manage it as a liability. This is not to say that technology should be treated as a liability; on the contrary, the management of technology should be as if its value declines over time.

So as to put this concept into perspective, the legacy of banking technology is rooted in the high capital equipment cost that was an investment with a useful lifespan, requiring maintenance and support personnel. Thus, the typical classification of technology as an asset depreciating over time while providing a mechanism for improved information flow. However, technology is advancing at an accelerated rate, making older technology not only less valuable, but commanding a higher cost to maintain.

Despite the rapid decay of technological value, technology is still regarded as an essential asset of the organization, one without which it cannot function. The idea of treating technology as a liability is not an oversimplification of the balance between technology investment and technology deployment; it is merely to say that the technology should be viewed and managed differently from the way in which it was managed in the past.

This can be seen in the following example: there is a fundamental difference between the strategy of an equity fund manager and a bond portfolio manager. Both specialists are managing assets with strategies that come from two very different philosophies on investing. Taking these conditions into account, the management of the technology liability will be different from core back office systems to end user or consumer devices.

If one considers that consumer retail delivery devices, such as PDAs, PCs, WAP phones and many others, will continue to experience a high turnover due to the nature of the innovation of devices and the demand for new technologies by consumers, it can be concluded that the delivery of retail banking products using these technologies will have a half-life much shorter than a core processing system. Simply, the rate of the half-life of technology is proportional to the distance to the end user. Core systems are replaced at a rate of five to ten years and retail end user technologies range from six months to four years.

The key althought to consider when treating the management of technology as a liability is that each technology should be handled according to its application to the business process that it serves and linked to a realistic expectation of a phased retirement. Again, the closer a technology is to the consumer, the faster the rate of decay and the greater the tendency to overmanage the asset. For example, a consultant was engaged to review the operating cost of the technology group within a large bank, and found an ongoing cost of warehousing a stockpile of outdated PCs because they were a depreciated asset.

The cost of warehousing these non-functioning computers, coupled with the cost of the labour associated with inventorying and tracking these assets, was greater than the new replacement value. Put simply, for the amount of money being spent on storing these outdated PCs, they could be purchasing new ones, as indeed they were.

Pervasive computing amplifies the fact that technology is ever changing. A general rule can be applied to thinking about managing pervasive technologies: the closer the technology is to the end user, the more it will be subject to change. Therefore, the key to providing pervasive technology services is a robust architecture that anticipates a continuous change of delivery platforms. The by-product of combining pervasive computing with evolving Internet technologies is to rethink core banking operations and redesign how banks work.

THE DARK SIDE OF NEW TECHNOLOGY

It is not hard to imagine a darker side to pervasive technologies as the intrusion into everyday life moves from something controlled by a consumer to an action regulated by a governing authority. Combinations of technologies have been coupled together to allowing a pet owner to pinpoint a lost pet using GPS technology.

A pet owner can elect to have this technology implanted under the skin of a cat or dog (in the case of farmers, sheep, cattle, horses) to determine where an animal is located if it becomes separated from the owner. Several organizations have discussed making this technology available to parents, allowing a similar transponder to be implanted under a child's skin to eliminate the problem of missing or abducted children. It is not beyond the range of Orwellian thinking to imagine the next evolution of this technology – a governing authority requires the insertion a GPS chip under the skin of citizens to monitor their actions and whereabouts. Regardless of the intent of these technologies, they will continue to raise questions about ethics, morality and social consciousness, creating new social responsibilities for business while redefining the relationship between technology and a diverse global population.

For financial services firms, another dark side looms in the distance. In a connected environment in which a customer's home provides massive amounts of usage data, for example lights, computer use, phone use and other data-supporting activities, the need to secure and encrypt this data arises because a criminal monitoring the data will know exactly when people are not home.

From a positive viewpoint, a variety of these GPS technologies could be employed in the physical world and cyberspace to track a variety of illegal activities, in order to reduce money laundering and drug trafficking, for example. As governments continue to develop new responsibilities for financial services providers to know the sources of depositors' funds, these technologies have an enormous potential to be used as a regulatory mechanism.

Regardless of the final evolution of the pervasiveness of technology, its potential over time to alter the social contract between employees and employer, taxpayers and governments, customer and financial services institutions is as predictable as the effect of radio, television and the PC.

The adoption of a technology will fundamentally interrupt the traditional relationships between parties and market forces, and, as has been proven, a planned design will not be able to reconfigure the way in which these relationships are maintained and executed. In conclusion, the implication to financial services is to develop a clear understanding of these trends, interpret how value can be added and create services that facilitate the transition.

9

Banking Trends and Deposit Insurance Risk

During the last decade of the twentieth century, the American banking industry and the global and domestic financial sectors have been undergoing major changes. These changes will profoundly affect bank regulation and deposit insurance as we enter the next century.

In recent years there has been unprecedented consolidation in the banking and thrift industries in the United States, and the move towards consolidation is also occurring in many other countries. Banks and nondepository institutions are competing with each other at an unprecedented level, and this is likely to continue, especially as banks receive additional powers to expand their product offerings and take advantage of their new powers.

Advances in technology have not only changed the economies of scale in banking but have also affected customers' expectations and demands for services. Increased globalization of economic activity has increased the competitive nature of financial services while at the same time making banks more vulnerable to developments in other countries.

The key questions are whether the current system of bank regulation and supervision allows for adequate risk assessment and monitoring to protect the government's interests as deposit insurer and whether the appropriate market incentives exist to promote the appropriate degree of risk taking by banks. As we enter the twenty-first century, it is the changes in the competitive pressures faced by banks and thrifts, the shift in the size distribution of financial institutions, and the increasing role of technology and globalization that are of greatest significance to the deposit insurance system.

Competition from nonbank firms has caused banks to shift away from lending as their dominant revenue-producing activity and shift into many other activities. Similarly, with the advent of improved technology, and especially the internet, geographic barriers and locational advantages have begun to break down.

More important, with the increased flow of information, and the reduction in search costs that have accompanied the spread of the Internet, comes the ability of depositors to move deposits almost instantly and with reduced transactions costs at the margin.

The net effect of these changes is to increase banks' exposure to the risk of liquidity pressures. For small banks technological change has meant a more competitive and complex business both operationally and financially. Of greater interest from a deposit insurance perspective, however, is the implications of these changes for large banks.

DEVELOPMENTS IN BANKING

Consolidation

The banking industry in the United States has undergone unprecedented consolidation during the past fifteen years. In terms of the numbers of depository institutions, the United States had a relatively fragmented industry throughout much of its history.

The total number of banks and thrifts remained at approximately 18,000 from the mid1960s through the mid-1980s. With the exception of a few large money centre banks, the industry was largely made up of large regional banks and a very large number of small banks and thrifts.

Beginning with the banking crisis of the 1980's, the number of banks and thrifts has declined dramatically--from approximately 18,000 banks and thrifts in 1985 to 10,327 at midyear 1999 and the number of organizations owning banks and thrifts has declined from 14,775 to 8,441. While the number of firms in the industry has declined, the total assets of the industry grew during the past fifteen years by approximately 63 per cent to approximately $6. 5 trillion.

Accompanying the structural change in banking has been a dramatic shift in the basic nature of banking. During the past fifteen years borrowing by the nonfinancial business sector has grown by 155 per cent.

However, the share of these loans held by commercial banks declined by approximately three percentage points to 20 per cent.

Thus, despite a robust economy and strong commercial loan demand, banks are losing market share to nonbank competitors. The end result of this shift has been that banks have had to rely on noninterest income (fees) to bolster revenue growth.

As a result, noninterest income as a per cent of net operating revenue grew from 29.6 per cent in 1984 to 40. 2 per cent at midyear 1999. This greater reliance on other sources of income changes the risk profile of banks and thus has implications for the way banks are supervised. In addition to the shrinkage in the number of banks, there has been a decided shift in the concentration of assets in the very largest institutions.

In 1984 the ten largest banking companies held approximately 19 per cent of the total assets in the banking and thrift industries; today, the ten largest firms hold slightly more than 39 per cent of total assets. The decline in the importance of small institutions relative to that of the largest banks.

Since 1996 the largest banking firm in the United States has had more assets than the aggregate total assets of all banks under $100 million. Moreover, since 1998 the three largest banks have had aggregate total assets greater than the combined assets of all banks with assets less than $1 billion. What is developing is an industry that resembles a barbell with the vast majority of banks at one end and the very largest banks at the other end.

Bank Activities

A cursory review of balance-sheet data for the largest banks indicates some of the changes that are occurring as we enter the twenty-first century. With the increased competition from nondepository institutions for loan business has come a significant decline in net interest income and a rise in noninterest income as a percentage of total income.

With the doubling in the share of total assets held by the banks in the ten largest banking organizations, to 39. 2 per cent, their share of net interest income has also increased from 21 per cent in 1984 to 35.9 per cent in mid-1999. However, mirroring the trend in the industry as a whole, noninterest income has become a greater share of total income--growing for the ten largest banking companies to 47. 7 per cent of total income from 31. 1 per cent fifteen years ago.

During this period, noninterest income for the industry as a whole grew from 29. 6 per cent of total income to 40 per cent. Although a significant portion, approximately 14 per cent, of noninterest income comes from trading income, this relative share has not changed significantly during the past fifteen years. Rather, banks have moved into other fee-generating activities, which add to the complexity of banking and place new demands on the regulators seeking to monitor risk.

Of particular note has been the growth in off-balance sheet activities at commercial banks. Two significant areas of growth are loan commitments and off-balance sheet derivatives. While the ten largest banking organizations have always had a significant share, just under half, of the outstanding loan commitments, they totally dominate the derivatives activity of banks and thrifts with approximately 90 per cent of the total. What is perhaps more important is the size of these activities when compared to the total on-book assets of banks.

At midyear 1999 the ten largest banking companies had total booked assets of $2. 56 trillion, and their unused loan commitments were $1. 89 trillion. However, even more significant is the volume of off-balance sheet derivative activity at these bank holding companies. As of June 30, 1999, the banks in the ten largest banking companies reported off-balance sheet derivatives with a notional value of $29. 9 trillion, or more than ten times their total book assets. These changes in the financial profiles of the large banks are consistent with changes in the nature of banking and the competition banks face in their traditional lending activities.

In addition to off-balance sheet assets, banks have expanded into new activities either directly, through the bank, or indirectly, through subsidiaries Of the bank or affiliates in a holding company.

These activities have encompassed the fields of insurance sales and securities sales and underwriting. This expansion of product lines has resulted from banks using the considerable leeway that exists under current law. As the debate on financial modernization evolves, it is likely that banks will receive expanded powers and banks will shift even more heavily into nonbank activities.

Globalization

Aside from the changes in bank balance sheets caused by domestic competition, the larger banks have adapted to the increased globalization of economic activity that has occurred in recent years.

While foreign lending by U. S. banks declined during the 1980s and early 1990s in response to the debt of less-developed countries (LDCS) and domestic banking crises, foreign lending has increased at an average rate of approximately 12 per cent per annum since 1993.

Moreover, the share of foreign lending by the largest banks increased during this period. While data on cross-border lending and local currency loans made by foreign branches of U. S. banks capture the direct global activity of U. S. banks, it does not reflect the international exposure inherent in domestic lending to multinational corporations and other firms reliant on international trade. Banks are no different than their customers in becoming more vulnerable to economic shocks in other parts of the world. In fact, to see how interdependent financial markets have become, one need look only at what occurred in U. S. credit markets as a result of the Russian debt default in October 1998. In addition to the effect of globalization on the asset side of the balance sheet, large banks continue to rely on foreign deposits as a significant source of funds. Foreign deposits constitute slightly more than one-third of total deposits at the ten largest banks and thrifts and approximately 25 per cent of total assets.

This reliance on foreign liabilities increases the global exposure of the largest banks. Not only are large U. S. banks reliant on foreign sources of assets and liabilities, but one of the largest banks, Bankers Trust, was acquired by Deutsche Bank, a large German bank.

The trend towards consolidation and international acquisitions of large banks is one that appears to be continuing in Europe and elsewhere and will likely increase the global nature of banking.

Technological Change

The financial sector has undergone significant change with advances in technology, as has much of the economy. As computer and communication technologies have improved, the ability of business and individuals to move funds both bilaterally and through clearinghouses has become effortless and almost instantaneous.

Advances in software and hardware have led to the creation of powerful tools that allow banks to value individual customer relationships, identify customer needs, and cross-sell products and services. Employees answering phones who have on-line access to customer and bank product information can meet many customer needs over the phone. Geographic boundaries have been further eroded by the access provided by the internet.

The youth of today, who are so accustomed to using the internet to communicate with friends, do research, and purchase goods, will very likely use their computers for banking transactions--potentially making the bricks-andmortar branch eventually irrelevant.

IMPLICATIONS FOR DEPOSIT INSURANCE

The changes occurring in banking have significant implications for bank regulation and for the deposit insurance system. Both the changes in the structure of the industry and the changes in the composition of banks' portfolios raise questions about the riskiness of banking and the long-term health of a deposit insurance scheme that relies on an insurance fund.

Although one might argue that the goal of regulation should be to avoid any risk to the deposit insurer, this would be poor public policy. If banks are performing their economic role of intermediation and serving the needs of the community, they will take risks. Similarly, in a competitive system, we should expect to see firms enter and exit the banking industry and this implies that there will be bank failures in the normal course of economic activity.

The role of deposit insurance is to protect small depositors, maintain public confidence in the banking system, and minimize the broader economic consequences that can accompany bank failures. However, the existence of deposit insurance reduces market discipline and may also create a moral hazard problem for troubled institutions.

Since insured depositors have no incentive to monitor and discipline management, government supervisory oversight tries to offset the risks posed by moral hazard. The question is whether the present approach to supervision is appropriate given the changes that have occurred in banking.

From a deposit insurance perspective, the consolidation in the banking industry during the past several years has increased the risk of insolvency of the Bank Insurance Fund (BIF). In a study using Monte Carlo simulations, Robert Oshinsky (1999) found that consolidation activity of the 1990s has "increased the risk to BIF.

" He concludes that "the health of the BIF has become more and more dependent on the health of the top 25 banking organizations, and future insolvency may be deeper, and harder to emerge from, than in the past. "Clearly the transformation of the banking industry into a small number of megabanks and a large number of significantly smaller banks raises issues for a deposit insurer. In theory, the reforms adopted as part of the Federal Deposit Insurance Corporation Improvement Act (FDICIA) and the subsequent enactment of national depositor preference should prevent the deposit insurance fund from becoming insolvent by shifting losses to uninsured depositors and nondepositor creditors.

However, in all likelihood, there would be massive shifts of uninsured deposits (including foreign deposits) from any large bank perceived to be in danger of failing. Insured deposits and secured borrowings would replace these liabilities, resulting in greater losses to the insurance fund. It is clear that the current system of bank supervision and risk assessment is appropriate for smaller banks; however, with the increased complexity of banking, especially at the very largest institutions, there will be a need for bank supervision and regulation to evolve as well.

BANK SUPERVISION AND REGULATION

Bank supervision and the process of risk monitoring by bank regulators has traditionally been focused on outcomes rather than on bank prospects. Supervisory oversight relies primarily on onsite bank examinations and offsite monitoring of bank conditions through the evaluation of financial reports and public disclosures.

Examiners can confirm the accuracy of financial reports issued by a bank as well as review private information in assessing the condition of the loan portfolio. In addition, examiners assess the adequacy of the bank's internal controls and risk-management procedures.

The examination process consists of an examination report containing narrative comments by the examiner and a rating of the bank. While examiners will frequently comment on the future prospects of the bank, the resultant rating system, the CAMEL rating, yields a rating of the condition of the bank that is ex post rather than ex ante. The major focus of supervision has been to evaluate the adequacy of capital after making adjustments for changes in market conditions and the credit quality of the loan portfolio. Most of this analysis is a reflection of the condition of the bank at a specific point in time. While some of the market and credit-risk models used by large banks and their regulators attempt to capture sensitivity to changes in interest rates and economic conditions, it is not clear that these give sufficiently accurate assessments of the risk exposure of a large complex institution.

Models to assess interest rate sensitivity are based on sufficient data to give a fairly reliable assessment of the sensitivity of a bank's financial condition to changes in rates. However, credit-risk models are constrained by a lack of historical loan performance data and information on many bank borrowers.

Moreover, when one incorporates the risk exposures associated with the international activities of larger banks, traditional examination techniques are unlikely to provide a true risk assessment suitable for deposit insurance purposes. Part of the problem may be that most examinations are not performed for the purpose of providing the deposit insurer with information needed to assess the overall risk posture of the insurance fund or to determine the relative long-term risk posed by an individual institution to the fund. While the CAMEL ratings are supposed to reflect, to some degree, the risk of failure, it is viewed as a relatively short-term prospect.

Clearly banks rated at 4 or 5 are considered to pose a significant risk of loss to the fund based on the deterioration in financial condition. Nevertheless, the primary purpose of examination is not risk assessment from a deposit insurance perspective. For example, the Manual of Examination, issued to all Federal Deposit Insurance Corporation (FDIC) examiners, indicates that safety-and-soundness examinations are performed for several purposes.

- Maintain public confidence in the integrity of the banking system and in individual banks
- Determine a bank's adherence to laws and regulations
- Protect the financial integrity of the deposit insurance fund by preventing problem situations from

remaining uncorrected and deteriorating to the point that a cost is borne by the insurance fund

- Supply the supervisor with an understanding of the nature, relative seriousness and ultimate cause of a bank's problems, and thus provide a factual foundation on which to base corrective measures.

It should be noted that the FDIC is the primary federal regulator for state-chartered banks that are not members of the Federal Reserve System, and most of these banks are relatively small institutions.

The Office of the Comptroller of the Currency (OCC) charters and supervises national banks and distinguishes the objectives of bank supervision between those that are applicable to small and large banks.

In supervising community banks, the OCC's objectives are to:

- Determine the condition of the bank and the risks associated with current and planned activities
- Evaluate the overall integrity and effectiveness of the bank's risk management systems Enforce banking laws and regulations

Attempt to achieve correction of deficiencies discovered during examination. The OCC considers banks with total assets greater than $1 billion to be large banks and, for administrative purposes, places the supervision of thes banks under an assistant deputy comptroller in a district office or, if the bank is larger than $25 billion, a large-bank deputy comptroller in Washington, D. C. Although the objectives of supervision are essentially the same for large banks as for small ones, the OCC does include the risks originating in subsidiaries and affiliates in its objectives for large banks and uses significantly different examination techniques for larger banks.

The OCC's examination focus for large banks is more risk focused than it is for small ones. The examiners focus on a bank's internal policies, procedures, and models to rate the riskiness of the various activities of large banks. While the examination process may not be focused solely on the condition of the bank, the assignment of ratings appears to be. This is especially true with respect to ratings that result in a downgrade that might result in further supervisory action. Since bank supervisors must be able to support their recommended actions in a legal proceeding, they must rely on current facts rather than perceptions about the future.

The focus on outcome-based risk assessment and analysis of riskmanagement systems works well for small banks given that the failures of small banks pose minimal risk to the deposit insurance fund. However, examination and supervision that focus on current conditions and risk-management systems may not translate into a complete set of information from which one can realistically assess the risk that an individual large bank poses for the insurance fund.

As banks have become more complex in terms of their global exposures, securities market activities, and the sheer magnitude of their operations, it has become more difficult for examiners to make an accurate assessment of an institution's total exposures at any point in time. Moreover, there is a clear distinction between the risk profile of an institution and the probability of near-term failure. An assessment of how well a bank manages risk is not a measure of its risk to the deposit insurance fund.

As we enter the twenty-first century, alternative means for assessing the riskiness of banks will have to be found. Some of these will augment existing supervisory and regulatory approaches while others should replace current methodologies. Given the size and complexity of large banks and thus the range of exposures they face, regulators will need to recognize the implications of economic trends for risk exposure.

This is especially true for deposit insurers who must develop quantitative measures of their own risk exposure. Regulators need to go beyond a current valuation of assets and an assessment of a bank's internal riskmanagement and monitoring capabilities. Greater attention needs to be paid to developments outside the banking industry and the potential risk exposures these developments hold for bank portfolios and earnings performance. The most obvious such exposure, and one currently incorporated into bank supervision in the

United States, is bank sensitivity to changes in interest rates. Other broader economic exposures that need to be focused on are country exposures both from a credit perspective and an operational perspective. Regulators should be monitoring economic and political developments in countries where large banks have credit exposure and branch and subsidiary operations.

Similarly, regulators should monitor trends in their own national and regional economies and make assessments as to the implications of potential change for the risk profile of large banks. Trends in commodity prices and industry performance can have a significant effect on the risk profile of an individual bank that goes beyond the effect on individual loans to firms in the industry. Thus, regulators need to understand these trends if they are to assess the overall exposure of a change in prices on a bank's portfolio.

An example of a large bank where this type of analysis would have proven useful was Continental Illinois National Bank (CINB). While it has been widely perceived that CINB's problems, and subsequent need for FDIC funds in 1984, resulted from their ill-advised purchase of energy loans from Penn Square Bank (which itself failed in 1982), the problems came from a deeper dependence on trends in oil prices. CINB believed that oil prices would rise to $60 per barrel, from a peak of $40, and engaged in a broad range of lending to firms that would prosper if energy prices rose.

Aside from loans to firms in the oil and gas business, the bank made loans secured by tankers, new container ships that while slower than older ships were more energy efficient, and non-energyrelated loans to companies in foreign countries whose economies depended on the price of oil. An analysis of the bank's portfolio and its sensitivity to changes in the price of oil and other economic events might have detected the degree of risk in CINB well in advance of the bank's problems. In response to the growth and increasing complexity of large banks, supervisors and insurers must develop new sources of information and analytical techniques to allow them to evaluate the effectiveness of management practice and measure the risks that accompany the broadening of managerial spans in growing institutions. This analysis should become more prospective than the current supervisory analysis, which is very sensitive to current bank performance. In effect, supervisors need to look at bank management in the same way as equity and credit market analysts do. They need to assess management performance and practices against those of other banks.

An additional source of information that can be used to assess the risk associated with a specific bank, or group of banks, is financial market data. Market participants, whether they are holders of subordinated debt or equity investors, are continuously assessing the future earnings potential and financial condition of a firm.

Several recent studies have shown that external stakeholders are able to evaluate risk effectively. Market information that reflects stakeholder expectations can be used by regulators to assess expectations of both the future earnings of publicly traded banks and the certainty with which the market believes the earnings stream will be achieved. The prospects, performance, and risk takings of the largest banks are monitored by a large number of research staffs at investment banking and brokerage firms as well as by institutional investors.

These analysts are not only assessing a single institution but are also making comparative judgments. Interest rate differentials between institutions on similar classes of debt clearly provide an indication of the market's view as to the relative risk of default. Similarly, relative equity price data provide insights into the market's expectations as to relative future earnings flows and the likelihood of success in achieving a specific level of future earnings.

A frequent criticism of the use Of market data is the paucity of such data for small banks and the burden that would be imposed on small banks if they were required to issue subordinated debt. However, from an insurance perspective, market data are available for the larger banks and, as argued above, these are the ones that pose the greatest risk to the deposit insurance fund. While in many ways the set of market data is superior to examination data in that it is ex ante, it should be recognized that markets assess the prospects for banks given that the current system of examination and regulation is in place.

A recent study conducted by John S. Jordan (1999) found that the supervisory process contributed to the market's assessment of banks in New England. Related literature (for example, Berger, Davies, and Flannery 1998) suggests that supervisory assessments, based on recent examinations, may be superior to those of stock market participants in assessing future performance.

Another study found that negative information uncovered by examiners is not generally reflected in market pricing until subsequent quarters. Bank examiners have an advantage over market participants in that they have access to private information about the loan portfolio and can provide the market with this information by making banks write off loans or increase loan-loss provisions.

On the other hand, market participants may be better than examiners at assessing management strategies and execution and the risks associated with prospective earnings. Equity markets are concerned with outlook for institutions, particularly the trade-off between risk and return. Debt markets and examiners tend to focus on the risk of default. While the likelihood of default is a significant risk to the insurance fund, it is not the sole determinant of the risk profile of the fund.

A well-capitalized bank that is not in imminent danger of failing but engages in risky lending still poses some level of risk to the deposit insurance fund and affects the overall risk profile of the fund. Market data allow one to distinguish the relative risk between two well-capitalized and profitable institutions.

In addition to improving risk assessment by using market data, bank regulators should study the effects of changes in technology and the risks and regulatory issues that will arise from technological change. Improvements in computer and telecommunication technologies have made banking services available across geographic borders, both within nations and globally. Clearly, the ability of consumers to bank, from their homes, with banks anywhere in the world should cause a rethinking of the definitions of banking markets for competitive analysis.

Similarly, the ability of depositors of all sizes to move money quickly and over great distances raises issues of the stability of core deposits and the increases likelihood of liquidity pressures on banks that are perceived to be financially distressed. The internet allows the rapid spread of both accurate and inaccurate information about financial institutions and thus increases the likelihood of bank runs, rational and irrational.

Perhaps of even greater interest is the ability of banks to solicit high-cost insured deposits over the internet, either as a substitute or complement to deposit brokers, as a means of funding rapid growth. Similarly, loan origination and solicitation over the internet raises a host of consumer compliance issues. Bank regulators and supervisors will need to monitor developments in electronic banking and funds movement technologies in order to anticipate problems, detect high-risk strategies by rapidly growing banks prior to examination, and address consumer issues that arise from electronic commerce.

Perhaps most important, from a policy perspective, is that regulators and deposit insurers will likely have shorter lead times within which to react to emerging problems in larger banks. The rapid flow of information accompanied by the ease of moving funds is likely to decrease the market's reaction time to real or perceived problems, and regulators are more likely to confront liquidity problems.

The combination of the existing examination approach with a monitoring system that relies on financial market assessments of future bank prospects should give the deposit insurer a better assessment of risk than does the present approach, which relies almost exclusively on examinations. By combining market information obtained from stock prices, relative, yield data, on bank debt, private, information obtained by examiners, and offsite monitoring tools, bank regulators and deposit insurers should be able to assess better the risk and prospects for large banks and control better the exposure of the insurance fund.

With the increase in the international activities of both domestic and foreign banks, not to mention their customers, there is a greater need for information about both the foreign banks that operate within a country and the foreign activities of domestic banks. As more of the larger banks are owned by foreign institutions, deposit insurers and regulators will have to have a greater understanding of the totality of the institution and its risk exposures.

Given the differences in treatments of deposits across borders, in regulations regarding permissible activities, and the ease With which depositors are able to move funds in and out of banks, deposit insurers need to gain access to significantly more information than is currently available about the international activities of banks.

There needs to be a greater sharing of information among all bank regulators and deposit insurers. While efforts have been under way to standardize fundamental regulatory standards, such as capital requirements, more work needs to be done to facilitate the free flow of information regarding the condition, risk profile, and activities of all banks.

Possibly an international body could be created to serve as a vehicle to facilitate the sharing of information among deposit insurers. In order that the financial markets can better assess the condition of large institutions, efforts should continue to increase the transparency of foreign bank financial statements as well as the international activities of all banks.

10

Market Discipline for Banks

A requisite condition for achieving efficiency in all types of market transactions is a form of money that provides a safe and efficient means of payments. In addition, macroeconomic stability requires a supply of money that contributes to sustained high levels of employment and output, price stability, and a satisfactory rate of economic growth.

In a rapidly changing institutional environment, how can banks as moneycreating institutions balance their innovational searches for profitmaximizing organizational structures and products with the social need for a money that is safe, efficient, and optimally supplied?

Certainly, this is not a new question. There were two important questions in banking: What system of banking will be most advantageous to the public and how can banks be rendered most profitable to the stockholders? Hildreth's answer to both was for the government to allow free competition in banking. Similarly, modern free-banking advocates argue that greater reliance on "market discipline" to regulate banks is the best way to deal with modern problems of inflation and financial instability, and to meet the challenges presented by financial innovations that affect the means of payments.

Some proponents of market discipline claim that central banks acting as monetary authorities would not be needed if governments observed a strictly laissez-faire policy towards the provision of all financial services. They predict the natural emergence of private arrangements to ensure that monetary services can be safely and efficiently left to competitive private enterprise. For example, Lawrence White claimed that replacing "a state monopoly central bank" with the provision of monetary services by free market institutions would prevent the type of inflation and deflation periods that were caused by "unbridled flat money" under the central bank during the 1970s and 1980s. White rejected both "rules" and "discretion" as being the proper regulator of the money supply, arguing instead that a free market approach to banking automatically constrains the money supply.

In that extreme form, market discipline means total reliance upon competitive market forces imposing losses and ultimately failure on suppliers that do not operate efficiently. In contrast, the traditional view has been that the banking system must be largely insulated from market discipline. Beyond the question of whether private monies can provide a universally accepted means of payment, there is the need for optimality and stability of supply.

Even in nonbanking sectors, where it is widely accepted that the social interest can be served by the regulating force of market competition, no theory of competitive markets promises market stability. At best, the static Marshallian theory of perfectly competitive markets only ensures that in the "long run" market price and quantity will move to an equilibrium that maximizes net consumer welfare (maximizes the combined consumer/producer surpluses).

Of greater relevance is the Schumpeterian theory of dynamic competition in which innovational shocks exert positive long-run effects but create instability in the short run. Significantly, financial innovations play a large a role in Schumpeterian dynamics.

Historical Experiences

Nonetheless, the theoretical literature on free or laissez-faire banking and arguments for its potential applicability in the present time continue to grow. Some advocates of free banking argue that its viability has been demonstrated by historical experiences. According to White, the Scottish experience with free banking in the eighteenth and nineteenth centuries provides "a vindication of free banking in theory and in practice and a rehabilitation of the advocates of free banking". Larry Sechrest asserts, "In many writer's minds, the theoretical case for free banking has been intimately tied to the alleged success in Scotland".

The American experience with free banking before the Civil War traditionally has been interpreted as demonstrating the need for a central bank and rather extensive regulations of commercial banking.

Free-banking advocates, however, claim that the traditional view ignored the successes and incorrectly viewed the failures as endemic to free banking. The theory of free banking to identify the institutional features of a system in which market forces are supposed to:

- Ensure that banks operate with safety for depositors,
- Provide a stable and efficient universal system of payments, and
- Achieve macroeconomic goals of price stability, a high and stable employment level, and a satisfactory rate of economic growth. The Scottish and American experiences with free banking are outlined. In both cases, banks issued notes that circulated as the major form of currency. There was, however, a third case of less-regulated banks that engaged in deposit banking and did not issue bank notes. In the late 1800s and early 1900s, the New York state banking laws allowed trust companies to operate as commercial banks without having to meet the same regulations. The experiences of those trusts are reviewed, and the dangers of insufficient regulations in more modern times are illuminated.

INSTITUTIONAL FEATURES OF FREE BANKING

George Selgin and Lawrence White conceded, in 1994, that identifying "the likely institutional arrangements of a laissez faire monetary regime requires imaginative speculation. Trying to assess the desirability of the hypothesized institutions only compounds the speculation". White described free banking as "the system under which there are no political restrictions on the business of issuing paper currency convertible into full-bodied coin". Sechrest offered a more complete list of the conditions necessary for free or laissez-faire banking, including

- No central monetary authority;
- Unrestricted freedom of individual private banks to issue bank notes as well as demand deposits;
- Banks free to pursue whatever policies they find advantageous in issuing liabilities and holding asset portfolios, subject only to the general legal prohibition against fraud or breach of contract;
- Unrestricted entry into the banking business, and banks free to open or close branches; and
- A complete absence of all of the following: interest controls on loans and securities, restrictions on investment in any particular industry, government deposit insurance, minimum capital or reserve requirements, and restrictions on the kinds of activities banks can undertake, such as investment banking.

The "Invisible Hand" in Free-Banking Theory

How is Adam Smith's famous "invisible hand" supposed to work under a system of free banking? If banks are free to issue their own notes, what assurance is there that those notes will circulate as currency--or that an optimal supply of money will be provided?

As suggested in White's depiction of free banking as involving paper banknotes convertible into "full-bodied coins," free-banking theories usually require some sort of commodity monetary standard. In that regard, they are basically following Adam Smith discussion of Scottish banknotes in Wealth of Nations in which banknotes substituted for specie and were convertible upon demand for gold or silver. In Smith's view, banknotes were a social improvement because they substituted a less costly "instrument of commerce" for a "very expensive one". People accept notes because they are confident the notes can be redeemed at any time for specie. The core thesis of market discipline-free banking advocates is that depositors are sufficiently rational; they have sufficient information to know which banks offer safety for their depositors and holders of notes and which do not. Banks falling into the latter category will quickly fail.

Bankers are rational enough to know that depositors will withdraw funds if the banks are perceived to be unsafe. Competition for depositors and the need to keep notes in circulation force each bank to operate within a safe zone relative to the amount of risk that depositors and note holders are willing to assume.

Banks that are willing to take greater risk on the asset side will have to reward depositors with higher interest rates or lose deposited funds. An optimal supply of money is ensured under the law of reflux, or the principle of adverse clearings. The general theory of free banking holds that the convertibility of inside money (notes or deposits issued by banks) into outside money (specie) restrains the supply of currency and deposits to optimal levels.

With the existence of a clearinghouse arrangement, all banks agree to accept notes issued by other banks. The principle of adverse clearings predicts that banks will quickly return other banks' notes to be redeemed in specie. It is impossible to oversupply paper currency and create monetary inflation unless all banks act in concert.

THE FREE-BANKING EXPERIENCE IN SCOTLAND

Much of this theory is based on the institutional system that evolved in Scotland in the 1700s and early 1800s. We begin this discussion with a brief review of the institutional developments in Scottish banking from its beginning in 1695 to 1845, the period within which free banking in Scotland began and ended.

Scottish Banking: 1695-1845

The development of banking in Scotland began in 1695 when the Bank of Scotland was created by an act of the Scottish

Parliament. The bank was a public corporation, with a provision requiring that the shares be freely bought and sold at the going market price (although two-thirds of the shares had to be held in Scotland).

It was granted a twenty-oneyear legal monopoly on banking and the right of note issue. Stockholders were given limited liability, and the dividends on bank stock were free of any taxation during that twenty-one-year period. With headquarters in Edinburgh, the bank opened branches in four Scottish cities.

In contrast to the Bank of England, the Bank of Scotland did not act as the government's financial agent and had no connection with the management of the public debt. On the contrary, lending to the state was forbidden. It was intended to be a purely commercial bank, providing secured loans to merchants and noblemen and discounting commercial bills. While it began accepting deposits (paying no interest), the real basis for its extended business in the early years was the issuing of notes in making loans and advances on discounted bills.

Almost immediately, the Bank of Scotland faced an attack from the Darien Company, a Scottish trading company that had intended to engage in banking operations and opposed the chartering the Bank of Scotland. By issuing its own notes, Darien acquired large quantities of the Bank of Scotland's notes which it presented for redemption in specie, creating a liquidity crisis for the new bank.

The Bank of Scotland's efforts to gain support from London failed because the Bank of England's own financial difficulties forced it to suspend payments partially in May 1696. The Bank of Scotland managed to survive by a partial call on subscribed capital and by calling in loans. By August 1697, the Darien Company's own financial difficulties forced it to cease the attack.

One consequence of the attack was the closure of the branches the Bank of Scotland had established in Glasgow, Aberdeen, Dundee, and Montrose. Until 1704 the Bank of Scotland issued notes only in large denominations (five-pound notes were the smallest). In 1704 it began issuing one-pound notes, a move that opened the way for a greater extension of the note issue and the beginning of the displacement of coins in smaller transactions.

In December 1704, the bank was forced to suspend payments because of a specie shortage in England and Scotland caused by the war with France. Then rumors circulated in Scotland that the government was going to raise the monetary value of specie, people rushed to change their notes for specie.

In May 1705, payment on notes was resumed. In 1715 the bank again had to suspend specie payments for eight months as a result of the Jacobite rebellion. During that crisis and its aftermath, the bank's twenty-one-year monopoly of corporate banking in Scotland ended, but the bank seems to have made no effort to gain its renewal.

In 1727 the Royal Bank of Scotland, also located in Edinburgh, was chartered by an act of the British Parliament. The Bank of Scotland, known as the Old Bank, had vigourously sought through political means to prevent the creation of the second public bank. The Royal Bank immediately launched an attack against the Bank of Scotland in the hopes of either destroying it or forcing an amalgamation on terms favourable to the new bank.

It began to exchange its notes for large quantities of the Bank of Scotland's notes and presented those notes for redemption in specie. For several years, the two banks engaged in a note "duel. " At one point, the Bank of Scotland suspended payments, called in loans, made a 10 per cent call on stockholders, and even closed for several weeks in 1728. Its notes continued to circulate at face value even during the suspension.

After a note holder won a suit against the bank for failing to honour the promise given on the face of its notes, the Bank of Scotland began to insert an "option clause" on its printed notes, with the option being a six-month delay with an annual interest rate of 5 per cent. While the act that created the Bank of Scotland had provided "summary diligence" in redeeming its notes in specie on demand, that provision did not extend to other banks. Opposition to option clauses led the British Parliament to pass an act in 1765 that made summary diligence enforceable for all banknotes and prohibited option clauses.

Two banking innovations occurred during the note duel of 1728. The Bank of Scotland began actively to solicit deposits by offering interest on the balances. The Royal Bank developed a more flexible method of lending in a cash advance, the forerunner of the overdraft.

The Bank of Scotland had required that an approved loan be taken fully in notes. Under the cash advance, a line of credit would be approved, with the merchant taking only that part which was needed at the moment, thereby minimizing the interest cost on loans.

Each of the Edinburgh banks formed partnerships to create new banks in Glasgow to promote circulation of their notes. Those banks, which began issuing their own notes, were able to survive despite note duels launched by the two Edinburgh banks. Another new bank which opened in Aberdeen in 1747 was excessive in issuing notes, and by 1753 it had been drained of its specie and forced to close.

A third Edinburgh bank emerged when the British Linen Company, which was started to promote the linen trade as wholesalers, began issuing non-interest-bearing banknotes, payable on demand. The company, which started the first successful branch banking, expanded so vigourously that it had the largest circulation of banknotes by 1845. Its charter, however, could be reviewed at any time after its initial thirty years, rendering it vulnerable to political attacks from rival banks.

In 1784 the company petitioned the government for a permanent charter to allow it to operate as a public bank. Political pressure from the Bank of Scotland and the Royal Bank prevented any such charter from being granted. Finally, in 1813, British Linen was granted a charter with limited liability for its stockholders. According to White, free banking in Scotland really began in 1765, although the meaning of "free" was highly qualified. A number of small private and provincial banks entered the industry in the late 1750s and 1760s. Some of the new banks issued notes in small denominations (in fractions of a pound). After being petitioned by Scots, the British Parliament prohibited the issuance of notes denominated less than one pound in Scotland in the same act that prohibited option clauses.

While that act imposed the two regulations, both of which met with Adam Smith's strong approval, the concept of "free banking" was instituted as the right of note issue was made universal. After their early efforts at "note dueling" failed, the Bank of Scotland and the Royal Bank began routinely to accept each other's notes to be returned for redemption in specie. The motive was economic self-interest since.

that arrangement made banknotes more acceptable to the public. In the 1770s, the Bank of Scotland instituted the Scotland note exchange. All notes were accepted at par and redeemed through a twice-weekly exchange of notes. Membership in the exchange became recognized by all banks as a "valuable brand-name capital asset". The Ayr Bank failed after issuing notes on bad credit. Since other banks held few of its notes, its failure had little negative effect on the Scottish banking system.

To bolster public confidence in banknotes, attract depositors, and put their own notes in wider circulation, the Bank of Scotland and the Royal Bank advertised that they would accept the notes of the defunct bank. There was little risk involved since the unlimited liability of the Ayr Bank's 241 shareholders forced them to bear all the losses. Claims of creditors and note holders were eventually paid in full.

In 1810 the Scottish banking system was still dominated by the three Edinburgh banks. The Bank of Scotland again had opened branches, which by 1810 numbered twenty. The Royal Bank had no branches but developed correspondent relationships with provincial banking companies. The number of Scottish banks had reached its all-time high of thirtyseven, but the provincial banks exhibited a firm life cycle associated with the limited opportunities for large-scale banking in small market areas. According to S. G. Checkland, those banks were governed by a kind of logic curve. In response to a local need, a new bank would be launched with a good deal of optimism. Based on a note issue, it would have little difficulty in becoming established and would flourish for a time, reach a certain size, and then stagnate, falling behind the needs of the growing community, though usually continuing to be profitable for the partners.

A new bank would then be launched, which would go through the same cycle. The limitations on provincial banking included management inadequacy (local banks became content with a modest scale of trading and relatively safe profits) and a lack of sufficient capital because it was not sought on a large scale.

Such banks also needed an Edinburgh connection. Some scholars argue that free banking in Scotland actually existed only during the era of joint-stock banking, which began in 1810. The term "joint-stock banking" perhaps needs clarification. Stockholders of the three "chartered" Edinburgh banks--the Bank of Scotland, the Royal Bank, and (after 1813) the British Linen Bank--were granted limited liability.

A number of provincial banks had been organized as joint-stock banks, but their charters were terminable after twenty-one years. The new joint-stock banks that emerged after 1810 were different by virtue of being larger in capitalization, number of stockholders, and branch activity. In actuality, these joint-stock companies were partnerships with hundreds of partners since the stockholders were not granted limited liability.

In 1830 the Scottish banking system consisted of the two "public" banks (the Bank of Scotland and the Royal Bank), the British Linen Company, two new joint-stock banks with national branches, and the provincial banks, a total of thirty-six separate banking enterprises. Only the two public banks had any considerable capital until the new joint-stock banks began.

Apart from a suggestion in 1825-1826 that one-pound bank notes be dropped, which was successfully opposed in Scotland, the government made no effort to alter or control the Scottish banking system and continued to insist on the conditions of free banking. At the same time, market forces were at work, which led to the standardization of types. Between 1831 and 1850, there was a large turnover of banking concerns.

Seventeen banks were begun but thirty-six were either closed or taken over. The joint-stock companies surpassed the public banks as the dominant element in the system, with nearly 60 per cent of paid-up capital and accounting for over two-thirds of the Scottish note issues.

The free banking era in Scotland came to an end in 1844-1845, when the British Parliament imposed control on the increase of banknotes by Scottish banks. The nineteen Scottish note-issuing banks were allowed to continue issuing their individual notes, but any new Scottish bank would have to gain the cooperation of the Bank of England to provide notes that the bank could then issue.

A Successful Experience with Market Discipline?

According to White, Scotland achieved "success with laissez faire banking," achieving "remarkable monetary stability" without a central bank or monetary policy, and with virtually no political regulation. Because Scottish banks were less affected by periods of "commercial distress," Scottish industry seemed to have been less affected than industry in England.

White interpreted the entry of the British Linen Company into banking as an illustration of the freedom of entry under the free-banking system and the failure of the Ayr Bank as an illustration of the effectiveness of market discipline. White's interpretation of the Scottish free-banking experience as representing a positive case for modern free banking has been viewed favourably by a number of free-banking advocates.

Unquestionably, the Scottish banking system did function reasonably well relative to other banking systems of the time. But the real issue is whether it demonstrated an effective reliance on market discipline. That devolves into two related questions. Did the Scottish free-banking system really represent laissez-faire banking, void of any centralized system and regulation? Did the Scottish banking system really perform as effectively as suggested by White?

A Centralized System

While the institutionalized and unified Scottish "note circle" has been viewed as providing an automatic control over excessive issuance of banknotes through the very rapid return of notes to offending banks, it was not a sufficient condition for stability.

Rather, the Bank of Scotland and the Royal Bank informally provided central bank services and discipline over the other Scottish banks. Both public banks made redemption demands with large quantities of notes to control banking behaviour. The Bank of Scotland in particular pressured provincial banks and especially those in the lesser burghs to restrict note issues.

It would agree to accept a bank's notes only if that bank agreed to be reasonable in issuing its notes. On those that did not, the Bank of Scotland made sudden demands for redemption of large quantities of notes. While it left the policing of the system largely to the Bank of Scotland, the Royal Bank assumed the equally important central banking role of providing credits to and holding balances for other banks.

The Scottish banking system was centralized in yet another way: through a heavy dependency upon the Bank of England for liquidity needs. Scottish banks held little specie reserves and quickly sent any excess gold to London. This was possible because, although notes were legally redeemable in specie upon demand, Scottish banks had several ways of obstructing redemption.

"It is plain from the formidable range of devices for forcing notes into circulation that the holding of bank notes by Scotsmen was not merely a 'psychological' preference, made possible by literacy and enlightenment". By the late 1700s, Scottish banks had developed several means of maximizing note issues; for example, by putting pressure on firms that borrowed from them to push the circulation of their notes, and by minimizing the specie they paid out. Checkland describes the Scottish system as "one of continuous partial suspension of cash payments", which "contributed greatly to Scottish banking success".

The public banks usually took up the notes of insolvent banks to avoid any threat to public acceptability of banknotes in general. As we noted earlier, there was little risk involved because of the unlimited liability of owners.

Scottish banks learned early on to depend on London and, in particular, on the Bank of England for liquidity. That took the form of holding government securities as assets that could be sold quickly, creating credits on their London correspondents. Thus, the pattern had become in a real sense a centralized one.

Stability and Optimality in Operations

Scottish banking in the period from 1745 to 1772 faced two familiar challenges. One was an administrative need to learn how to organize banks so they would be profitable for the owners. The second was a policy need to develop an understanding of the effects of the banking system on the economy, and vice versa.

A natural harmony of interest was not necessarily forthcoming. "Because the game was a competitive one, and often fiercely so, bankers in their search for profitable business might place the economy, and their own part in it, in jeopardy.... Forming new institutions and adopting new practices in a fully competitive situation was risky and often ruthless business".

A fundamental question about market discipline is whether the market is perfectly competitive or oligopolistic. While theoretical arguments of efficiency can be made from competitive market models, it is difficult to make a case that competition in oligopolistic markets tends to maximize efficiency. That is important because the Scottish banks exhibited a definite tendency towards an oligopolistic market structure. While economies were not sufficient to allow a natural monopoly situation to develop, they were substantial enough that small banks were squeezed out by broadly branched bank companies. A characteristic of oligopoly is that it encourages collusion rather than competition, and there is evidence of such behaviour on part of the Scottish banks. During

the financial boom of 1836, the Scottish bank in conclave agreed to raise the lending rate to 5 per cent and to increase the borrowing rate by a half-per cent. In so doing, they were acting "in the hope that the present understanding may continue and that no change may be made without mutual notice.

The claim of stability in Scottish banking is challenged by the large turnover in the industry. Of the 109 banking firms that began operating before 1845, only 20 were still operating in 1845. Nineteen of those issued notes, and nine had entered the industry rather recently. By 1810 Scottish banks had to be as concerned about sudden withdrawals of deposits as about runs on their notes.

In the heyday of Scottish free banking, 1831-1845, the weaknesses of the provincial banks were exposed by successive financial crises, and the banks were either taken over by larger banks or closed. Checkland described the establishment of new banks as in part "the children of the speculative urge" and credited the Scottish banks, especially those in Western Scotland, with contributing to the "speculative excesses" of the boom of 1825 by "over-generous credit extension". Even the Bank of Scotland tended to ride with the boom, along with other banks "finding it increasingly difficult to distinguish real business from speculation".

The degree of innovation in bank operations is also in some doubt. Since Adam Smith is often regarded as the original theorist of market discipline, his theory of bank management is quite relevant. He argued that banks should be very cautious in their operations, restricting their loans and advances to short-term commercial loans that are repaid quickly. Free entry into banking was not a sufficient condition in itself to ensure vigourous innovative performance by any of the banks. The cautious management practices followed by Scottish bankers gave rise to several kinds of restraints on banks financing the growth needs of the community. One was the trend towards the greater safety of operating on a relatively modest scale. The other was turning towards investments in government securities.

Scottish Free Banking was Not Laissez-Faire Banking

Scottish free banking was definitely not laissez-faire banking. Three important regulations were in place after 1765: the prohibition on option clauses, the prohibition on small notes, and legal ceiling interest rates. After 1714 Scottish banks usually charged the upper limit of 5 per cent, referred to as the "legal rates of interest".

In Wealth of Nations, Adam Smith had given bankers advice on how to vary their lending and note issuance modestly under normal conditions. As the industrial revolution took hold in the early 1800s and the Scottish economy began experiencing periods of economic expansion that accelerated into booms, Scottish banks found themselves in a difficult situation.

Unable to raise interest rates on loans above legal levels, banks had little incentive to expand their lending. Raising interest rates on deposits to prevent a sudden wave of withdrawals would reduce the margin between the cost of deposits and the rate on loans. At the same time, banks were being pressured by the business community to increase loans, a pressure that Smith warned banks to resist in Wealth of Nations.

Individual banks, however, found themselves unable to reduce lending because to do so would have negative impacts on the business community. As Checkland noted, a bank would suffer heavy losses "if it so acted to bring the structure down".

To some extent, this was a problem of legally imposed interest rate ceilings, which also limited competition for deposits. At the same time, it was also a problem imposed by the lack of an effective monetary policy. Checkland summed up the situation as follows: "Each bank, therefore, though it might attempt to control lending, was ultimately ineffectual in this, and was forced to increase advances until the system produced crisis, detonated by the failure of some component businesses, and soon threatening all".

The three Edinburgh "chartered" banks enjoyed privileged positions. An especially important one was the limited liability enjoyed by their shareholders while shareholders of all the other banks were subject to unlimited liability. Sechrest correctly observed that unlimited liability was a significant regulatory barrier to entry.

He also noted a longstanding government instruction to customs officers to accept only notes of the chartered banks in payment of duties. To that we would add Adam Smith's statement that princes could create a certain value to paper money by making taxes payable in that money.

THE FREE-BANKING EXPERIENCE IN THE UNITED STATES

Economic historians usually date the free-banking era in the United States as beginning in 1838, when New York enacted legislation that permitted granting a bank charter to any group of citizens that could meet a set of legal requirements. Prior to that, bank charters were granted by special act of the state legislature on the basis of a demonstrated need for a new bank and evidence that the applicants were fit persons to operate a bank.

Critics alleged that political corruption in the granting of bank charters had resulted in many undercapitalized and poorly managed banks. Although Michigan had enacted free-banking legislation in 1837, that law had serious flaws. Interestingly, New York and Michigan have been judged by historians as representing the successes of free banking and worst failures of free banking, respectively. With the New York law providing a model, eighteen states enacted some Variation of free-banking legislation before the free-banking era ended with the creation of the National Banking System in 1863.

According to Hugh Rockoff, little or no "free" banking was done in nine of those states. Among the states in which free banking was active, six experienced problems with "wildcat" banking, while three had some of the "soundest" banking of the era.

The initial free-banking legislation was a response to the Panic of 1837 and the subsequent economic depression which in length and severity was one of the worst in American history, lasting until 1843. Developments in banking and federal treasury policies in the United State during the 1830s were important contributing factors.

Between 1830 and 1837, the number of state banks had doubled, and their note expansion had tripled. After President Andrew Jackson vetoed the bill that rechartered the Second U. S. Bank in 1832, treasury deposits in that bank were drawn down. Initially, the treasury funds were transferred to seven banks in Philadelphia, Baltimore, Boston, and New York, six of which were considered to be Jackson's "pet" banks. By 1836 treasury funds were on deposit with thirty-three banks. In part, this was a consequence of Congress's passing an act that restricted deposits in any one bank to no more than three-fourths of that bank's capital.

In 1836 the large federal government surplus was transferred to the states, which drained specie from banks in the northeast, especially in New York. Banks in New York suspended specie payments in May 1837, and banks in other regions followed suit. By October, a regional imbalance had developed.

More funds were to be paid out to Northern states than were deposited with Northern banks. While just the opposite was true in the South, funds could not be transferred from the Southern banks because they had suspended specie payments and the U. S. Treasury could not accept their notes. The specie problem was intensified when Jackson issued the Specie Circular in 1836, which required that payments for federal lands be made in specie. The suspension of specie payments in 1837 and the depression that followed the Panic of 1837 provided the immediate impetus for a general revision of state banking laws that was intended to ensure that banks would follow more conservative policies. Bank reform was a major economic issue, but there were very divergent opinions on the appropriate reform measures.

When New York enacted freebanking legislation, three different views on banking prevailed. One group, reflecting the Jeffersonian agrarian philosophy, was opposed to all banks. A second group favoured no increase in the number of bank charters awarded by state legislatures, that is, a continuation of the status quo. A third group, the free-banking advocates, wanted "to throw open the business of banking, like all other mercantile business, to free competition".

Despite the efforts of a political coalition of the first two groups, aimed at preventing any easing of the requirements for starting banks, New York's free-banking law was enacted in 1838. Under that law, any applicant would be granted a charter to open a bank by meeting certain requirements, which included a minimum capital stock of at least $100,000 and the submission of semiannual reports to the state comptroller. Applicants were not required to demonstrate a need for the bank or that they were fit persons to operate a bank.

Shares were transferable and shareholders were given limited liability. Banknotes were engraved and printed by the state comptroller. By depositing collateral security in the form of bonds of federal or state governments or mortgages, free banks would receive notes of equal amounts that they could put in circulation through loans or discounting bills. Banks received the interest on the deposited securities as long as their notes were redeemed in specie on demand. If a bank failed to redeem its notes, the trust fund would pay and the deposited securities would be sold. Initially, a specie reserve of 12. 5 per cent for banknotes was imposed, but that requirement was later removed.

In enacting free-banking laws, the primary concern of the states was to maximize the freedom of banking while protecting the note holders against losses in the case of bank failures. No protection was provided for either depositors or stockholders. In most cases, note holders were given first lien on bank assets if notes were not redeemed. As was the case with Scottish free banking, whether free banking in the United States was a successful experience with market discipline essentially devolves into two questions: To what extent did the freebanking system comply with the laissez-faire requirements specified by advocates of market discipline and were the experiences with free banking ones of success or failure?

American Free Banking Laissez-Faire Banking?

The free-banking era has been described as a "conscious attempt to introduce the principle of laissez faire into banking". Bray Hammond assests that "[f]ree banking was an application of laissezfaire to the monetary function", but Hammond also saw fit to qualify that statement with a quote from a 1849 report by Millard Fillmore, then the comptroller of New York, that "the free-bank system. . . takes its name from the fact that all are freely permitted to embark in it who comply with the rules prescribed".

The rules that required banks to have minimum levels of capital stock, to deposit securities with the state agency before they could issue banknotes, and to make regular reports kept the free-banking system from being one of laissez-faire. To enforce those rules, state bank examiners came into existence, and they visited banks without warning to verify their accounts and assets.

Thus, the "free" in free banking meant only that new banks could be started without having to convince legislators that a need for another bank existed. This was a change from a public utility (natural monopoly) concept in which a community need had to be demonstrated as well as the fitness of the owners to operate a bank.

It was not, however, according to Rockoff, a change to regard banking as ordinary business. The state necessarily became involved not only in ascertaining that minimum capital requirements had been met, but also in accepting and holding the deposited securities and in printing and engraving the banknotes. Rockoff has noted the possibilities of damage clauses in he form of a provision that authorized the banking authority to assess the bank and pay note holders a certain penalty--the "normal rate of interest"--for the failure of the bank to redeem its notes in specie. Such clauses would have effectively provided a type of insurance for note holders similar to deposit insurance, which is incompatible with laissezfaire banking (and which modern advocates of free banking abhor).

Generally, free-banking laws provided for double liability of stockholders. A true laissez-faire approach would have meant unlimited liability of stockholders, but Rockoff has argued that it might have hindered the accumulation of capital in banking, citing the case of Georgia's free-banking law which did provide unlimited liability. In addition, state banking laws that limited branch banking were not affected by the free-banking legislation.

"Wildcat Banking" or Successful "Market Discipline"?

In 1840 R. Hildreth, perhaps the most articulate advocate of free competition in banking during that era, expressed both confidence and realistic expectations about the impact of New York's free-banking law. He declared that the law "has ensured for the system of free banking a fair trial. Nor does its success, or its speedy introduction into the other states, appear to be doubtful". At the same time, he cautioned against undue optimism:

That the system of free banking will at once put an end to all fraud or mismanagements, that it will prevent fluctuations in trade, or will introduce a mercantile millennium, it would be ridiculous to imagine. Fraud, mismanagement and fluctuation are incidental to all business transactions.

But as free competition in every other branch of trade has been found beneficial, and has afforded a certain degree of protection against these evils, so free competition in banking must and will be attended with the same results. In 1848 British economist J. R. McCulloch, a strong advocate of tight regulations on the issuance of banknotes, expressed the view that free banking in America represented the "worst parts of the American banking system". Hindsight of the entire era of free banking only reinforced that perception. Since the late 1800s, historians have generally viewed the free-banking experience as a failure.

Margaret Myers, for example, stated, "The ease of obtaining charters in many states and the inadequate restrictions in many charters were important factors in the unsatisfactory performance of the American banking system during much of the nineteenth century,". She also noted the ineffectiveness of the enforcement of the requirements imposed on free banks.

The protection provided for note holders and depositors of free banks was often "more apparent than real; the tales of the bank examiner trotting along the main highway in his buggy from one bank to the next, while an Indian runner raced through the woods bearing the justcounted gold to the next bank on the examiner's list, are probably not completely apocryphal".

Within a year of the passage of Michigan's free-banking law, "more than forty banks had been set up under its terms. Within two years more than forty were in receivership". Most of the notes of Michigan's wildcat banks ultimately lost all of their value. The free-banking act of 1837 was repealed two years later.

Michigan passed a new free-banking act in 1857, which might be interpreted as a demonstration of the recognized successes of free banking in other states. But the experience under the 1837 law certainly gave free banking its first notoriety. Contemporary accounts suggest that Michigan banks monetized state debts by buying bonds with their notes, then disappearing; used kegs of nails and broken glass with layers of coin on top as specie reserves; and engaged in multiple counting of the same specie reserves.

Rather than limiting the amount of paper currency, free banking meant "in effect, an indefinite and unlimited number of banks". Free banking was "American democracy's choice of a permanent policy of monetary inflation--a policy that assures plenty of funds for all who wish to borrow, prices that rise in the long persistently though haltingly, and a dollar that never ceases for long to shrink in value". Rockoff contends that the traditional view rests on purely anecdotal evidence of a small number of stories about wildcat banking. Similarly, the popular belief that banking is inherently unstable is based on historical events of which American free banking is considered to be the worst case.

While they have conceded that free banking did have its problems, they also have argued that it was not as chaotic as believed. Free-banking experiences provide no compelling evidence of any inherent instability, which Rolnick and Weber define as producing bank runs or panics. Economic shocks caused many banks, including free banks, to fail, but did not lead to bank runs or panics. On the other hand, data cited show that a high percentage of free banks closed, ranging from a low of 36 per cent in New York to a high of 86 per cent in Indiana.

A smaller percentage failed to redeem their notes at par, ranging from 8 per cent in New York to 56 per cent in Minnesota. Note holders' losses were smaller than many had estimated and that, based on time in circulation, free banks' notes were relatively safe. Hence, they contend that it is misleading to characterize the overall free-banking experience as a failure of laissez-faire banking.

Yet, their argument clearly concedes that the entire banking system was unstable, which favours the traditional view that a central bank was needed. It is noted that "wildcat banking" occurred in only some of the free-banking states. By his definition, "wildcat banking" meant not only that banks issued notes that they could not continuously redeem in specie, but also that those banks came into existence as the result of a liberal entry provision under free-banking laws.

Rockoff attributed the differences in experiences among states under superficially similar free-banking laws to several factors. The most important was that eligible bonds (or other securities such as mortgages) were accepted as collateral for notes at inflated legal values rather than true market values.

Wildcat banking generally occurred because where the market values of bonds were less than their par values, banknotes could be issued in larger amounts than were safe. There was also the problem of the link between the deficit-spending policies of states, which affected the supply and quality of bonds, and the volume of banknotes issued by the free banks. In some cases, legislators failed to realise that, by allowing banks to deposit bonds of other states, the issuance of banknotes in their own state was tied to the deficit-spending policies of other states.

Similarly, Rolnick and Weber found that that decreases in the market values of bonds of Southern states left banks holding those bonds with insufficient reserves to back their notes. The research conducted by Rockoff, Rolnick, Weber, and others helps to explain why free banks in some states were more fragile than free banks in other states, but it offers no evidence that supports the argument that market discipline provides adequate assurance of stability, safety, and optimality in the supply of money.

Even if free banks in a number of states performed no worse than other banks, the system as a whole failed repeatedly. The traditional view that the system needed a central bank remains the only compelling interpretation of the historical experience with free banking in Scotland and the United States.

The Suffolk Banking System

The argument that unregulated banks will not increase the money supply to inflationary levels rests on the belief that private clearinghouses for banknotes provided effective checks in Scotland and in New England from 1825 to 1858 under the Suffolk banking system.

In 1824 the Suffolk Bank of Boston formed a coalition with the other Boston banks to create a fund to be used to purchase country banknotes and return them for redemption. Their intent was to eliminate the competition from notes of country banks circulating in the city. Failing to achieve that, the other banks in the coalition suggested that the Suffolk Bank accept deposits of and clear at par all country banknotes that participating banks chose to deposit. Country banks could participate by maintaining permanent non-interest-bearing deposits with Suffolk or another Boston member of the Suffolk system, and additional non-interest-bearing accounts with Suffolk that were sufficient on average to redeem their deposited notes.

Like the Bank of Scotland and the Royal Bank, the Suffolk Bank essentially became a private regional central bank, offering loans to members of the system in addition to providing clearinghouse services. In holding member bank deposits and clearing member banknotes, the Suffolk Bank was able to monitor and influence member banks' activities. The Suffolk Bank essentially became a natural monopolist in clearing banknotes, realizing economies of scale and enhancing its profits through exploiting economies of scope.

The Suffolk Bank's role as a private central bank demonstrated the need for a central bank, but the Suffolk system ended in 1858, which illustrated the unreliability of private arrangement to conduct the public services of a central bank. The natural monopoly interpretation appears validated by the Suffolk Bank's response to the competition created by the chartering of the Bank of Mutual Redemption in 1855. In 1858 the Suffolk Bank announced that it was withdrawing from clearing notes for country banks and did so in 1860. There appeared to be room for only one clearing bank, which confirms the interpretation of a natural monopoly.

UNREGULATED TRUSTS IN NEW YORK

Finally, we turn to a historical case in which the banks involved did not issue banknotes. In most states in the latter half of the nineteenth century, trust companies operating as fiduciary institutions chartered by state governments were also allowed to engage in commercial banking.

By 1875 the Bankers' Magazine was complaining that trust companies in New York were doing banking business without being subject to the restrictions of banking laws. The trusts had a comparative advantage over both national and state banks in "deposit currency" as they were not subject to reserve requirements and had greater freedom in lending, particularly with reference to real estate. In 1889 the Bankers' Magazine complained that trusts were dependent on reserves of associated banks while competing with banks for general deposits, and warned that at some point the trusts would prove to be a source of weakness to the banking system.

Complaints from banking interests about unfair competition from the trusts increased in the 1890s as their numbers rose and their total deposits and lending expanded rapidly. Trusts actively solicited deposits by paying interest, something the banks did not do. In 1898 the Commercial and Financial Chronicle sarcastically observed that the trusts were experiencing "wonderful growth" by offering rates on deposits of up to 5 per cent when call loan rates were 1 ½ per cent or less. A general incorporation law for trusts enacted in New York in 1887 and amended in 1892 encouraged the growth of trusts by placing them on the same footing as banks with regard to loans and discounts but with no supervision or reserves requirements.

In other states, courts nullified laws that prohibited or limited trusts engaging in banking. Those who advocate dependency on market competition to regulate banks must recognize that large banks may collude to prevent competition. The response of large banking interests to trusts in New York provides a case example. In the absence of a central bank, banks had to clear their checks on their own.

The New York Clearing House Association, organized for the purpose of clearing checks between members, was "dominated by the more conservative and solidly entrenched institutions which were either within the Morgan sphere of influence or the National City Bank sphere of influence or were in substantial accord with those financial powers". The management of the Clearing House had the power to dictate terms to the lesser banks in times of crisis. To suddenly deny a bank access to the Clearing House services effectively meant closing that bank. Most of the trusts were not members, but many cleared their checks through member banks. The

Clearing House management regarded the exemption of trusts from reserve requirements as both unfair and a danger to the banking system.

In 1899 it moved to adopt rules requiring that trusts clearing checks through member banks submit to examinations, provide weekly statements, and maintain a cash reserve starting at 5 per cent of deposits and rising to 10-15 per cent of deposits. The trusts resisted, arguing that most of their deposits were time deposits, whereas banks had largely demand deposits, and thus did not need liquid reserves. In 1905 the trusts withdrew from the Clearing House and cleared their checks by messengers.

There is no doubt that trusts played a major role in the Panic, but historical accounts differ on the nature of that role. The panic was caused by legislation enacted in New York that required trusts to maintain 10-15 per cent reserves against aggregate deposits.

The withdrawal of funds on deposit with the New York central city reserve banks by the trusts to meet the required cash reserves caused a liquidity crisis. As the central city banks lost reserves, they restricted lending, which resulted in a liquidity crisis in the stock market in the spring of 1907. The tightening of reserves caused the fall panic of 1907 because it had eliminated the elasticity of credit at a time when fall crop-moving demands for funds in the interior occurred.

In early 1908, the law was amended to apply reserve requirements only to the trusts' demand deposits. Smith (1928) claimed that not a dollar of deposits in trusts was lost during the panic. A different interpretation reveals serious weaknesses in the whole banking system, including behaviour spawned by the absence of effective regulation which allowed stock market speculators to put banks at risk.

Two speculators, F. Augustus Heinze and Charles W. Morris, the latter a notorious crook, gained control over a number of banks and trust companies by "chain banking," which used a variation of "check kiting." Money was borrowed to buy controlling shares in a bank, which would be used as collateral against a loan from that bank to buy controlling shares in another bank, and so on. The less regulated trusts were especially well suited for that operation. In 1907 Heinze and Morris attempted to corner the market in United Copper stock with the support of the Trust Company of America, the Lincoln Trust, and the Knicker-bocker Trust.

When their attempt was foiled by John D. Rockefeller's Standard Oil group, depositors began withdrawing funds from the Mercantile National Bank, which was controlled by Heinze and Morris. While the Clearing House came to the bank's aid, the management publicly announced that Heinze and Morris must be removed from banking.

That announcement increased public unease, and the bank was forced to close. Pressure then mounted on the three trusts affiliated with the Heinze-Morris group. The large Knickerbocker Trust Company faced heavy withdrawals of deposits and was forced to close. Subsequently, the Trust Company of America, located on Wall Street, faced a run, as did the Lincoln Trust Company.

J. P. Morgan and his group were reluctant to bring the aid of national banks to the trusts, viewing the situation as a "trust company" panic to be left to the trusts to resolve collectively.

Although Morgan and his group had used the trust companies earlier in a scheme that allowed insurance companies to multiply assets and evade laws that regulated insurance companies, they were ready to allow them to fold as banks. The head of the Rockefeller group's National City Bank convinced Morgan that failure of the large trusts would hurt the national banks.

Ultimately, Morgan forced his will on the presidents of the trust companies, and they subscribed to a loan fund of $25 million to save the Trust Company of America. Morgan's decision to protect that institution has been interpreted as one of conniving self-interest.

Trust Company of America was holding as collateral against a loan the controlling stock in an iron and steel corporation that Morgan wanted. When Morgan was ultimately able to purchase that stock at a fraction of its market value, public suspicion arose that he had engineered the panic for that purpose. The events surrounding the Panic of 1907 illustrated how much more complex and interrelated the banking and financial system was in the early 1900s than it was in the eras of free banking in Scotland and the United States.

In the aftermath, trust companies became as regulated as banks, and the Federal Reserve Act was passed in 1913 in recognition that the American banking system needed a central monetary authority.

11

Corporate Governance of Banks

THEORY VS. EVIDENCE

Bank regulators once had a relatively easy task of supervision when banks were small and banking consisted of accepting short-term deposits and making short-term loans. That is no longer the case. Today, bank regulators must deal with complex global megabanks and new technologies that are rendering government regulation inept and ineffective. They hope that private market regulation, or market discipline, can help them discharge their supervisory responsibilities. Market discipline and the extent to which it works.

Specifically, it deals with the concept of private market regulation and how it relates to banks; principal agent conflicts; the evidence about the successes and failures of market discipline, as well as the suggested use of subordinated debt; and the requirements for market discipline.

PRIVATE MARKET REGULATION

Private market regulation, or market discipline as it is commonly called, comprises the mechanisms that signal the behaviour of firms to holders of debt and equity who, in turn, affect the franchise value of the firm and influence its future behaviour. A key feature is that market discipline is expected to influence future behaviour.

This is in contrast to the use of the term by some bank regulators who focus primarily on the cost of borrowing. The franchise value aspect of private market regulation is exemplified in stock markets, such as the New York Stock

Exchange. Stock market prices are considered "efficient" because they reflect all information contained in past stock price movements, they reflect the published information, or they embody all available information. The efficiency occurs because the listed firms are relatively transparent, and they are monitored continuously by securities analysts, the media, and investors.

Changes in stock prices signal stockholders' reactions to current earnings announcements and expectations of future earnings. Although U. S. stock prices are reasonably efficient, stock market anomalies, such as the weekend effect, the January effect, and others suggest that they are not as efficient as previously thought.

Nevertheless, institutional investors that hold about 65 per cent of domestic stocks do impose some market discipline. Institutional investors and stock market activists played a major role in the corporate shake-ups of Eastman Kodak, General Motors, Sears Roebuck, and International Business Machines in the 1990s.

In a speech, Federal Reserve Board Chairman Alan Greenspan examined historical evidence from U. S. banking history and concluded that in the future, as in the past, we need to place greater reliance on private market regulation. No chartered banks in the United States failed until massive fraud brought down the Farmers Exchange Bank in Rhode Island in 1809.

Thereafter, a series of macroeconomic shocks--the War of 1812, the depression of 1819-1820, and the Panic of 1837--resulted in large numbers of failures. In the absence of those shocks, the stability of the banking industry reflected private market discipline. With respect to current times, he concluded that rapidly changing technology is rendering much government regulation irrelevant.

In many countries-- Germany among them--supervisors have traditionally held the opinion that too much reliance on disclosure is detrimental, since it could cause depositors to react in destabilizing ways and make it more difficult to resolve a bank's difficulties quietly. But as a supervisor's primary task is not getting banks out of trouble but preventing them from getting into difficulties in the first place, it would be counterproductive under today's conditions not to allow the disciplinary forces of the market to assist supervisors to the fullest extent possible in ensuring sound and prudent banking.

Using clearinghouses and exchanges as examples of self-regulation, Greenspan stated that the self-interest of industry participants generates private market regulation. They establish margins and capital requirements to protect the interest of their members.

What he failed to say is that there is continuous monitoring by participants because of their daily transactions. Moreover, their debts are cleared at the end of the day or shortly thereafter. This differs significantly from monitoring that is provided by holders of long-term debts who receive interest payments twice a year.

Debt holders also act in their own self-interest. Riskier thrifts had to pay higher rates and attracted smaller amounts for uninsured deposits. When the market judges a bank to be in dire trouble, market participants may cause a substantial loss of deposits, or cause the bank's stock price to fall, which may result in a change of management or ownership, or even the closing of the bank. While that may be true, the bank was already in "dire trouble" before the market recognized the problem.

Increased emphasis has been placed on market discipline to provide corporate governance for banks. One reason is the widening gaps of knowledge and information between the participants in global financial markets and the regulatory and supervisory authorities. Andrew Crockett, general manager of the Bank of International Settlements (BIS), states that regulators are finding it increasingly difficult to keep up with a complex and rapidly changing financial system.

They believe that is "useful--perhaps necessary-to get the market itself involved in the regulatory process". According to William McDonough, president of the Federal Reserve Bank of New York, "[A]s financial institutions and their activities become more complex, diversified, and global in nature, I believe that market discipline will become an even more important ally of the supervisor than it is now". Recent federal legislation has placed greater emphasis on the role of market regulation.

Provisions of the Federal Deposit Insurance Corporation Improvement Act of 1991 (FDICIA) impose higher capital standards which shift more risk to shareholders. In addition, changes in depositor preference for payoffs puts creditors and uninsured depositors behind insured depositors if a bank is liquidated.

The notion that banks should issue more subordinated debt to the public also has been suggested as a means of establishing market discipline. Finally, president of the Federal Reserve Bank of Minneapolis, favours amending the FDICIA to address the too-big-to-fail issue, to let uninsured depositors know that they would suffer some losses.

He argues that this would increase market discipline. Regulators favour market discipline because it reduces governmentdirected investment and reduces subsidies and safety nets, along with the moral hazard problems associated with safety nets. Accordingly, in January 1996, New Zealand's Reserve Bank regulators placed greater reliance on market discipline increased public disclosure by banks, increased accountability of bank directors and management, and reduced prudential supervision. While the initial reports of the new approach are encouraging, it should be noted that New Zealand is a small country and seventeen or eighteen of the nineteen banks are foreign owned.

Thus, New Zealand's Reserve Bank "free rides" on the home-country bank supervisors. Moreover, there have been no bank failures in several decades. Therefore, without a severe economic downturn or crisis, it is not possible to judge the effectiveness of the market system.

PRINCIPAL AGENT CONFLICTS

Government regulation of banking firms differs substantially from private market relationships. Governments have taken a creditor position and bear some of the default risk. It follows that safety and soundness regulations are designed, in part, to protect their creditor position. In addition, governments' primary motivation in regulating banks is to prevent widespread financial market failures. Accordingly, bank regulators examine banks to obtain audit information, regulatory discipline information, and private information about the banks' condition.

The private information from CAMEL rating downgrades revealing unfavourable information about the bank condition was substantial. On the other hand, supervisory assessments of bank performance are much less accurate overall than both debt and equity market assessments in predicting future changes in performance.

Confidential supervisory information on bank ratings improved the forecast accuracy of variables critical to the conduct of monetary policy. In contrast to inside information provided by bank examinations, private market regulation stems from decisions of investors that are reflected in security designs and prices.

The motivation of these investors is assumed to be wealth maximization. The oversight of banks could be improved if federal supervisors incorporated more market information into their analysis and action plans. The conflicts between principals and agents are discussed below in the context of control mechanisms.

Index